Metropolitan College of NY
Library - 7th Floor
60 West Street
New York, NY 10006

BORDER BROKERS

CHRISTINA M. GETRICH

BORDER BROKERS

*Children of Mexican Immigrants Navigating
U.S. Society, Laws, and Politics*

THE UNIVERSITY OF
ARIZONA PRESS
TUCSON

The University of Arizona Press
www.uapress.arizona.edu

© 2019 by The Arizona Board of Regents
All rights reserved. Published 2019

ISBN-13: 978-0-8165-3899-7 (cloth)

Cover design by Leigh McDonald
Cover photo by Matthew C. Wright

Publication of this book is made possible in part by the proceeds of a permanent endowment created with the assistance of a Challenge Grant from the National Endowment for the Humanities, a federal agency.

Library of Congress Cataloging-in-Publication Data are available at the Library of Congress.

Printed in the United States of America
♾ This paper meets the requirements of ANSI/NISO Z39.48-1992 (Permanence of Paper).

CONTENTS

List of Illustrations	*vii*
Preface	*ix*
Acknowledgments	*xiii*
Introduction	3
1. Increasingly Anti-immigrant Public Policies and Their Impact on Mixed-Status Families	37
2. Conceptualizing Citizenship and Illegality	59
3. Contending with the Repercussive Effects of Illegality and Deportability	91
4. Embodying and Contesting the Effects of Racialized Enforcement	117
5. Tracing Different Trajectories of Transborder Life	140
6. Brokering Belonging in the Shadow of the State	169
Conclusion	197
Appendix A: Conducting Research with Borderland Young Adults	*209*
Appendix B: Participants	*217*
Abbreviations	*219*
Notes	*221*
References	*225*
Index	*245*

ILLUSTRATIONS

1. The westernmost segment of the U.S.-Mexico border ending in the Pacific Ocean, dividing San Diego and Tijuana — 26
2. A typical home in the southeast San Diego barrio — 30
3. The barrio, in the shadow of San Diego and encroaching development — 32
4. The second layer of border fencing and stadium-style lighting in the San Diego sector of the border — 46
5. A young protestor demonstrates his Mexican and American heritage and pride during the immigrant rights protests of 2006 — 60
6. Protestors at the May 1 "Day Without an Immigrant" protest at the U.S.-Mexico border — 81
7. A uniformed Border Patrol officer stands guard by an apartment complex and shopping mall close to the border on the U.S. side — 102
8. Approaching the San Ysidro Port of Entry from the U.S. side — 119
9. Approaching the inspection booth at the San Ysidro Port of Entry from the Mexican side of the border crossing — 128
10. A Border Patrol sports utility vehicle stands guard at Friendship Park on the U.S. side of the U.S.-Mexico border — 201

PREFACE

During the fifteen years that I have been working on this project, immigration policymaking has increasingly become an almost daily news headline—somewhat ironically, given the lack of any actual federal immigration-reform legislation being passed during this period. Rapidly changing developments regarding immigration make it inherently challenging to write a book on the topics of immigration policies, border enforcement practices, and the life experiences of members of mixed-status families. Indeed, changing circumstances have on several occasions forced revision to parts of the manuscript that become suddenly out of date or not in alignment with the new sociopolitical realities of the moment. I have attempted to keep the book current with general changes and developments throughout the production process.

As this book goes to press, we will be approaching the midpoint of the Trump presidency; during this interval, significant changes to immigration have been taking place through executive orders, congressional budget allocations, and changes to how immigration policies are executed. Indeed, even without making major official legislative changes, Trump is nonetheless "building a border wall that no one can see" by wielding executive authority to make major bureaucratic changes such as ending the provisional residency of Deferred Action for Childhood Arrivals (DACA) recipients and Temporary Protected Status (TPS) holders (Sacchetti and Miroff 2017) and expanding enforcement targets, sharpening enforcement tools, and widening enforcement locations (Murray 2017).

Even apart from attempting to track these shifting practices, there is some intrinsic difficulty in capturing what is actually transpiring during Trump's presidency as it relates to immigration. Though some of his stated positions have remained firm and consistent, such as the construction of the border wall, others, such as his position on the future of DACA, have been quite fluid. Another challenge of this time period is that so many different immigration-related topics have taken turns commanding headlines; this book does not provide a comprehensive analysis of all of these topics. For instance, major changes have occurred with the refugee program, asylum-seeking processes, and family separation and detention, none of which is my focus here. Muslim immigrants have been targeted in new ways through the "Muslim ban" executive order (now codified by the Supreme Court), which is certainly indicative of a larger anti-immigrant impulse that has flourished anew with Trump. This book does not provide a comprehensive analysis of all of the changes to immigration policy introduced by Trump or, for that matter, by his predecessors; rather, I focus mostly on the policy topics that most relate to my population of focus—mixed-status families living in the U.S.-Mexico borderlands.

Given the unpredictability of the Trump presidency writ large, it is also difficult to anticipate what is yet to come; thus, I have not attempted to make prognostications and have limited my policy recommendations, as it is not clear what is even feasible now or in the near future. This prolonged state of uncertainty, however, is precisely what is stoking a continuous state of fear in immigrant communities nationwide, a condition that is increasingly being recognized as a public health crisis by scholars (Dreby 2015a, 174; Lopez et al. 2017), physicians and health-care systems (Artiga and Ubri 2017; Stein 2017), and even those in the media (Richards 2017; Rodriguez 2018).

Notwithstanding these constraints, the benefit of this book and my research design is that it is not constructed simply to offer a snapshot of current immigration policy conditions; rather, it provides a longer-term context for viewing immigration policies and enforcement practices that have for decades shaped the lives of children in mixed-status families. Indeed, long before Trump, borderland mixed-status families were being subjected to intensifying surveillance and enforcement pressures in their communities and the resultant deportation fear. Though my participants' current realities are unquestionably being shaped by today's policies and practices (including the lack of comprehensive immigration reform, which continues to plague many of their families), this book provides a longitudinal portrait of the effects of immigration policies and enforcement practices on the lives of children who grew up in mixed-status families and came of age during a time of increasingly restrictive immigration policies. Thus, the book not only speaks to the potential fate of mixed-status families under Trump but also provides a perspective on the longer-term effects of immigration policymaking over the last thirty years. By focusing on the resilience and agency of the young adults who grew up in structurally vulnerable mixed-status families, I hope to demonstrate their potential for helping to improve circumstances for immigrant families and communities as we work toward a better future.

ACKNOWLEDGMENTS

FIRST OF all, I would like to thank the young adults and their families whose life experiences this book chronicles. They have shared their struggles and successes with me with great openness and sincerity, and I am immensely indebted to them for all that I have learned from them. It has truly been a pleasure to watch them grow up and become impressive adults, and I feel fortunate that I have been able to see them and maintain relationships with them over time. I also relish in being able to follow all of the latest developments in their adult lives in real time via social media; as I wrote these acknowledgements, one just walked the stage to get her master's degree in counseling with her proud family cheering her on, while another celebrated her first Mother's Day with her own mother, and yet another spent the afternoon just eating tacos and hanging out with his brother in Tijuana. Seeing these moments flash by has served as a frequent and valuable reminder of the triumphs and normalcy of life amid challenges and strife. I would also like to thank my sister, Diana, for facilitating my initial access to the center where this project was initially conducted and introducing me to the families who came to be featured in this book. I also thank center staff for their support during my fieldwork and for sharing their insights into my participants' lives.

Next, I would like to thank my mentors and colleagues for their guidance and support. I am particularly appreciative of Louise Lamphere for her steadfast belief in me and for always inquiring with great interest about what I am working on. Louise's indefatigable dedication to her students and to the discipline of anthropology is truly inspiring. I also thank my other committee members, Carole Nagengast, Les Field, and Nancy López, for their contributions to my dissertation project and encouragement as I completed it and beyond. I have also been fortunate to have an incredibly supportive set of graduate school colleagues throughout my academic journey, foremost among them my cherished cohort-mates and dear friends Lisa Hardy, Nicole Kellett, Marie Sardier, and Gwen Saul. They have been wonderful sounding boards for ideas related to this project that I have been working through for years and, more importantly, have been my social support network since we were lucky enough to find ourselves in graduate school at the same time and place. I also thank Michael Adair-Kriz, Jara Carrington, Lara Gunderson, Ruth Jolie, Miria Kano, Patrick Staib, Gabriel Torres, and Marnie Watson for their engaging discussions and friendship during graduate school and afterward. I also would like to acknowledge Debbie Boehm, Sarah Horton, Julia Meredith Hess, Andrew Sussman, and Catie Willging for their much-appreciated mentorship and enthusiasm about my work and professional development. I have also benefited from fruitful conversations about my research with Jacque García, Angélica Solares, and Estela Vásquez and am grateful for their ongoing friendship. At the University of Maryland, College Park, I would like to thank my colleagues Andrea López and Thurka Sangaramoorthy for their productive exchanges as I drew this project to a close and for helping to keep me sane throughout the tenure process, as well as Janet Chernela, Judith Freidenberg, Barnet Pavao-Zuckerman, and Paul Shackel for their guidance and mentorship. I also wish to acknowledge UMD graduate students Kaelin Rapport, for his assistance in organizing bibliographies and performing literature searches, and Emilia Guevara, for many interesting talks about second-generation life, Mexico, and other related topics.

I was fortunate enough to receive generous funding for this research project from many organizations over the years. My preliminary and initial dissertation fieldwork was funded by several mechanisms through the University of New Mexico between 2004 and 2008, including three Graduate Research and Development Grants; a Student Research and Allocations Committee Grant; and a Research, Project, and Travel Award. The primary fieldwork for the project was funded by a National Science Foundation Doctoral Dissertation Improvement Grant (2006–2007), and the write-up was supported by the Louise Lamphere Ortiz Center for Intercultural Studies Public Policy Fellowship (2006–2007) and an American Association of University Women American

Dissertation Fellowship (2007–2008). I also greatly benefited from participating in the Fourth Annual Summer Institute for International Migration, Social Science Research Council / UCSD Center for Comparative Immigration Studies. During the summer institute, I was able to get valuable feedback on these research findings from leading scholars in the field as well as a cohort of junior colleagues and have the opportunity to take a Border Patrol tour, during which I took some of the pictures included in this book. The follow-up research was supported by my start-up funds from the Anthropology Department and a grant from the Consortium for Race, Gender, and Ethnicity at the University of Maryland (2014–2015).

I am also grateful to the University of Arizona Press for their early and sustained interest in this project. I thank Senior Editor Allyson Carter in particular for her input and guidance on the project throughout the process; Editorial, Design, and Production Manager Amanda Krause for keeping everything humming along; Art Director Leigh McDonald for her diligence and patience in developing the book cover; and Marketing Manager Abby Mogollon for her work on promoting the book. I also thank Copy Editor Amy Maddox for her careful and thorough treatment of the manuscript and Amron Gravett for her excellent index. I also appreciate the recommendations made by the two anonymous reviewers, which greatly improved the manuscript.

I must also acknowledge my first (and longest-standing) editor, my father, Rich Getrich. I can remember first asking him to edit a paper for me in high school; he asked me to bring him his (literal) red pen and gave the paper back to me covered in red, which was incredibly humbling. Since then, he has always been eager and ready to break out his (now electronic) red pen and improve on whatever I send him. He has slogged his way through many drafts of this material at this point and still always has helpful and valuable insights to offer. He also is not afraid to tell me when something is crap, though in the most constructive and loving way possible. I wish to thank my mother, Judy, for sharing with me her passion for working with immigrant populations as an ESL teacher and for always being so enthusiastic about our shared interests along my academic journey. I also am grateful to her for inculcating in me both an ability to empathize with people from different backgrounds and a strong sense of social justice. Certainly her mother, Mary Roberts, also shaped these propensities and passions and was a strong female role model for me growing up. I am also appreciative of the teaching and writing skills my mom has passed down to me, inherited in part through my grandfather, Charles Roberts. He was an esteemed reporter and talented writer, and I hope I have carried on his legacy.

I also thank the rest of my wonderful family for always supporting all of my endeavors, including this project, which has occupied my life for so many years. As I already mentioned, I am grateful to my sister, Diana, for facilitating access to my fieldwork site in the first place, but also for being so instrumental in shaping my path beyond that. My interest in Mexican immigration began and the seeds of this project were sown when she moved to Tijuana and crisscrossed the U.S.-Mexico border for many years before settling on the San Diego side; she introduced me to this place that has become my second home, including the fascinating aspects of borderland culture and the indignities of what takes place there that lit a fire in me. I feel fortunate to be able to share so much with her as well as her children, Bryan and Ariana, whose lives also have been fundamentally shaped by being born and living there. Both of them made my fieldwork memorable, and I can still picture them so clearly playing with my research participants as young children.

Though he reentered my life during the final phases of this project, I am immensely grateful for all of the love and support that my partner, Matt Kacenga, has provided me and for helping to keep me grounded when work and life get overwhelming. I found myself wrapping up this book focused on children and families at an interesting time in my own life journey, as I awaited the birth of our child, Marisa Shea. At the end of my pregnancy as I finalized the book, Trump's heartless and downright cruel separation of young children from their parents at the border was implemented as a part of his "zero tolerance" immigration policy. The Trump administration's actions commanded the news cycle and prompted the general citizenry to finally pay attention to and be indignant about the phenomenon of family separation that has long been taking place in our country, including, in a different form, among longer-term residents and their U.S.-born children. Part of me feels angst over bringing our child into a society that has been so cruel to immigrants and their children and has inflicted such suffering and pain on them, though another part draws inspiration from the young adults I have written about here, who have fought so hard for justice and the recognition of the dignity of their families and communities. I am hopeful that our child—and, indeed, their children as well—are able to live in a future U.S. society that is characterized by greater tolerance and equity.

BORDER BROKERS

INTRODUCTION

BORN AND raised in San Diego, Isabel Clemente is the oldest daughter of Mexican immigrant parents who are from the same neighborhood in Tijuana, about fifteen miles away from their San Diego home across the U.S.-Mexico border. Her parents met when they were teenagers, and after getting married they decided to cross the border to join his sisters in Southern California, even though her mother was hesitant about leaving her large extended family. Despite the proximity of their hometown, Isabel's undocumented parents have for twenty years been unable to cross the heavily surveilled border to see the rest of their Mexico-based family. Even though they could not go, Isabel's parents ensured that she and her two younger siblings regularly visited their extended family in Tijuana throughout their childhood by sending them across with family members who had legal immigration status and could cross. Growing up, the girls enjoyed spending time with their extended family, though Isabel reflected that "it always felt like something was missing" being there without her parents.

Each time she waited in line to cross the border to return to the United States, Isabel also experienced profound anxiety about interactions with antagonistic border officers. She remembers that she "would always get terrible butterflies in [her] stomach" as she waited in the border crossing line, afflicted by the fear that something going awry might ultimately lead to her parents being deported. Although she is a U.S. citizen, these deportation fears also shaped her daily life in southeast San Diego, where she and her family members went about mundane tasks like walking around the neighborhood, shopping for necessities, and going to work on public transportation under the surveillance of the U.S. Border Patrol, whose ever-presence and pattern of ethno-racial profiling plagued her neighborhood for the last two decades.

Carlos Franco grew up down the street, in the same barrio as Isabel, with his parents and three siblings. His parents are from the same rancho in central Mexico, San Antonio, though they met in San Diego, where they each had independently followed migration pathways established by their family networks. Carlos and his siblings' countries of birth crisscrossed as their parents migrated back and forth in the mid- to late 1980s: his eldest sister was born in San Antonio, and then his older brother in San Diego; Carlos was born in San Antonio, and then his youngest sister was born in San Diego once the family had established itself there more firmly. Carlos characterized life in the United States in the early years as "hard" for his family, saying "My mom and the three of us had to go back to Mexico because they couldn't keep up here until my dad was able to get a good job." Despite these early challenges, though, Carlos states, "I couldn't have asked for a better childhood. The neighborhood I grew up in was poor, but I had a lot of friends. And my parents always tried their best—they wanted the best for us."

One major—and hugely consequential—difference between Isabel's and Carlos's family trajectories is that Carlos's parents were among the 2.7 million previously undocumented immigrants who were able to regularize their immigration status through the Immigration Reform and Control Act (IRCA), which Congress passed in 1986, the very year that Carlos was born. Carlos likewise was able to adjust his status through his parents. Thus, Carlos did not grow up with the same angst, fear, and uncertainty that so pervaded Isabel's childhood; he was able to maneuver through his life and neighborhood more securely. Carlos's family was also able to go back to their beloved San Antonio "every year since we got our papers." These regular trips allowed him to forge a meaningful connection to the town and members of its expansive transborder network, including his wife, Melissa, who grew up in Texas but whom he met in San Antonio during the town's annual festival when he was a teenager. He and Melissa now go back to the town's annual festival with their parents as well as with their own three children.

Upon first glance, Beto García's story mirrors Carlos's in that he was also born in central Mexico to parents from the same rancho who moved to San

Diego to join extended family. However, unlike the Francos, neither García parent was able to regularize their immigration status through IRCA. Therefore, like Isabel, Beto grew up grappling with the implications of illegality alongside his parents and an older and younger sibling, who were all undocumented. Unlike Carlos and Isabel, Beto and his family were prevented from taking regular trips back to his hometown or even to nearby Tijuana; as he reflected as a teenager, "It was hard not having that option." When his mother made the difficult decision to go back to tend to her ailing parent, she was caught and sent to a detention facility, an episode that still haunts her in many ways, as she is now "in the system." Though she ultimately reunited with the family in San Diego, they continued to contend with the collective uncertainty of potentially prolonged family separation.

The Garcías' worst fears were realized when Beto was twenty: his older brother, Luis, was picked up by the Border Patrol just down the street from their house and ultimately deported. Though Beto had been able to regularize his immigration status by marriage, his first trip back to Mexico since he was three years old was not the grand homecoming he had idealized when he first described what it would be like to me when he was a teenager; rather, the purpose of the trip was to take his brother clothes and household items and help him get established in his new life in Tijuana, a city completely unfamiliar to both brothers because they had never been able to go growing up because of their status. At that point, Beto became the connection bridging divided family members on different sides of the border who could no longer see each other, emerging in his new familial role as a border broker.

MIXED-STATUS FAMILIES IN THE UNITED STATES

This book chronicles the lived experiences of the children of Mexican immigrants—like Isabel, Carlos, and Beto—who grew up in mixed-status families and came of age in the U.S.-Mexico borderlands. Mixed-status families are families that contain a combination of U.S. citizens, legal immigrants, and unauthorized[1] or undocumented immigrants (Fix and Zimmerman 2001). At the turn of the twenty-first century, one in ten children in the United States belonged to a mixed-status family.[2] In California, that number was even higher; three in ten children belonged to such family units (Fix, Zimmerman, and Passel 2001, 15).

When I first met Isabel, Carlos, and Beto and started conducting research on them and their families in 2004, mixed-status families had just started coming to the attention of policymakers and the general public. As the subsequent decade unfolded, comprehensive immigration reform stalled, creating even more mixed-status families as avenues for undocumented immigrants to regularize their statuses remained elusive. Mixed-status families also commanded increasing attention as more comprehensive data documenting their characteristics emerged. By 2010, 16.6 million people in the United States were estimated to live in mixed-status families (Dreby 2015a, 5; Taylor et al. 2011; Zayas 2015).

Living within mixed-status families are an estimated 5.1 million children, some 4.1 to 4.5 million of them U.S. citizens (Capps, Fix, and Zong 2016; Dreby 2015a, 5; Taylor et al. 2011; Zayas 2015). To encapsulate the commonplace presence of citizen children in mixed-status families, Dreby (2015a, 5) highlights that "numerically speaking, today you are about as likely to know a child living with a stepfather as you are to know a child living with an unauthorized parent." Nearly one million noncitizen children also live in mixed-status families (Capps, Fix, and Zong 2016), underscoring that their configuration is often more complex than just citizen children with undocumented parents. Further, noncitizen family members' immigration statuses may change over time, introducing new gains in membership or vulnerabilities to the family unit, as exemplified by Carlos's family.

Mixed-status families are complicated social units because individual members hold distinct immigration statuses; these statuses differentiate them in terms of their formal membership in society, eligibility for social and healthcare services, ability to work legally, and risk of being detained by immigration officials and/or deported. Per the Fourteenth Amendment of the U.S. Constitution, adopted in 1868, anyone born in the United States is granted citizenship through the jus soli (right of the soil) principle, regardless of the citizenship or nationality of the parents; all U.S. citizens are theoretically entitled to the full benefits and privileges of nation-state membership. However, despite the fact that statuses are conferred upon individuals and immigration policy focuses on individual subjects (Sassen 1996), parents' immigration statuses affect the lives of children living in mixed-status families tremendously.

Children growing up in mixed-status families often experience barriers to accessing services because undocumented parents are reluctant to approach public institutions, fearing that their children's use of benefits could jeopardize future immigration applications and carry a risk of deportation (Capps and

Fortuny 2006; Leiter, McDonald, and Jacobson 2006). Beyond services, children in mixed-status families are exposed to a number of risk factors that place them at a social disadvantage, including lower preschool enrollment, linguistic isolation, limited English proficiency, poverty, and reduced socioeconomic progress (Capps, Fix, and Zong 2016, 1–2). These cumulative disadvantages render mixed-status families in a position of structural vulnerability, as they are subjected to physical and emotional suffering in marked and patterned ways due to their subordinate position within social hierarchies (Quesada, Hart, and Bourgois 2011; Szkupinski Quiroga, Medina, and Glock 2014). Scholars and think tanks have increasingly been charting these vulnerabilities in the last two decades, during which mixed-status families have come to be more prominent and have faced exclusionary immigration policies and enforcement practices at federal, state, and local levels.

The change in political leadership ushered in by President Trump in January 2017 has made mixed-status families more vulnerable than ever, as parents and noncitizen children have been targeted in new ways, including during their regular check-ins with immigration authorities and while engaging in everyday activities like going to school and church. Despite the official position that Trump would continue former president Obama's practice of specifically targeting those with criminal records, it has become increasingly clear that ICE is arresting anyone they encounter out of status, including those who are not even their nominal targets (Murray 2017). Indeed, the news is saturated with daily stories of the latest immigrants who have been detained and/or deported, families that have been torn apart, and the tragic effects of these deportations on the children who remain behind. Thus, an examination of the longer-term effects of mixed-status families' structural vulnerabilities—and strategies for overcoming them—is instructive in helping us to understand what is yet to come for these latest targets of aggressive immigration enforcement tactics deployed by the government.

INVESTIGATING HOW YOUNG ADULT CHILDREN OF IMMIGRANTS NAVIGATE ILLEGALITY OVER TIME

This book examines how the children of Mexican immigrants grappled with the immigration policies that framed their mixed-status family's lives as they came of age in the increasingly anti-immigrant U.S. society of the late twentieth and early twenty-first centuries. I argue that illegality has deleteriously impacted the lived experiences and incorporation pathways of these young adults, but that over time they have also developed competencies for brokering inclusion for themselves and their family members. The book contributes to the growing literature on the impacts of immigration policies and enforcement practices on mixed-status families (Castañeda, 2019; Dreby 2015a; Gomberg-Muñoz 2017; Gulbas and Zayas 2017; Schueths and Lawston 2015; Zayas 2015) and is situated "at the nexus of the public sphere of immigration policy and the private lives of families" (Dreby 2015a, 9; see also Boehm 2012, 9).

Scholars have recently asked probing questions about the fate of these "forgotten citizens" (Zayas 2015) and the longer-term implications of having "parents without papers" (Bean, Brown, and Bachmeir 2015). This book examines these questions by following ethnographically the lives of these children as they transitioned from adolescence to adulthood. Although we know about how immigration policies shape young children's developmental trajectories (Yoshikawa 2011), as well as their preadolescence and adolescence (Dreby 2010, 2015a), we know much less about how children from mixed-status families experience and engage with these policies as they mature and become adults. Further, as citizens who have secure immigration status, are bilingual, and have greater knowledge of how U.S. social systems operate, we also do not know about the potential roles they may play in buffering the effects of and contesting policies that target members of their mixed-status families.

This book also contributes to the well-established literature on immigrant "illegality" (DeGenova 2002; Menjívar and Kanstroom 2014).[3] Illegality refers not only to the processes by which state regimes create "legal" and "illegal" subjects (Boehm 2012, 13) but also to how individuals navigate "the dichotomous states of being allowed or unallowed, legitimate or illegitimate, during their daily lives" (Dreby 2015a, 1). Specifically, I examine how illegality pervades the lives of U.S. citizen children from mixed-status families in the U.S.-Mexico borderlands. To examine illegality and related phenomena like deportability—or the ever-present fear of deportation (DeGenova 2002)—I foreground how these young adults understand what it means to belong and how growing up in mixed-status families shapes their subjectivities. As Park (2005, 26) observes, surprisingly little scholarship on the children of immigrants has been explicitly focused on their own perspectives and subjectivities.[4] I also highlight how they have maneuvered these policies and practices, coming to advocate on behalf of their less-secure family and community members over time. As Suárez-Orozco and Suárez-Orozco (2001, 117–18) noted long ago, "The story of today's immigrant children is not complete without reference to their consciousness and agency."

As enforcement has become the cornerstone of U.S. national and, increasingly, state and local immigration policies, it is also important to understand how this policy approach frames the lives of the children of immigrants. Examining the lives of my participants within the San Diego–Tijuana borderlands enables us to observe the magnified effects of immigration policy and enforcement practices on mixed-status families, given that targeted enforcement (in the form of Operation Gatekeeper) has pervaded the region since the mid-1990s. This "Gatekeeper generation"—children who literally grew up under the gaze of the state[5]—has, over time, developed particularly keen insight into how state power operates and how to navigate it. Insights gleaned from their experiences and perspectives are instructive for understanding the longer-term impact of immigration enforcement on mixed-status families as it has expanded significantly in scope, moving into the U.S. interior and infiltrating communities nationwide.

This book makes several contributions to scholarship on the effects of U.S. immigration policy and enforcement practices. First, it foregrounds how the children of immigrants understand illegality and experience its imprint on their lives. I examine how, as teenagers, my participants first came to understand state categorizations such as "citizen" and "undocumented immigrant" and ultimately reinscribed them to better fit the circumstances of their lives by distinguishing between those who "had papers" and those who did not (Getrich 2008). I situate their initial understandings of these categories temporally during their adolescence, when they participated in the immigrant rights protests of 2006—the first form of political engagement for many—but also in the subsequent decade.

My second objective is to examine the lived and embodied experiences of state immigration policies and enforcement practices on these young adults. I demonstrate how illegality, and the condition of deportability that accompanies it, has shaped their families' configurations, settlement and mobility patterns (both in the United States and Mexico), economic prospects, stability and security, and health and well-being over time. I also describe how my participants "shared in the fear" of their vulnerable family members and friends as they contended with the constant surveillance of the Border Patrol. However, because of the racialized system of "policeability" (Rosas 2006b) that predominates in the borderlands—and, increasingly, nationwide—my participants have also regularly been directly targeted by Border Patrol and CBP agents in their barrio and while crossing the international border, despite being citizens (Getrich 2012). These encounters produced fear and embodied distress in them as they grew up and transitioned into adulthood. However, over time, my participants have also cultivated strategies for resisting the state's intrusion into their and their family members' lives.

The third objective of this book is to highlight the emerging brokering roles that my participants cultivated as they transitioned into adulthood. I call attention to the state's role in shaping participation in transborder life for second-generation young adults; for some with families divided by the border, the state can also *necessitate* participation in it. As U.S. citizens with the ability to cross the international border, my participants have emerged as linchpins of families with complex transborder configurations. Beyond their role in buffering state-produced separation, my participants are also carrying forward the brokering roles that they developed within their families into adulthood. As adults, they are bridging immigration-related gaps for their families more privately and advocating broadly for their communities through their professional jobs as social workers, lawyers, and educators.

This book is a portrait of the lives of citizen children (Zayas 2015, 4) and their mixed-status families spanning more than a decade, coinciding with a period of intensifying anti-immigrant and anti-Mexican sentiment. It is based on ethnographic fieldwork conducted with an initial sample of fifty-four young adults whom I met while volunteering at a nonprofit organization in southeast San Diego, and a smaller cohort of thirteen of them whom I have continued to follow over the subsequent decade. (See appendix A for a description of research methods and appendix B for participant characteristics.) Foregrounding the subjectivities and agency of these young adults, I illuminate how they have developed competencies for brokering inclusion for themselves and their family members over time. The book engages with and builds upon theories about *second-generation incorporation, state power and illegality,* and the *brokering roles* of young adults in immigrant families. It also adds to a robust literature chronicling the richness of everyday life in the U.S.-Mexico borderlands, spanning from Martínez (1994) to Vélez-Ibañez and Heyman (2017). In the borderlands, immigration policies and enforcement practices are experienced particularly acutely and family life is often lived across borders—both by choice and by necessity.

THE INCORPORATION PATHWAYS OF
SECOND-GENERATION YOUTH

Though attention to children of immigrants has shifted more recently to the mixed-status families in which they often live, there is long-standing interest in the fate of the children of immigrants, also known as the second generation.[6] The children of immigrants are a demographic of increasing size and importance in U.S. society, comprising nearly a quarter of all U.S. children in 2014 (Urban Institute 2016). Between 1970 and 2005, the share of children with at least one immigrant parent more than tripled, climbing from 6 to 21 percent (Capps and Fortuny 2006). California has the largest statewide concentration of children of immigrants at 48 percent; San Diego also has one of the largest concentrations of a metropolitan area at 44 percent (Urban Institute 2016).

Given their demographic prominence, the integration of the contemporary second generation is an important topic for policymakers and researchers alike (Alba, Kasinitz, and Waters 2011, 763). The literature on this "new" second generation emerged from sociology in the early to mid-1990s and focused principally on the topic of assimilation among the post-1965 children of immigrants. Sociologists sought to refine the classic model of "straight-line" assimilation—by which immigrants were thought to become more similar to natives over time in norms, values, and behaviors—to explicate the different pathways that were emerging with this new second generation. Whereas previous waves of immigrants had been predominantly European, the Hart-Cellar Act of 1965 abolished the national origins quotas that had favored Europe and opened up migration from Africa, Asia, Latin America, and the Middle East (Kasinitz, Mollenkopf, and Waters 2004, 1).

Gans (1992) was the first to "turn traditional assimilation theory on its head" by arguing that members of the second generation who were restricted by a lack of economic opportunities and racial discrimination might experience downward mobility relative to their parents (Kasinitz et al. 2008, 7). Gans (1992) laid out the possibility of a "second-generation decline" among the children of poor immigrants of color. An even more influential framework for understanding divergent adaptation outcomes for the second generation emerged in segmented assimilation, elaborated by Portes and Rumbaut (2001) and Rumbaut and Portes (2001) in their seminal volumes stemming from the Children of Immigrants Longitudinal Study (CILS).

Segmented assimilation focuses on the location in the socioeconomic hierarchy that particular groups of children assimilate to and the assets or structural vulnerabilities influencing their positions. It delineates three divergent pathways: smooth transition into the mainstream, selective acculturation accomplished by drawing upon ethnic communities' resources, and downward assimilation to an oppositional culture (Portes and Rumbaut 2001). These pathways are thought to diverge based on the human capital of an ethnic group, its context of reception, family structure, and other community factors related to social capital formation (Smith 2008). Among all of the different ethnic groups examined, Mexicans were pegged as the group most "at risk" of falling into the third path due to their low human capital, a negative context of reception, and fewer supportive social practices and organizations (López and Stanton-Salazar 2001; Perlmann and Waldinger 1997). Given these factors and the size of the Mexican population in the United States, they were deemed to be a case of "unique importance" (López and Stanton-Salazar 2001, 58).

Into the 2000s, a second wave of scholars critiqued segmented assimilation. Some argued that its focus on outcomes obscured the processes by which children came to understand who they were and the "active efforts" they took to "shape the terms of their own integration" (Park 2005). Others critiqued the predominant focus on ethnicity at the expense of race, gender, and class as important variables influencing second-generation pathways (Aparicio 2007; Fouron and Glick Schiller 2001; Golash-Boza 2006; Kasinitz, Mollenkopf, and Waters 2004; Levitt and Waters 2002; López 2004; Smith 2006; Smith, Cordero-Guzmán, and Grosfoguel 2001; Waldinger and Feliciano 2004). Scholars also argued that segmented assimilation did not adequately account for the effects of ethno-racial discrimination and racialization (Espiritu 2003; Golash-Boza 2006; Park 2005; Smith, Cordero-Guzmán, and Grosfoguel 2001, 12–13).

More recently, scholars examining undocumented and 1.5-generation young adults have pointed out that there has been inadequate attention to legal status as an important axis of stratification (Abrego 2011, 339; Menjívar 2006, 1006–7). Indeed, legal status is an important factor shaping young adults' "blocked paths" to incorporation (Abrego and Gonzales 2010; Gonzales 2016; Gonzales, Terriquez, and Ruszczyk 2014). Legal status is not merely an "integration handicap" for immigrant parents; it can also permeate across generations, potentially disadvantaging their children and even grandchildren (Bean, Brown, and Bachmeir 2015, 6–7). Beyond that, the prevailing focus on how different ethnic groups were "making it" in U.S. society also did not capture second-generation participation in transnational life for those who possessed a status that enabled them to travel across borders (Fouron and Glick Schiller 2001, 63; Levitt and Waters 2002; Smith 2006).

As a metacritique, scholars pointed out that the initial scholarship on the new second generation may have been overly pessimistic (Alba, Kasinitz, and Waters 2011; Kasinitz et al. 2008; Waldinger and Feliciano 2004). While they acknowledge that concern over the prospects of today's second generation was "warranted," Waldinger and Feliciano (2004, 395) found little evidence to support the downward assimilation hypothesis among the Mexican second generation. Alba, Kasinitz, and Waters (2011) also concluded that "the kids are (mostly) alright." Even more "cautiously optimistic" about the fate of second-generation New Yorkers, Kasinitz et al. (2008, 397) found that second-generation youth from a variety of backgrounds have advanced educationally and occupationally beyond their parents' generation while intermixing culturally and socially with other groups to create a vibrant youth culture. They argue that particularly in multicultural New York, they may actually have a "second generation advantage," picking and choosing from both their parents' and U.S. cultures.

In 2005, as I began my fieldwork, I sought to reconcile the ongoing debate about the trajectories of the Mexican second generation—which was trending more toward the decline scenario at that point—with my experiences and observations about the lives of the children I was getting to know. Like Smith (2008, 272), I did not witness oppositional attitudes and blocked pathways emerging among my second-generation Mexican[7] participants in the way that segmented assimilation predicted. Though I did note the presence of many well-documented structural barriers, like poor neighborhoods and low-performing schools, the children I was working with were not falling prey to gangs and crime and their parents had actively pursued and forged opportunities for their children.

What was *quite* apparent to me from the beginning that I did not see articulated in the literature on the second generation was the deep imprint of the state on their lives, specifically related to immigration. Portes and Rumbaut (2001, 46–47) highlight the role of governmental policy in shaping the context of reception for different groups. Yet they focus on the conditions under which immigrants arrived and were initially received, not adequately accounting for the ongoing influence of the state on the everyday lives of immigrants and their children. State immigration categorizations clearly determined immigrant parents' economic, social, and political incorporation and influenced their everyday lives. These limitations also clearly impacted my teenaged participants as well, as they took on after-school jobs to help contribute to household expenses, traveled without their parents throughout California and Mexico, and, once they turned sixteen and got their licenses, drove around family members who could not drive.

These limitations featured into everyday discussions around the center where I met them, if in coded or indirect ways (through statements like, "She can't go on the field trip to L.A. because of *her situation*"). Indeed, high school was the time when many came to realize specifically what these immigration-related restrictions meant because of the practical limitations they introduced not only for their family members but also for their friends. Beyond that, it became clear to me that simply by living in the neighborhood, these teenagers had regular, and largely negative, interactions with agents of the state—even as they walked to the center for after-school programming on any given day and encountered Border Patrol agents along the way. Given that San Diego was one of the research sites for Portes and Rumbaut's landmark CILS study, the omission of state power was especially notable.

While large-scale survey studies like CILS have provided invaluable data on larger trends and set the stage for understanding the trajectories of second-generation young adults, they provide less in-depth insight into the complex lived experiences of the second generation, shaped not only within schools, neighborhoods, and workplaces, but also in the shadow of the state as they come of age contending with the fallout of their family members' legal vulnerabilities and exclusion. To examine this fallout and its reverberations, it is also important to track changes within mixed-status families' circumstances over time since the policy context has evolved so dramatically in the last twenty years. CILS set an important precedent by including three time points in their longitudinal design—eighth/ninth grade, eleventh/twelfth grade, and young adulthood—underscoring the importance of documenting life-course transitions. Yet these three time points still do not provide all of the context we need to understand second-generation young adults' transition to adulthood.

Life-course scholars typically define the transition to adulthood in reference to five milestones or markers: completing school, moving out of the parental home, establishing employment, getting married, and becoming a parent (Gonzales 2011, 604; Waters et al. 2011). These markers may apply to a normative U.S. young adulthood, taking place between the ages of eighteen and thirty-five—although they are also under debate as today's young adults are finding it increasingly hard to achieve them (Waters et al. 2011). Broader changes in gender norms, marriage practices, schooling, and entry into the labor force also shape the transition into adulthood and have blurred the traditional line between adolescence and full-fledged adulthood (Waters et al. 2011, 1–2).

For my participants, markers of adulthood are even more complex; they are much more oriented toward their families of orientation and, indeed, directly implicate the state. For instance, how does getting a job as a young adult so you can finally help your undocumented parents stabilize economically fit the traditional milestones? What about becoming the highest wage earner in your household since your parents are relegated to working in the informal economy? How might we make sense of second-generation young adults using their local knowledge to help family members find safer ways to get to work that circumvent the Border Patrol? And finally, what about the fact that while some young adults look forward to turning twenty-one so that they can legally enter a bar and spend their money on alcohol with their friends, others save their money and look forward to that landmark birthday so they can hire a lawyer and finally sponsor their parents' immigration applications? Though some might see these phenomena as delays or forces impeding my participants' transition to adulthood, they are the realities of living within a mixed-status family and actually demonstrate quite a bit of adult maturity and dedication. Thus, to truly make sense of the incorporation trajectories of many second-generation youth, it is imperative to consider how the state has shaped their family lives.

MIXED-STATUS FAMILIES' LIVED EXPERIENCES OF ILLEGALITY

Indeed, the state has played a far-reaching role in shaping the incorporation trajectories of the children of immigrants in ways that have not been fully explored. Alba and Waters (2011, 5) recognize that their comparative analysis of the second generation in the United States and Western Europe largely sidesteps the state, commenting that "the role of state policy and law . . . is obviously consequential and thus to some extent agenda setting for second-generation integration." State power is also far-reaching in determining the context of reception for immigrants and their children over time, both at national and, increasingly, local levels. Abrego (2011, 364) points out that the legal context of reception "merits a closer, more detailed examination as a factor that powerfully determines immigrants' incorporation experiences."

The legal context is particularly important as a backdrop for assessing how state regimes create "legal" and "illegal" subjects (Boehm 2012, 13) and determining the implications of these categorizations for mixed-status families. DeGenova (2002) first put forth the construct of "illegality," referring to the socially, politically, and legally produced condition of immigrants' legal status. He argues that illegality is the product of deliberate immigration lawmaking that has codified immigrants' exclusion to sustain a legally vulnerable reserve of labor while rendering them in a state of protracted and enduring vulnerability (DeGenova 2002, 439–40). Though processes of illegalization steadily operated throughout the twentieth century, a new chapter commenced with IRCA in 1986 as immigrants who were ineligible or arrived after its passage found themselves with no avenue through which to regularize their statuses.

It was during this immediate post-IRCA period that my participants were born, between 1986 and 1992—some to parents who had been able to take advantage of IRCA and were now lawful permanent residents (LPRs); others to LPR-undocumented couples who were in the process of petitioning for the other spouse (generally, a mother); and some to parents who were—and continue to remain—undocumented. The academic examination of illegality emerged through ethnographically grounded studies of lived experiences of undocumented immigrant adults as they navigated their statuses within "spaces of non-existence" (Coutin 2000).

It is precisely through these lived experiences of *children* in mixed-status families that I consider the ways in which illegality and navigating these spaces of nonexistence has shaped their lives over time. When my participants were toddlers and preschool-aged in the early 1990s, immigrants (among them, their parents and family members) became the targets of new initiatives and restrictions—especially in California, the birthplace of anti-immigrant policymaking (Pastor 2018). The 1990s were a period of flux in California, during which economic restructuring (toward a global corporate model), a deep economic recession, great demographic change, natural disasters, and riots all hit the state hard (García Bedolla 2005, 21). Stemming from these changes, an "outbreak" of "historically unparalleled concern" about the U.S. government's ability to police the U.S.-Mexico border and prevent unauthorized immigration from Mexico and California emerged as an epicenter of this debate (Nevins 2002, 2).

To address this heightening concern, the U.S. government launched the border enforcement initiative known as Operation Gatekeeper in 1994. Operation Gatekeeper implemented a strategy known as "prevention through deterrence," attempting to redirect migratory pathways through more treacherous terrain via a massive infusion of resources to the border, including the deployment of Border Patrol agents and the use of new surveillance technologies (DeLeón 2015; Nevins 2002). This new approach represented a major shift; previously, as parents of the families with whom I conducted research recalled, the border had been a fence with gaping holes that had been much easier to cross. Gatekeeper ramped up enforcement at the border, though the Border Patrol also became a conspicuous fixture in borderland communities. Deportability started to factor more prominently into everyday life, unquestionably affecting undocumented parents the most, but also deeply impacting their children's mental and physical health as they contended with deportation fear (Dreby 2012, 2015a; Zayas 2015).

As my participants made their way through elementary school, immigrant family units also became explicit policy targets. On the heels of Operation Gatekeeper, in 1994 California voters passed Proposition 187, a ballot initiative that targeted undocumented immigrants' use of public education, health, and social services. Though ultimately declared unconstitutional, it set the stage for future legislation, including the federal Personal Responsibility and Work Opportunity Reconciliation Act (PRWORA) of 1996. Though not limited to immigrants, PRWORA restricted their public benefit access exclusively to those who had resided in the United States under qualified status for five years or more (U.S. Department of Health and Human Services 2012). Congress also passed the Illegal Immigration Reform and Immigrant Responsibility Act (IIRIRA) and the Antiterrorism and Effective Death Penalty Act (AEDPA) in 1996; together, IIRIRA and AEDPA served to more explicitly link immigration to criminality by increasing penalties for illegal entry, making more crimes subject to deportation, stripping immigrants of legal rights (including the right to due process), and making even LPRs more vulnerable to deportation (Castañeda 2006; Oboler 2006). These provisions broadened and elaborated the scope of illegality for immigrants and those associated with them—like their children (DeGenova 2006, 79).

This increased association of immigrants with criminality had ramifications for my participants' lives as they continued through late elementary and middle school. Being detained became a more commonplace occurrence within their extended families and social circles. And the Border Patrol continued to ramp up its presence in the barrio, constantly looming around the corner. Given that it is impossible to ascertain people's immigration status simply by their physical appearance, my participants were also treated as "presumptively illegal" within this larger system of racialized governance (Harrison and Lloyd 2012, 379; Menjívar and Kanstroom 2014, 13; Rosas 2006a). This stringent policing meant that some families started opting out of activities like going to family gatherings and nearby beaches, which became increasingly risky, or going to Disneyland in the greater Los Angeles area, which involved passing through a Border Patrol checkpoint. Indeed, my participants started cultivating an increasing awareness of the limitations that undocumented people they knew faced.

My participants were in middle school and early high school on September 11, 2001. In the aftermath, border enforcement came to be redefined as a national security issue under the newly formed DHS. For those who were able to cross the border and did, the wait times crossing back from Mexico became longer and longer, meaning that their families were less inclined to go and those who did were also subjected to more intense inspection. As my participants became teenagers, they became even more aware of what having undocumented status meant, particularly as some of their friends were unable to participate in symbolically and practically important rites of passage like getting a driver's license. Those who were able to get their licenses found that they needed to give rides to family members and friends without proper documentation. Some teenagers also started working to help contribute to household expenses, taking on adult responsibilities at an early age.

In 2004 when they were in high school, I first set out to ascertain how they understood and experienced living in their mixed-status families, as there was increasing recognition of the prevalence of these family units. As the purview of illegality scholarship has expanded, there is increased recognition that it is experienced differently by gender, life-cycle stage, and generation (Menjívar and Kanstroom 2014, 7). Indeed, young people have their own subjective understandings of state categorizations and what they mean in their lives (Boehm 2012, 127). At that time, there was much less attention to how illegality impacted children in immigrant families—both noncitizens and citizens alike. Yet clearly illegality had already impacted their mobility locally and across the border, as well as their sense of security and well-being. Important questions were emerging about how these children made sense of the increasing influence of legal status on their everyday lives (Dreby 2015a, 174) and processed vitriolic messages made by politicians and others about their families (Zayas 2015, 57).

Because of their connections to immigrant family members and friends, my participants had a strong defensive reaction to the passage of the Border Protection, Anti-terrorism, and Illegal Immigration Control Act of 2005 (H.R.

4437) when they were in high school and I was conducting fieldwork. H.R. 4437 proposed to change being undocumented from a civil offense to a felony and to criminalize those who knowingly aided or assisted them in entering or remaining in the United States. Like many nationwide, my participants were prompted into action once they found out about its passage in the spring of 2006, organizing through social media and participating in protest activities. Taking place at a pivotal moment in their adolescence, the protests provided them a platform for critiquing the policies that had been increasingly affecting their mixed-status families. After the 2006 protests, undocumented youth and youth living in mixed-status families came to play an even more prominent role in the immigrant rights movement (Nicholls 2013). Many of my participants were in college then and continued to build on the legal consciousness (Abrego 2011) that they had cultivated during the immigrant rights protests. Others were less formally engaged in the movement but continued to pay close attention to immigration developments and advocate for their family members and friends. They also witnessed the disappointing failure of immigration reform at the federal level—despite several attempts at its passage—during this period.

After he was elected president in 2008—the first time the majority of my participants who were citizens were eligible to vote—Obama continued with raids and also increased deportations overall to levels well beyond his predecessors (Zayas 2015, 18), earning him the infamous moniker "deporter in chief." Under Obama, enforcement programs like Secure Communities and 287(g) agreements allowed linkages to be created between local police agencies and the FBI and DHS. Beyond significantly increasing deportations of people with no or only minor infractions, these state-local linkages set the stage for unpredictable and stressful interactions with police and further exacerbated the climate of fear in immigrant communities (Dreby 2015a, 25). Though enforcement became a "mobile technology" as techniques perfected at the border were exported to the U.S. interior (Inda and Dowling 2013, 10), border enforcement remained strong as my participants and their families continued to be subjected to it.

Despite the major uptick in immigrant detention and deportations, Obama provided some relief for undocumented young adults in the form of Deferred Action for Childhood Arrivals (DACA), which he established through executive order in June 2012. DACA is a form of prosecutorial discretion that provides legal work authorization and deferral of deportation for qualifying undocumented young adults. DACA has allowed recipients to secure new jobs and higher wages, obtain driver's licenses, open bank accounts, and get credit cards (Wong et al. 2016). Some of my participants' family members, like Beto's younger brother, and many of their friends and peers who were now in their twenties were able to benefit from DACA. At DACA's five-year anniversary on June 15, 2017, President Trump stated that the program would remain; by September 5, however, he announced that he would be rescinding the program, leaving the fate of some 800,000 young adults in limbo.

Trump also quickly issued two new executive orders—one focused on interior enforcement and the other on border enforcement—signaling that enforcement would remain a priority of his administration. Trump changed the Obama-era focus on those with criminal backgrounds to all immigrants without status, meaning that a wider range of individuals would be detained and deported, ensuring further family separation for members of mixed-status families (Murray 2017). The structural vulnerability of undocumented immigrants, liminally legal immigrants (Menjívar 2006) like DACA recipients, and mixed-status families is more acute than during the previous thirty years. Yet the infrastructure for these developments under Trump was already carefully laid during the thirty years of immigration policymaking that preceded him.

During those thirty years—the span of my participants' lives—the immigration policy context has become more exclusionary and aggressive toward immigrants of all statuses and, by extension, their children—even those born in the United States. Mixed-status families have become increasingly marginalized and vulnerable as enforcement (at the border and within communities nationwide), detention, deportations, and prolonged family separation have become increasingly the norm for mixed-status families. Literally every day that I worked on this book, another story emerged about the latest deportation occurrence that resulted in yet another mixed-status family being torn apart, ever more callously and viciously than the last.

While these developments have been new and unprecedented in many communities nationwide, large-scale enforcement, deportation fear, and the vulnerability of mixed-status families have long been a way of life in the U.S.-Mexico borderlands. Border enforcement has been heavily concentrated at border crossings and in nearby communities for more than two decades. Yet during this time, children in mixed-status families have been growing up, coming of age, and learning to live under these very challenging circumstances. Even if their immediate family members are squared away in their status, *every single* individual with whom I conducted research had someone in their lives whose status rendered them vulnerable. Beyond that, regardless of status, my participants have had to deal with the ever-presence of border enforcement and persistent anti-immigrant fervor swirling around them.

As I have followed my participants over the last decade, I have seen firsthand their struggles in contending with immigration-related vulnerabilities and how very quickly they had to grow up. Now adults, they unquestionably bear the scars of these immigrant policies and enforcement practices. But during this time, I have also observed that despite the significant constraints the U.S. state has placed on their family's lives, negative predictions of their downward assimilation have not borne out. Instead, over time, they have developed competencies for brokering between their families, friends, and communities and broader social institutions, including the state immigration bureaucracy. Indeed, it is precisely because of their unique local knowledge bases, experiences interacting with the state, and transborder competencies that they have been able to emerge as grounded and skilled brokers.

YOUNG ADULTS' BROKERING WORK

There has been increasing attention paid to the ways that young adults navigate the larger immigration systems that structure, divide, and constrain their lives and those of their family members (Abrego 2014; Boehm 2012, 2016; Coe et al. 2011; Coutin 2016; Dreby 2012, 2015a; Heidbrink 2014; Hess 2009). Scholars have foregrounded the agency that children have asserted whether they are "on the move" (Boehm 2012; Heidbrink 2014) or "staying put" (Boehm 2012), stuck in immigrant detention (Heidbrink 2014) or ultimately "exiled home" (Coutin 2016). Boehm finds that children's actions are oftentimes mediated by adults, meaning that theirs would be best characterized as an "embedded agency" (Boehm 2012, 115; Ortner 1996, 13). However, Heidbrink (2014, 14) contests the construction of the child as dependent, arguing that such a vision "stands in marked contrast to the integral roles children often assume in familial decision-making processes as well as the decisions they make as individual social actors."

Indeed, the children of immigrants do frequently take on active roles in family life—often by necessity. Literature on children in immigrant families has documented the crucial contributions they make to the smooth functioning of the family unit overall (Dorner, Orellana, and Jiménez 2008; Katz 2014; Kibria 1993; Menjívar 2010; Orellana 2001, 2009; Orellana, Dorner, and Pulido 2003). Oftentimes children's "everyday work" starts with translating and interpreting as their fluency and familiarity with U.S. social norms outpaces that of their immigrant parents (Dorner, Orellana, and Jiménez 2008; Katz 2014). However, in the process, these children come to serve as intermediaries between their families and the outside world, including in health care, social service, and school settings (Bloemraad and Trost 2008, 511; Katz 2014, 17; Kibria 1993; Menjívar 2010; Orellana, Dorner, and Pulido 2003; Orellana 2001, 2009). In these encounters, children become "experts" in charge of negotiating their families' well-being and integration into U.S. society (Orellana 2001, 378).

Though some have questioned if children's brokering can adversely impact their schooling and developmental processes (Dorner, Orellana, and Jiménez 2008; Dreby 2015a) or represent a role reversal that undermines parental leadership and authority (Dreby 2015a; Foner 2009), others have pointed out that it can serve to strengthen children's loyalty, commitment and responsibility to their family and community (Menjívar, Abrego, and Schmalzbauer 2016, 118; Pallares and Flores-González 2011, 172). While this robust literature has documented children's brokering work in a range of settings, there has been only minimal attention paid to the work that children have performed specifically in relation to the state (Orellana 2009; Orellana, Dorner, and Pulido 2003). Children's brokering work vis-à-vis the state includes more everyday, passive activities, such as translating official letters received in the mail, as well as more specialized, heightened encounters with authority figures in welfare, social security, and immigration offices (Orellana, Dorner, and Pulido 2003, 519).

Further, there is scant attention given to the brokering roles that children continue to play within their families as they transition into adulthood. Indeed, their already-established roles within the family and experiences in this capacity may very well translate into adult caregiving responsibilities. U.S.-born children often have a form of security and privilege—U.S. citizenship—that may allow them to perform particularly effectively in their role as broker. For instance, a U.S. citizen who turns twenty-one may petition for the lawful permanent residency of their parents by filing paperwork with U.S. Citizenship and Immigration Services (USCIS). Such an action often entails significant effort in securing a lawyer and financial hardship for the adult child, and it can undoubtedly be read as an act of devotion and commitment to family.

But as I describe, many of my participants articulated broader commitments to their community, both through volunteer work they undertook and through their professional jobs as social workers, nonprofit employees, lawyers, educators, and customer relations specialists. In these roles, their bilingual-bicultural competencies, problem-solving skills cultivated within their families, and intimate knowledge of life in the borderlands are assets. In the increasingly anti-immigrant political climate in which my participants came of age and continue to live, their contributions to their families and communities are only more crucial. Over the decade plus in which I have been observing my participants' lives, I have documented how they understand the constraints that shape the lives of their families and community members and how they have ultimately come to assert agency through their brokering roles.

In the process, I have witnessed the ways in which my participants have navigated boundaries between opposing categories like "immigrant" and "citizen" and "Mexican" and "American" that divide members of their families in both symbolic and practical terms. As Kasinitz et al. (2008, 12) pointed out, members of the second generation must balance between categorizations of foreignness and native-born entitlement and negotiate insider-outsider statuses regularly in their daily lives. In some characterizations, the second generation may be regarded as being caught "between two worlds"; indeed, as Kasinitz et al. (2008, 13) argue, "Having a foot in both worlds may make one unable to sit comfortably in either." Some of my participants have espoused this sentiment at different points in their lives, particularly during adolescence as they sought to make sense of the anti-immigrant sentiment swirling around them.

However, an alternative view of their positionality is that the children of immigrants may be particularly adept at performing the "boundary work" (Lamont 2000; Lamont and Molnár 2002; Park 2005, 63) required to maneuver between these categorizations. The classificatory boundaries that social actors create require that they tease through similarities and differences between them and others in a relational manner (Barth 1969; Lamont and Molnár 2002, 171). My participants' boundary work involves making sense of the seemingly fixed boundaries between binaries like citizen/noncitizen and American/Mexican. Their boundary making challenges these taken-for-granted social categories in not only symbolic but also practical terms. As Fassin (2011, 214) points out, the sociology of boundaries and the anthropology of borders developed as distinct fields out of different intellectual traditions, with the former focused more on social constructs establishing symbolic differences and producing identities, and the latter focused more on territorial limits defining political entities and legal subjects. Yet, he argues, immigrants (and I would argue, their children) "embody the articulation of borders and boundaries," meaning that the two should be more comprehensively linked (215).

In the late 1980s and 1990s, theorizing about border crossings and cultural hybrids became popular as scholarship about the border region proliferated

(Anzaldúa 1987; Rosaldo 1989; Vila 2000). Though border crossing and hybridity are certainly apropos metaphors for these young adults, it is also the case that, as Vila (6, 15) argues, these concepts need to be ethnographically evaluated and situated in the structural conditions border residents encounter (see also Heyman 2017). In the case of my participants, the border and the reinforcement of boundaries of difference that accompany it have a tangible and high-stakes presence in their lives. They literally cross the U.S.-Mexico border, which forces them to confront state practices of categorization and division as they come to understand how people are treated differently based on their status. They also regularly have encounters with agents of the state—Border Patrol and CBP officers—who police these boundaries of difference, sometimes with traumatic results. And indeed, as they have grown and matured, they have developed competencies for contesting these systems of classification and negotiating these encounters.

While brokering these borders has sometimes been challenging for these now-adult children of immigrants, I will demonstrate how they have cultivated a particular ease in shifting back and forth across boundaries and borders (Suárez-Orozco and Suárez-Orozco 2001, 114). Indeed, it is precisely because of their unique subject positions as the citizen children of immigrants that they are able to perform their border-brokering work. Massey and Sánchez (2010, 14) highlight the boundary work performed by natives in creating mechanisms that facilitate or inhibit interactions with immigrants that serve to incorporate or exclude them; I argue that the children of immigrants who occupy this positionality are particularly well situated to perform this border-brokering work. They are active agents in negotiating, constructing, and elaborating their own identities (Massey and Sánchez 2010, 16); however, they are also actively involved in forging belonging for their family and community members. In addition to the ability to mediate these boundaries of difference, these young adults also possess a specialized skill set for negotiating them based on growing up in the borderlands. Thus, the geographic location in which they have come of age has also been incredibly important in shaping their competencies for brokering inclusion.

THE U.S.-MEXICO BORDERLANDS

As Wilson and Donnan (1998, 4) argued two decades ago, "The anthropological study of the everyday lives of border communities is simultaneously the study of the daily life of the state, whose agents there must take an active role in the implementation policy and the intrusion of the state's structures into people's lives." Indeed, state power in border communities has long been a tangible reality, framing the conditions of everyday life for residents of all statuses. In this book, I highlight what it is like to grow up under these conditions, particularly when close family members possess immigration status limitations that render them particularly vulnerable. Even for those who are citizens, like Isabel, the state is still an unmistakable nuisance, impeding their ability to circulate without harassment within their neighborhoods and cross the border freely.

Yet the borderlands not only are characterized by the presence of the state and forces that divide, as policymakers and the popular media insinuate, but they also are a region with deep historical and contemporary interconnections that supersede the state (Alvarez 1991; Heyman 1991; Vélez-Ibañez 1996). For those who are able to cross freely, like Carlos, they allow for the opportunity to embrace community, family, and social life in both places. By highlighting key features of the region as filtered through the life experiences and perspectives of my participants, I seek to portray the complexity of life in the U.S.-Mexico borderlands. Here, I describe the San Diego–Tijuana borderlands, San Diego County, and the barrio where I conducted my initial research, as well as provide a sketch of my participants and their families.

THE SAN DIEGO–TIJUANA BORDERLANDS

The U.S.-Mexico borderlands (also referred to as the border zone or transborder region) describes the geographical zone that encompasses people living on both sides of the territorial boundary between the United States and Mexico. Martínez (1994) identifies the "core" of the U.S.-Mexico borderlands as a corridor of forty-nine U.S. border counties and thirty-six Mexican municipios (municipalities), though his vision of the "greater" borderlands encompasses the U.S. states of Texas, New Mexico, Arizona, and California and the Mexican states of Tamaulipas, Nuevo León, Coahuila, Chihuahua, Sonora, and Baja California (41). Vélez-Ibañez (2017) has recently termed the greater borderlands as the Southwest North American (SWNA) region to underscore its long history of interconnections and the arbitrariness of the international geopolitical boundary. He argues that the SWNA is characterized by its unique ecology of deserts, valleys, rivers, mountain ranges, flora, and fauna; an interdependent political economy based on diverse and complex modes of production; and "cultural bumping," through which peoples from different cultures regularly meet and interact (12, 24). Vila (2000) highlights the wide range of subcultures that interact on both sides of the border, capturing the complexity of identity construction in the borderlands.

In 2010, an estimated fourteen million people lived within border counties and municipios, fairly evenly divided between Mexico (7,304,901) and the United States (7,303,754). In the broader border *area*—100 kilometers / 62.1 miles north and south of the international boundary, as defined by the La Paz Agreement—the population was 31,015,457 (17,048,419 in Mexico and 13,967,038 in the United States; Wilson and Lee 2013, 10). The nearly two-thousand-mile-long U.S.-Mexico border is also dotted by thirteen border *cuates*, or twin cities (Kearney and Knopp 1995). At the westernmost segment of the border, abutting the Pacific Ocean, are the twin cities of San Diego and Tijuana, whose downtowns are less than nineteen miles apart. The San Diego–Tijuana conurbation, or binational metropolis, is one of the largest sets of *cuates*, with five million residents (Williams et al. 2017).

FIGURE 1. The westernmost segment of the U.S.-Mexico border ending in the Pacific Ocean, dividing San Diego (foreground) and Tijuana (the other side of the fences).

The passage of the North American Free Trade Agreement in 1994 more deeply integrated the transborder economy and spurred the flow of commercial goods and people. The binational metropolis has a $230 billion economy and some two million workers, many of whom cross the border daily to commute to work (Williams et al. 2017). Crossers make their way through ports of entry—the physical checkpoints through which cargo and visitors entering the United States pass (Heyman 2004, 303). California has a total of twenty ports of entry, including airports. The San Ysidro Port of Entry, the busiest land border crossing in the Western Hemisphere, sees 120,000 passenger vehicles, 63,000 pedestrians, and 6,000 trucks pass through its gates each day (Williams et al. 2017). A second local port of entry, Otay Mesa, was originally constructed to divert commercial traffic from San Ysidro but has expanded significantly in passenger vehicle and pedestrian traffic. Indeed, many border residents craft dynamic cross-border livelihood strategies, diversifying their economic opportunities (Chávez 2016). Beyond work, residents from both sides are connected through tourism, shopping, health care, education, and family. Márquez and Romo (2008, 1) highlight the uniqueness of the space in which policies and larger structures of power intersect so markedly with family and everyday life.

While San Diego and Tijuana are, in many respects, a contiguous urban zone, the cities are also very distinctly demarcated by the international boundary. The border region has long been shaped by the asymmetrical relationship between the United States and Mexico, forged through warfare; the legal dispossession of land, water, and rights of Native Americans and Mexican frontier people; and processes of capitalist agricultural and industrial development (Heyman 2017, 45–46). The border region illustrates the "contradiction, paradox, difference, and conflict of power and domination in contemporary global capitalism and the nation-state" (Alvarez 1995, 447).

Border crossings are highly regulated at ports of entry operated by the coercive apparatuses of the state (Heyman 2017, 49; Lugo 2000). One of the most salient local inequalities centers on who is able to cross the border. Anyone from the United States with a valid passport can cross into Mexico; however, a more limited set of individuals are able to cross into the United States, stratified by citizenship status, race, class, age, and gender (Chávez 2016; Heyman 2017, 51). As Heyman notes, human mobility at the border is "partially legal and favored, partially illegalized and persecuted" (50). In addition to voluminous authorized border crossings, San Diego was traditionally a principal entry point for unauthorized crossing before Operation Gatekeeper launched in 1994, shifting the migration flow eastward to more remote desert and mountain terrain. In the current policy environment with deportation front and center, Tijuana is now home to many repatriated deportees (Chávez 2016, 15), many of whom formerly lived in Southern California and await visits from those family members who can legally cross.

The highly integrated economies and societies, large volume of border crossers (authorized and otherwise), presence of massive ports of entry, and visible enforcement infrastructure make immigration a particularly salient regional issue. Daily stories about the border saturate local news stations and the local newspaper, the *San Diego Union-Tribune*. The border also has an unmistakable visceral presence the closer you get to it. As you approach it from either of the two major southbound freeways on the U.S. side, you start seeing more of the ubiquitous white-with-green-trim sport utility vehicles circulating, and then hear the sound of helicopters circling above. Just as you are greeted by the enormous Mexican flag waving from across the border in Tijuana, it is impossible not to also notice the three-tiered fences and stadium-style lighting that mar the hillside and divide the cities. Approaching the port of entry itself by freeway, signs warn you that it is the "last USA exit." You can see vehicles being corralled to cross over to Tijuana and glimpse those returning to the United States, waiting in even longer lines. The border is a prominent feature of everyday life in southern San Diego County—and, over time, an increased presence throughout it as well.

SAN DIEGO COUNTY

San Diego County is the southernmost county in California and the state's second-largest in size behind Los Angeles County; in 2016, its population was estimated to be 3,317,749 (United States Census Bureau 2016). The city of San Diego—the county seat—is often referred to as "America's Finest City" due to its abundant sunshine, mild year-round climate, and plethora of beaches, water, and land activities. San Diego also has a strong military presence—seven bases are located throughout the county with some 148,000 employees. Another 146,000 civilians also work for private-sector defense companies in support of the military, a major economic contributor to the regional economy (Griswold del Castillo 2007, 2). Seniors (over the age of sixty-five) also have become an increasingly visible demographic presence in the county, with almost 500,000 living in greater San Diego in 2000 (3–4).

The combination of military personnel and retirees have formed a more conservative political electorate that is less focused on marginalized groups in the county, like Latinxs (Griswold del Castillo 2007, 3; López and Stanton Salazar 2001, 63). Anglos, as they are known locally, have controlled San Diego since 1848 and predominated local power structures (Griswold del Castillo 2007, 5). Since California became part of the United States, Latinxs have been subjected to social and geographic segregation, economic discrimination, and political exclusion (García Bedolla 2005, 26). This historical memory of exclusion remains and continues to affect Latinxs' engagement with the U.S. political system (35). Yet Ortiz (2007, 129) points out that despite this history of formal political exclusion, it would not be accurate to characterize Latinxs in the area as politically apathetic, as they "forged a record of consistent multidimensional activism" in the last few decades of the twentieth century and into the twenty-first century—including very actively during the immigrant rights protests of 2006 and in the present as political debates about increased border enforcement recur.

San Diego is home to several million Mexicans and Chicanas/os, whose descendants founded the city in 1769; yet there has been a tendency to ignore and devalue these origins (Griswold del Castillo 2007, 1). Hispanics/Latinxs compose 33.5 percent of the county population, which is the third-largest concentration of Latinxs in California, following greater Los Angeles and the San Francisco Bay area (López and Stanton-Salazar 2001, 62). Many South Bay cities have well-established Mexican neighborhoods whose origins date back to the Mexican Revolution (1910–1921), when people fled economic and political turmoil (63). Migratory pathways were also well established through the bracero program of the mid-twentieth century, which recruited laborers from west-central Mexican states like Jalisco, Michoacán, Guanajuato, and Zacatecas to work on short-term labor contracts, primarily in agriculture (Runsten 2005, 4). Many of these braceros remained in San Diego after the program ended, and relatives subsequently joined them throughout the remainder of the twentieth century.

After the bracero program ended in 1964, San Diego became a major destination for those migrating from southern and central states (Runsten 2005, 5). Since the 1970s, industries such as agriculture, hospitality, construction, and service drove in-migration to San Diego County from all over Mexico (Kiy and Woodruff 2005, vii). San Diego's proximity to Mexico makes it an attractive settlement choice for people who can and do cross the border frequently, as well as for people who seek the comfort of the Mexican goods and services that predominate. Within the county, Latinxs have primarily settled in barrios in the City of San Diego, South Bay communities like National City and Chula Vista, and North County communities like Escondido, Oceanside, and Vista (Runsten 2005, 34). Many of these communities are underserved in the areas of housing, education, and health services (Kiy and Woodruff 2005, viii).

THE BARRIO

The barrio where I conducted my ethnographic fieldwork in southeast San Diego is one such underserved community, though it is also one of its oldest, with a deep sense of history and pride. As you enter, you do not find the fantastic beaches or stellar scenic views for which San Diego is famous; in fact, industrial buildings block direct views of the ocean and prevent access to the water. In the shadow of the ever-rising and architecturally showy downtown skyline, most houses are modest, consisting of one-story buildings with small yards. Pit bulls

FIGURE 2. A typical home in the southeast San Diego barrio where this project was based.

rather than elaborate alarmed security systems are more likely to protect the property. Nonetheless, most of the houses are meticulously and lovingly kept, some painted with brilliant colors. An interesting mix of older model cars and large new SUVs and trucks coexist side by side. Many vehicles actually have Mexican license plates that read "BC Mex" (Baja California Mexico) or "Frontera BC" (border zone Baja California), indicating that many residents live at least part of the time in Mexico. The barrio is located some fifteen miles north of the U.S.-Mexico border. Weather conditions permitting, you can actually see to the city of Tijuana on the Mexican side.

The barrio is also one of the most quintessentially Mexican neighborhoods in San Diego. Lining the streets are businesses and houses of worship with signs in Spanish. Most of the people walking along the streets are talking in Spanish, and Spanish radio—broadcast from stations on both sides of the border—can be heard booming through the speakers of passing cars. The hub of the neighborhood is a large park where numerous social events take place, ranging from celebrations of Mexican Independence Day to lowrider car shows to protests on social issues like immigration. An unmistakable spirit of Mexican pride is evidenced in brightly colored murals that display the red, white, and green of the Mexican flag and imagery of Aztec warriors and Mexican folk heroes. Many of my participants are proud of their neighborhood; as Mateo noted, "When I tell people where I grew up, they're like, 'Oh man, how was that? Was it rough?' I have a lot of pride in this neighborhood. I love the community and all that it stands for. This is where I feel at home."

Despite its rich history and vibrant character, the neighborhood also faces challenges. Public safety is a concern for residents, with homelessness, drug use, and gang activity making the park and neighborhood somewhat unsafe. Residents also contend with industrialized air pollution, substandard housing, overcrowded schools, and inadequate health care and social services. The median household income of the neighborhood was estimated to around $26,761 in 2010, less than half of the countywide median of nearly $60,000; approximately 41 percent of the population lived below the poverty level (SANDAG 2017). Neighborhood residents are predominantly Hispanic/Latinx (72 percent), with 59 percent of residents aged five and over reporting using Spanish as the primary language at home (SANDAG 2017); fewer Latinxs overall live in the neighborhood than when I started my research in the mid-2000s, owing to the ongoing gentrification of the neighborhood as downtown San Diego has undergone extensive development. Luisa has noted that the barrio is increasingly "losing

FIGURE 3. The barrio, in the shadow of San Diego and encroaching development.

its homey touch" as outsiders move in. Some 27.7 percent of neighborhood residents are children under the age of eighteen (SANDAG 2017). In general, when sociodemographic characteristics are compared to the county overall, the barrio's population is younger (28 percent vs. 23 percent under eighteen), more likely to speak non-English languages at home (62 percent vs. 12 percent), have less than a high school education (40 percent vs. 15 percent), and live in poverty (41 percent vs. 12 percent).

THE PARTICIPANTS

In total, I conducted research in 2005–2006 with fifty-four second-generation young adults and their families. (See appendix A for more detail on my research methods.) Most parents had migrated from Mexico in the 1980s and 1990s and had resided in the United States for ten to twenty years by the time I met them. Most were also long-term residents of the barrio—more than half had lived there for more than ten years at that point. Thus, the families that I worked with had fairly established settlement trajectories. Their initial migration pathways followed fairly established gendered migration patterns (Boehm 2012); the fathers generally had arrived first, joining other family members already working in the United States and moving around for work during their early years. The majority of them were undocumented initially, though many subsequently became LPRs through IRCA in the late 1980s, with some naturalizing thereafter. The mothers arrived later, often joining family members, though not necessarily husbands, as many met their spouses in the United States. Most mothers regularized their statuses later in the 1990s and into the 2000s, though more of them than the fathers remained undocumented. Most of the parents completed their formal schooling in Mexico before immigrating, with middle school as the median level of educational attainment.

Most parents worked in immigrant-heavy industries like construction, landscaping, gardening, and food service. Many of the fathers had been at their jobs for years or even decades, and six had moved into supervisory roles. The majority of their households were also dual worker: 74 percent of mothers (twenty-five) worked outside of the home, in the areas of housekeeping, food service, factory work, and elder care. Despite their fairly established roots in the United States, many families did not report having strong support networks in place; some 38 percent of them reported having no family members living in San Diego outside of their spouses and children and indicated that they did not come into regular contact with anyone from their home communities. The majority were not part of large transnational communities (as discussed in chapter 5); indeed, in some cases, the lack of family presence in San Diego coupled with vulnerable immigration status rendered the family quite isolated (as described in chapter 3).

Though I wanted to understand more about the bigger picture of the parents' lives, my principal focus was on their children, forty-two high school students and twelve program alumni whom I met during my preliminary fieldwork (see appendix B for more information on participants). My participants ranged in age between fourteen and nineteen in 2005–2006. Most were U.S. citizens by birth, though three had been born in Mexico (one a naturalized citizen, one a resident, and one undocumented). The U.S.-born children were all born in California, the vast majority (83 percent) in San Diego. Four of them could be considered -1.5 generation, as they were born in the United States but spent time in their early childhood living in Mexico because of their family's immigration-related and/or economic hardships. Many of their siblings—particularly older ones—were not U.S. born; 21 percent of the families contained children who were born in Mexico but whose statuses ranged from undocumented to naturalized citizens. I also got to know some of my participants' siblings (both program participants and nonparticipants), even if I did not conduct formal research with them. In 2014, I conducted follow-up research with a smaller cohort of thirteen participants, going in greater depth into their adult lives. The book focuses principally on this cohort—such as Isabel, Carlos, and Beto, whom I introduced at the beginning—but also draws from some of the earlier fieldwork. *Border Brokers* follows the lives of these individuals to demonstrate how they have navigated immigration policies and border enforcement practices for themselves and their families over time.

ORGANIZATION OF THE BOOK

Border Brokers advances our understanding of the constraints being faced by the children of immigrants in U.S. society and the agency they assert in navigating those constraints as they mature into adults. The seminal scholarship on the fate of the children of Mexican immigrants made negative prognostications about their likely incorporation pathways and even their commitments to their families. *Border Brokers* contests these predictions by documenting processes over time through which second-generation young adults successfully broker their own belonging and that of their family members as active citizens and engaged community members.

The first chapter of the book lays out the increasingly anti-immigrant sociopolitical context in which these second-generation Mexican young adults came of age. I describe policy developments that have affected them and members of their mixed-status families over the last thirty-plus years, up to and including the current Trump era, with a specific eye toward Mexican immigrants and their children and the changing California context.

Next, in chapter 2, I present findings from the research. I start by looking back to examine how even as teenagers my participants understood categories like citizen and "illegal immigrant," given their complex positionalities within their mixed-status families. I review state categorizations produced by immigration law (i.e., citizen and unauthorized immigrant) as well as dominant discourses on immigration that reify social categories like "illegal aliens." I then describe my participants' own classification system that is more practical and inclusive but nonetheless also reflects internalized exclusionary messages about immigrant illegality. I contextualize these understandings amid the backdrop of immigrant rights protests of 2006, which allowed them to build their knowledge bases, raise their legal consciousness, and blossom into their roles as advocates "representing" their vulnerable family and friends who "didn't have papers."

In chapter 3, I consider how illegality and deportability shaped my participants' childhoods in the U.S.-Mexico borderlands, examining the "repercussive effects" (Comfort 2007) of illegality on their families. "Not having papers" was a clear axis of stratification between U.S. citizen children and their noncitizen family members; yet parents' vulnerable statuses also shaped my participants' lives in marked ways, including limiting their local mobility and transborder travel, fostering social isolation and increasing responsibilities at home, and affecting their well-being. My participants described "living those fears" alongside their immigrant loved ones, demonstrating how they too internalized and embodied these status-related vulnerabilities. My participants also have long been directly subjected to the racialized immigration enforcement practices that undergird the policing of illegality, which I highlight in chapter 4. As citizens, my participants should be insulated from mistreatment by immigration officials while crossing the border and maneuvering within their neighborhoods. However, participants recalled early and ongoing memories of negative encounters with the Border Patrol during which their membership was regularly questioned. These encounters reinforced a racialized form of belonging that had negative effects on them; however, participants have also cultivated strategies of resistance to contest them.

While chapters 2–4 are focused principally on the U.S. side of the border, chapter 5 shifts to my participants' engagement in transborder life in Mexico. Examining participants' transborder trajectories over time, it is clear that they remain actively engaged in transborder life, answering lingering questions about the durability of transborder life for the second generation. Participants whose family members had papers have been able to participate meaningfully in and embrace transborder life; meanwhile, others whose family members did not have papers had much more limited engagement in it. However, for those embedded within divided family units, restrictions on some family members can also *necessitate* participation in transborder life for family members who have papers. As U.S. citizens, young adults like my participants can and do serve as linchpins within these complex transborder family configurations.

Chapter 6 turns more explicitly to these brokering roles. Building on their burgeoning activism in the 2006 protests, participants started brokering on behalf of their families in institutional settings like schools and health-care clinics and even in navigating the state immigration bureaucracy. Now as adults, they recognize the resilience and problem-solving skills they refined within their mixed-status families, skills that have served them well in their adult lives. Some have put their skills to use privately within their own families, while others serve as professional brokers in careers as social workers, activists, and lawyers or by "giving back" to their immigrant communities as EMTs and early-childhood educators.

Border Brokers concludes by considering the constraints that second-generation border brokers continue to face in their efforts to buffer the negative effects of illegality and advocate for inclusion for their immigrant family members and friends. These U.S. citizens of Mexican descent are carrying a significant burden in contending with the fallout of our broken immigration system and grappling with the exclusionary policies that continue to place their families and community members in precarious circumstances. Instead of buffering these immigration policies, I argue that their brokering skills would be put to far better use in facilitating the incorporation of their family and community members. This book thus bolsters the call for comprehensive immigration reform that appropriately and humanely addresses the situations of mixed-status families and the young adults who help hold them together under incredibly trying circumstances.

1

INCREASINGLY ANTI-IMMIGRANT PUBLIC POLICIES AND THEIR IMPACT ON MIXED-STATUS FAMILIES

THE TRAJECTORIES of mixed-status families in U.S. society have been profoundly shaped by the increasingly exclusionary and punitive immigration policies and enforcement practices that emerged during the last thirty years. U.S. immigration policies have always been shaped by an exclusionary impulse, stemming back to the emergence of the United States as a nation-state in the late eighteenth century. The Naturalization Act of 1790 established that citizenship was to be the domain of free white men of good moral character, upholding prevailing racial, gendered, and class-based notions of belonging (Gomberg-Muñoz 2017, 21). By the late nineteenth and early twentieth centuries, the "legal edifice of restriction" was upheld through the "exclusion of Chinese, other Asians, and various classes of undesirable aliens (paupers, criminals, anarchists, and the like)" (Ngai 2004, 3). Immigration policy during this time served to realign and harden racial categories in the law (Haney López 1996; Ngai 2004, 7).

Despite these long-standing exclusionary structures, a new chapter of exclusion started in the 1990s with a series of harsh anti-immigrant policies that were "unusual in their scale and severity," targeting not only undocumented immigrants but also eventually "legal" immigrants and immigrant families as well. As Massey and Sánchez (2010, 2) argue, these punitive policies and practices have "erected needless and counterproductive barriers" to immigrant integration.

One distinguishing feature of this time period is that no large-scale pathway to legalization has opened up for undocumented immigrants since IRCA was passed in 1986. Immigrants who were able to regularize their statuses through IRCA have been able to make gains in employment, housing, mobility, health, and countless other realms of economic, social, and political life in the United States; these gains are evident in the Franco family, both among the parents and the four now-adult children who have found stability and upward mobility. Yet for immigrants who were ineligible for IRCA or arrived after 1986, they and their children have faced tremendous challenges in employment, housing, health, and overall security, as evidenced in the experiences of the Clementes and Garcías.

Many of the estimated eleven to twelve million undocumented immigrants nationwide, like the Clemente and García parents, are long-term residents who have strong family ties in the United States (Schueths and Lawston 2015); of these unauthorized immigrants, some 58 percent are Mexican (Dreby 2015a, 1). Whereas in the past these undocumented immigrants more easily could have demonstrated long-term residence and close family ties in the United States as mechanisms for legalizing their status, these avenues are no longer available (Gomberg-Muñoz 2017). Pathways to legalization are also particularly challenging for Mexicans (DeGenova 2004; Dreby 2015a, 1). These immigrants and their children have thus had to deal intimately with the fallout from the lack of comprehensive immigration reform at the federal level (1). This situation has placed mixed-status families in a position of structural vulnerability, imposing physical and emotional suffering on them in patterned ways (Quesada, Hart, and Bourgois 2011). Indeed, these structural vulnerabilities have only become accentuated over time as enforcement, detention, and deportation have taken hold as the hallmarks of U.S. immigration policy since the 1990s.

Beyond the lack of comprehensive immigration reform, the broader immigration policy context has also become increasingly injurious toward immigrants (of all statuses) and their children. The young adults at the center of this book were born in the late 1980s and early 1990s. During their lifetimes, anti-immigrant sentiment and the racialization of Mexicans have increased markedly, especially in their home state of California, the birthplace of anti-immigrant policies in the 1990s (Pastor 2018), and in their home city of San Diego, one of the primary areas targeted for border enforcement operations during the same period (Nevins 2002). Immigrants and their children have been framed in public rhetoric and media coverage as a threat to U.S. society and culture through popular framing metaphors like "tidal waves" and "battleground" (Chavez 2001, 2008; Massey and Sánchez 2010, 58). Mexicans have been portrayed in public discourse as quintessential "illegal aliens" (Chavez 2008, 3), a term that is particularly infused with racialized difference (DeGenova and Ramos-Zayas 2003, 3). My participants came of age in this stigmatized and racialized policy context in which they and their families have been under attack and have had their social legitimacy constantly questioned (García Bedolla 2005).

These perceptions of immigrants have also increasingly found their way into bills, laws, and state practices that have had very real impacts on the lived realities of these young adults and their families. Though many of the restrictionist policies emerging in the 1990s initially focused on undocumented immigrants, they eventually began to target LPRs, who found the protections of their statuses eroding as well (Massey and Sánchez 2010, 58). Now, the U.S. government is even denying passports to U.S. citizens of Mexican descent in the borderlands under the pretense of "citizenship fraud," undermining the privileges of citizenship and devaluing Latinxs' social membership (Sieff 2018). Instead of focusing on immigrant integration and promoting the "blurring of boundaries between immigrants and natives," Massey and Sánchez argue, "Economic, social, and political conditions have shifted so as to harden categorical divisions between immigrants and natives" (2010, 58). Into the 2000s, public policies ensnared not only undocumented and legal immigrants but also their native-born U.S.-citizen children, having tangible effects on their well-being (Dreby 2015a; Zayas 2015) and further hardening the boundaries of social belonging.

This chapter examines the broader immigration policy context that circumscribes mixed-status families, with particular attention paid to Mexican migration and conditions of everyday life in the U.S.-Mexico borderlands. Specifically, I highlight the public policy initiatives of the last thirty years as a backdrop for understanding the conditions under which my participants came of age. Before examining these more recent policy initiatives, though, I provide a brief background on the preceding century of Mexican immigration to establish the conditions that undergirded the policy developments toward the end of the century. Then, I provide a brief chronology of increasing exclusionism embedded within immigration and immigrant[1] policies (at national, state, and local levels), starting in the 1980s and going decade by decade to the present. I also describe how illegality has increasingly interfaced with public policy as a means of stigmatizing different segments of Mexicans in the United States, including the U.S.-citizen offspring of undocumented immigrants.

THE EARLY TO MID-TWENTIETH CENTURY: THE "REVOLVING DOOR" OF MEXICAN MIGRATION

Mexican migration to the United States has been shaped for more than a century by shifting U.S. immigration policies and practices (Massey, Durand, and Malone 2002). Among the first Mexican "migrants" to the United States were the seventy-five thousand to one hundred thousand Mexicans who found themselves suddenly residing in U.S. territory following the conclusion of the Mexican-American War in 1848, when the Treaty of Guadalupe Hidalgo ceded Mexico's northern province to the United States (DeGenova and Ramos-Zayas 2003; Gomberg-Muñoz 2017, 21). Mexicans began to move to the United States in the late 1800s and early 1900s, fleeing the dictatorship of Porfirio Díaz and the chaos of the Mexican Revolution (Ngai 2004, 52). During this period, U.S. restrictive actions to regulate migratory flows were few and inconsequential. In fact, quite the opposite occurred, as the U.S. government actively recruited Mexicans to fill the labor demand in the establishment of new industries and agriculture in the U.S. Southwest (DeGenova and Ramos-Zayas 2003, 4). Even the U.S. Border Patrol, created in 1924 nominally to prevent the passage of unwanted immigrants, long maintained the "revolving door" policy of the U.S. state (Calavita 1992; Cockcroft 1986; Martin 2002) by selectively enforcing the law depending on the varying labor needs of U.S. employers and occasionally in deference to electoral politics (DeGenova and Ramos-Zayas 2003, 4).

In the first half of the twentieth century, the demand for Mexican migrant labor corresponded to cycles of economic prosperity and turmoil (Carrasco 1997). In times of prosperity, Mexican laborers were welcomed and even encouraged to migrate. In times of economic hardship, however, the United States excluded and even expelled Mexicans. During the Great Depression in the 1920s and 1930s, Mexican laborers were perceived to be a drain on the economy and were sent back to Mexico, often absent due process in expulsion proceedings (194). From 1929 to 1934, the U.S. government forcibly "repatriated" nearly a million Mexicans, including not only Mexican nationals but also U.S. citizens of Mexican descent (Balderrama and Rodríguez 1995).

Following this period of exclusion, the pendulum swung the other way as the U.S. government began actively recruiting Mexicans through the bracero program in response to labor shortages generated by U.S. involvement in World

War II (DeGenova and Ramos-Zayas 2003, 5). The bracero program was a guest worker program that ran from 1942 to 1964. U.S. labor recruiters secured these largely male braceros in rural Mexico; the U.S. government then transported and delivered them directly to U.S. growers and ranchers (Calavita 1992, 1). Throughout the program, some 4.6 million Mexican nationals were admitted (Martin 2002, 1128), working in twenty-four different U.S. states (Calavita 1992, 1). The bracero program shaped the contemporary configuration of Mexican migration today, including establishing the pattern of male-led migration (Boehm 2012). In fact, the program sought out males while subjecting women to restriction or deportation as a means of discouraging permanent settlement and biological reproduction (Golash-Boza and Hondagneu-Sotelo 2013; Gomberg-Muñoz 2017).

As with demands for immigrant labor, the pervasiveness of anti-immigrant sentiment has historically ebbed and flowed with the health of the U.S. economy. During periods of labor shortage, the United States has "enthusiastically welcomed" immigrants (Carrasco 1997, 190). Correspondingly, anti-immigrant sentiment during these periods has been less prevalent, as immigrants are perceived to be productive additions to the economy. Alternatively, during periods of economic stress or labor surplus, immigrants in the United States are "subjected to particular cruelty" and have served as scapegoats for all of the country's woes (190). It is during these periods that anti-immigrant sentiment has been harnessed into new pieces of legislation (Massey and Sánchez 2010, 71–72).

Despite fluctuations in the U.S. economy and corresponding attitudes toward immigrants, a constant demand for Mexican labor has come to transcend these cycles as labor demands have expanded from the agricultural sector to a variety of other industries, including construction, food service, and housekeeping. Guest worker programs actively promoted during otherwise restrictive and anti-immigrant periods provide evidence of the embedded demand for immigrant labor in U.S. society (Chavez 1997). DeGenova and Ramos-Zayas (2003, 6) point out that Mexico in particular has "provided U.S. capitalism with the only 'foreign' migrant labor reserve so sufficiently flexible and tractable that it can neither be fully replaced nor completely excluded under any circumstances." Yet fluctuations in the economy are not the only force animating anti-immigrant sentiment, as a new framing of Mexican immigrants as a threat (Chavez 2008; Massey and Sánchez 2010) also emerged in the second half of the century.

THE 1960S: CHANGES TO THE SYSTEM AND THE PERPETUATION OF "ILLEGAL" IMMIGRATION

The United States entered into a new historical period with regard to immigration policy in 1965 when the Democrat-controlled Congress passed the Immigration and Nationality Act (INA), also known as the Hart-Cellar Act, abolishing the national-origins quota system that favored the admission of nationals from northern and western European countries. The INA, as DeGenova (2006, 71) points out, was an ostensibly egalitarian effort to dismantle the U.S. nation-state's overt racism in its treatment of immigrants. The act established a preference system based on family unification, economic needs, and foreign policy considerations. The INA ultimately ushered in dramatic demographic change as more immigrants from Asia, Africa, and Latin America started migrating to the United States (Kasinitz, Mollenkopf, and Waters 2004, 1).

Despite its apparent liberalizing tendencies, however, the act also sustained the long-standing regime of immigration restriction (Ngai 2004, 13) by imposing restrictions on one group that had not been subject to them before: Mexicans. Before 1965, DeGenova (2006, 69) observes, "There were absolutely no *quantitative* restrictions on 'legal' migration from Mexico at the level of statute, and none had ever existed. There had, literally, never before been any *numerical* quota legislated to limit migration from Mexico." The implementation of this quota for Mexicans thus represented a dramatic shift, and the consequences of the new restrictions weighed disproportionately on Mexico because of its overwhelming numerical preponderance among all immigrants (DeGenova 2006, 72–73). Before 1965, undocumented immigration was virtually nonexistent, as most migrants came as guest workers and permanent immigrants (Massey and Sánchez 2010, 73). But after, countries like Mexico with deep linkages to the United States saw their demand for U.S. visas quickly exceed the supply (Gomberg-Muñoz 2017, 29). Furthermore, the new law's more expansive and apparently liberal provisions for family unification were structured in a manner that made them less easily applicable to or accessible by Mexicans.

The Hart-Cellar Act codified the category of the illegal immigrant as someone who is not formally extended permission to reside and work in the United States; it was instrumental in constructing the "illegal alien" as a legal subject (Ngai 2004). Before its passage, discussion of the topic of "illegal" immigration seldom appeared in legislative debates (DeGenova 2005, 233). Once the Mexican quotas were established, however, some migrants from Mexico were classified as outside of this system and therefore illegal, setting the stage for illegal immigration emerging "as the central problem occupying immigration policy throughout the late twentieth century" (Ngai 2004, 14). DeGenova (2006, 61) points out the fundamental paradox with regard to Mexican migration—although no country has supplied as many migrants as Mexico, practically all of the immigration laws that have appeared since 1965 have sought to impose ever harsher restrictions on it by restructuring their status as "undocumented."

THE 1980S: INCREASING CONCERNS WITH "ILLEGAL" IMMIGRATION

After a period of relative quiet in the 1970s, the next monumental piece of federal legislation to address the nation's increasing concern with "illegal" immigration in the United States was IRCA, which Congress passed and President Ronald Reagan signed into law in 1986. IRCA for the first time made hiring undocumented workers illegal and punishable (Behdad 2005, 20). The act's architects believed that by legalizing scores of undocumented workers, strictly regulating workplaces, and tightening measures to keep out others, undocumented immigrants who were still living and working in the United States without papers would ultimately choose to go back home.

Though IRCA contained sanctions against employers who hired undocumented immigrants, the sanctions were largely symbolic as the employers were essentially immune from penalties due to legal loopholes that protected them from prosecution (Behdad 2004, 21, 190n26). In fact, some components of IRCA were actually proemployer. Responding to employers' multimillion dollar lobbying efforts, IRCA created or strengthened three special guest worker programs (Martin 1999, 147). Rather than punish employers, employer sanctions provisions prompted a "flourishing industry in fraudulent documents" that served to impose additional expense and greater legal liabilities on undocumented immigrants (DeGenova 2006, 77).

IRCA was inclusive in the sense that it granted legal status to undocumented immigrants who could prove that they had entered the United States before January 1, 1982, and had resided in the United States continuously since then. Somewhere between 2.7 and 3.1 million individuals were ultimately able to adjust their immigration status through IRCA (Massey and Sánchez 2010, 73). Mexicans comprised around 70 percent of the total applicant pool, with some states—like California—registering higher statewide percentages (DeGenova 2006, 77). Once immigrants had regularized their status, they were able to petition for additional family members because of family reunification priorities that had been established through the INA (Boehm 2012, 16), thereby extending the benefit of regularization to larger family units.

IRCA unquestionably benefited its recipients and their relatives through subsequent family reunification; however, it also effectively foreclosed legalization options for those who did not qualify or arrived after its passage (DeGenova 2006, 76). Millions of immigrants who were not able to legalize through IRCA were able to find employment despite the newly developed employer sanctions and remained in the United States without proper documentation. No comparable legalization program has been implemented in the three-plus decades since IRCA. However, the changes brought about through IRCA set in motion the large-scale condition of immigrant illegality as it exists in the present (Abrego 2014, 7). In the decade to come, undocumented immigrants came to face new types of legislative attacks as policies embraced a rising Latinx threat narrative (Chavez 2008; Massey and Sánchez 2010, 69).

THE 1990S: HEIGHTENING ANTI-IMMIGRANT SENTIMENT

The 1990s ushered in a new era of heightened anti-immigrant sentiment and unquestionably exclusionary policies, many of which emerged in California. The 1990s were a period of flux in California, during which economic restructuring (toward a global corporate model), a deep economic recession, demographic change, natural disasters, and riots all hit the state hard (García Bedolla 2005, 21; Pastor 2018). During this era, there was "a historically unparalleled level of official and public concern about the U.S. government's ability—or lack thereof—to police the U.S.-Mexico boundary and prevent unauthorized or 'illegal' immigration from Mexico" (Nevins 2002, 2). Public opinion polls from the early 1990s found that a majority of Americans favored tighter immigration restrictions; public sentiment also found political voice as anti-immigration groups became increasingly prominent. Politicians—particularly Republicans—also started making immigration a primary campaign issue (DeLaet 2000, 103).

The concern about immigration found firm footing in California in 1994 when voters passed with an overwhelming majority Proposition 187, a ballot initiative that aimed to restrict undocumented immigrants from accessing health care, education, and other public services and also required that law enforcement authorities, school administrators, and medical workers turn in suspected undocumented immigrants to federal and state authorities (Castañeda 2006, 153). Proposition 187, also known as the Save Our State (SOS) Initiative, was animated by the changing demographics of the state's population; whereas in the past mostly male workers had constituted a temporary low-cost labor force that was born and raised elsewhere, the more recent arrival and settlement of those laborers' wives, offspring, and unmarried sisters made a more notable fiscal impact on the state (Wilson 2000, 192, 196). The increasing presence of females and children fostered a new form of anti-immigrant sentiment that coalesced around their use of public resources and institutions (200). The Proposition 187 campaign also boosted xenophobic attitudes and galvanized anti-immigrant sentiment, particularly against Mexicans (Castañeda 2006, 153). In the next few years, California voters passed two other propositions that targeted immigrant families and played upon xenophobic fears: 1996's Proposition 209, which prohibited affirmative action (effectively restricting college access for Latinx youth from low-performing schools with de facto segregation), and 1998's Proposition 227, which severely limited bilingual instruction for children (García Bedolla 2005, 33).

In part as a response to the imagery of an "out of control border" generated by Proposition 187, Congress vigorously pursued a new strategy involving stronger surveillance and concentration of resources at the U.S.-Mexico border. The "geographical epicenter" of these concerns was San Diego (Nevins 2002, 2). Border enforcement strategies were first developed in the late 1970s / early 1980s through the adaptation of low-intensity conflict (LIC) doctrine techniques (Dunn 1996). LIC doctrine was created to establish social control over civilian populations in Latin American and other "third world" countries through the incremental introduction of force and coordinated efforts between police, paramilitary, and military forces (4). The extension of LIC techniques to the U.S.-Mexico border resulted in its steady militarization throughout the 1980s and early 1990s (3).

The former Immigration and Naturalization Service (INS) launched targeted operations in the form of Operation Blockade in El Paso in 1993 and Operation Gatekeeper in San Diego on October 1, 1994. Gatekeeper aimed to close the revolving door by forcing migrant traffic from dense urban areas to more remote terrain where crossing was less visible through an approach called "prevention through deterrence" (DeLeón 2015; Dunn 2010; Nevins 2002). Gatekeeper targeted what had been the busiest sector of the border through an infusion of resources and technology that included three-tiered steel fencing, stadium-style lighting, motion and sound detectors, infrared night scopes, and

FIGURE 4. The second layer of border fencing and stadium-style lighting in the San Diego sector of the border.

military-style helicopter patrols designed to reach remote locations (Dunn 2010; Inda 2006a, 2006b; Nevins, 2002). Additionally, federal agents became ever more reliant upon databases that monitored individuals' immigration transactions, created automated fingerprint records, consolidated intelligence at ports of entry, and linked immigration information to the national criminal database (Heyman 1999, 433–34).

Despite the dramatics of these operations, border enforcement has been recognized as largely ineffectual (Heyman 1998, 162; Suárez-Orozco 1998, 8), a poor deterrent for migrants (Andreas and Biersteker 2003, 4), and an enormous waste of taxpayer money (Massey, Durand, and Malone 2002, 140). Ultimately, these border operations have violated human rights (Dunn 2010; Fassin 2011); raised the costs and risks associated with crossing, forcing migrants to be ever more dependent on human smugglers; and made crossing more dangerous and deadly (Cornelius 2001; DeLeón 2015; Heyman 2014; Rosas 2006a). Immigrant deaths have skyrocketed, with a marked increase in deaths attributable to environmental causes like dehydration, heat stroke, or hypothermia (Cornelius 2001; Eschbach et al. 1999; Suárez-Orozco 1998). The strategy resulted in 4,600 recorded deaths between 1994 and 2007 (Dunn 2010, 2), though the actual number is estimated to be much higher. In 2007, thought to be a peak year for deaths, an estimated 827 border crossers lost their lives (Inda and Dowling 2013, 19).

In addition to augmenting border enforcement, several major federal laws that impacted mixed-status families also passed in 1996 that were unquestionably a legacy of Proposition 187 (Castañeda 2006; Nevins 2002; Wilson 2000). After Proposition 187, Congress and the White House came under increasing pressure to "get tougher on undocumented immigrants" (Nevins 2002, 87). With the support of the Republican-led Congress, President Clinton signed PRWORA into law in 1996. PRWORA targeted women and families, restricting access to public benefits (Medicaid, Medicare, Child Health Insurance Program [CHIP], income support, and food stamps) exclusively to immigrants residing in the United States under qualified status for five or more years (U.S. Department of Health and Human Services 2012). PRWORA represented the first time that citizenship was explicitly used as a factor in determining eligibility (Cacari Stone, Viruell-Fuentes, and Acevedo-Garcia 2007). PRWORA ultimately had a chilling effect on immigrant families' participation in these programs—even for eligible U.S.-born children of immigrant parents, as their parents did not enroll in services due to confusion regarding eligibility, concerns about the effects of welfare utilization on future opportunities in the

United States (such as family sponsorship or naturalization), reluctance to provide residency information for fear that the information would be accessed by the government, and feelings of suspicion that the programs were government-operated (Hagan et al. 2003).

Also in 1996, Congress passed IIRIRA and AEDPA, which together served to more explicitly link immigration to criminality (Castañeda 2006, 155; Oboler 2006, 16). In addition to further militarizing the border, IIRIRA increased penalties for illegal entry and passport and visa fraud and made more crimes subject to deportation. The law also stripped immigrants of their legal rights, including due process (Oboler 2006, 16), and made even LPRs more vulnerable to deportation (Castañeda 2006, 156). IIRIRA placed petty misdemeanors on the same level of severity as criminal acts and was also retroactive, meaning that an LPR could be deported for an extremely minor crime committed decades prior, regardless of their family ties or subsequent behavior (Gomberg-Muñoz 2017, 31). DeGenova (2006, 79) argues that these extensive provisions "significantly broadened and elaborated the *qualitative* scope of the law's production of 'illegality.'"

Together, the 1996 laws represented a dramatic shift in post–World War II U.S. immigration policy by redefining the social membership of immigrants and drawing an ever-sharpening distinction between citizens and noncitizens (Hagan et al. 2003, 445). The 1996 laws also served to narrow the grounds for the social inclusion of immigrants and their children. By the late 1990s, ideas about undocumented immigrants as undeserving and undesirable were well established, even though "legal immigrants increasingly were being tarred with the same brush" (Massey and Sánchez 2010, 70). Collectively, these policies have not ultimately acted as a deterrent or served to reduce unauthorized immigration; rather, they have led to the entrapment of undocumented immigrants as circular migration has become more costly and dangerous (58). They have also led to the phenomenon of families undergoing temporary or prolonged separations as the border has served to divide them (Abrego 2014; Boehm 2012, 2016; Coutin 2016; Dreby 2012, 2015a).

These policies do not affect children living in immigrant families merely by proxy, either; the children of immigrants are also direct targets. In the late 1990s, conservative members of Congress (especially the House) starting pushing to eliminate birthright citizenship for the children of undocumented immigrants. Proponents argued that citizenship should not be automatically granted to children born to undocumented immigrants, also referred to derogatorily as "anchor babies" (Chavez 2017). Bills to rescind birthright citizenship have been introduced periodically, though they have died without making it to a vote as they failed to gain general support. With each new incarnation, though, they have gained more cosponsors. Eliminating birthright citizenship would entail amending the Constitution; if successful, such an effort would be the first time in its history that the Fourteenth Amendment (the Constitution's basic guarantee of equal citizenship) underwent limitation (Delgado 1997, 320).

Interestingly, in an era committed to restrictive immigration measures, new guest worker proposals began to appear in Congress during the latter half of the 1990s. This contradiction reflects a larger historical pattern: "For almost as long as the United States has sought to enforce general restrictions on immigration, there have been parallel legal attempts to make formal exceptions for the admission of foreign workers" (Briggs 1987, 995). That guest worker proposals can concurrently exist with restrictive immigration and immigrant laws is further evidence that immigrant laborers are welcome, though their families—who represent longer-term settlement—are not. Even Pete Wilson, the ardent anti-immigrant politician who used Proposition 187 as his battle cry in the 1990s, was also traveling to Washington, D.C., in that era to promote a new guest worker program (Chavez 1997, 71).

THE 2000S: LEGISLATIVE IMPASSE AND THE SOLIDIFICATION OF THE DEPORTATION REGIME

At the turn of the new century, the 2000 presidential elections in both the United States and Mexico ushered in another round of discussion about immigration reform. Both newly elected U.S. president George W. Bush and Mexican president Vicente Fox favored a new guest worker program (Martin 2002, 1136–37), and pragmatic discussions about overhauling immigration policies proceeded between key U.S. and Mexican officials through the summer of 2001. Then the September 11 attacks occurred, completely refocusing the attention of the Bush administration. In the aftermath of 9/11, immigration became redefined as a national security issue (Jonas and Tactaquin 2004, 70; Oboler 2006, 15). The fact that the INS was abolished and its functions and units transferred to the newly created DHS in January 2003 strongly emphasized this reorientation (Inda 2006b, 153).

September 11 took place "against a backdrop of growing anti-immigrant hysteria" that had been building over the last decade and was "directed at all foreigners, documented or undocumented" (Massey and Sánchez 2010, 70). In addition to spurring the emergence of "a new and powerful form of patriotism," the events of 9/11 led to the enhanced power of state apparatuses such as the FBI, the CIA, and the INS (Behdad 2005, xi–xii). The "immigrants as a threat to national security" narrative became reified in federal legislation such as the 2001 PATRIOT Act, which authorized federal officials to detain a broad class of noncitizens without legal review and immediate disclosure of specific charges (Coleman 2007, 60). Border surveillance efforts also intensified after 9/11 when the "war on terror" soon became a war on immigrants. Ethno-racial profiling by law enforcement officials came to be seen as an acceptable means of protecting the homeland, despite its detrimental effects on Latinx and African American communities (Hernández 2008).

By the mid-2000s, Congress once again returned to tackling immigration reform. The U.S. Senate debated competing bills, but none ultimately gained the necessary traction to proceed. Meanwhile, the House moved forward with its own bill, H.R. 4437, passed in December 2005. H.R. 4437 proposed to criminalize not only undocumented immigrants but also those who knowingly aided or assisted them in entering or remaining in the United States, and to change being undocumented from a civil offense to a felony. H.R. 4437 was also punitive in other ways, outlined in a laundry list of provisions including further construction of the border fence, having the federal government take custody of undocumented immigrants detained by local authorities, mandating employers to verify their workers' immigration status via an electronic database, increasing the punishment for fraudulent documents, and increasing penalties for employing undocumented workers (Library of Congress 2005).

H.R. 4437's provisions were unabashedly anti-immigrant. The bill was so contentious that it served as the impetus behind the immigrant rights protests of spring 2006, the largest mass mobilizations on any topic since the 1970s, with an estimated 3.5 to 5.1 million participants nationwide (Zavella 2011, ix). Many of these protestors made claims as legitimate political subjects with rights despite not being official members of the nation-state, an important act of symbolic resistance (Inda and Dowling 2013, 27). In addition to immigrants and their family members, participants from unions, religious institutions, immigrant rights organizations, and the general public banded together to engage in public protest (24).

Since 2006, the proimmigrant movement has continued to strengthen (Schueths and Lawston 2015); indeed, undocumented immigrants and their advocates "have not simply accepted the new status quo" (Inda and Dowling 2013, 3). Building on momentum from the immigrant rights protests, undocumented youth and youth living in mixed-status families have propelled the immigration reform agenda forward in important ways (Nicholls 2013). These efforts have coalesced around DREAMer activism, which references different variations of the Development, Relief, and Education for Alien Minors (DREAM) bills introduced in the U.S. House and Senate since 2001. In addition to pushing for a path to permanent residency for those who came undocumented as young children, DREAMers have organized for status and tuition equity for undocumented students and broader efforts like driver's licenses for undocumented immigrants. Due to these young adults' activism, Schueths and Lawston (2015, 5) note, "Immigration stories, many on mixed-status families, have become a noteworthy media staple."

Yet despite this public push for inclusion for immigrants, enforcement as the primary immigration policy strategy only intensified after the nationwide immigrant rights protests as the "deportation regime" (DeGenova and Peutz 2010) solidified. In fact, enforcement is one of the few areas of immigration policymaking that garners bipartisan consensus (Dreby 2015a, 4). One new strategy with regard to immigration enforcement has been the expansion in the space of policing (Inda and Dowling 2013, 3). During the mid-2000s, the border became a "mobile technology," as techniques perfected at the border were exported by the DHS to the U.S. interior (10). Between 2006 and 2008 under President Bush, the DHS escalated its strategy of conducting high-profile workplace and home raids throughout the nation, attracting much attention in the press (Zayas 2015). A March 2010 DHS report demonstrated that officials carrying out these localized raids were not always properly trained; consequently, detainees' civil rights were systematically not protected (Preston 2010).

Children and families were also "collateral damage" (Inda and Dowling 2013, 1) in these raids, as undocumented parents were summarily deported and separated from their citizen children without being able to ensure that they were properly cared for. Children experienced trauma-related reactions after their parents' deportation, including anger, anxiety, the inability to eat or sleep, and withdrawal. Capps and his colleagues have estimated that for every two undocumented immigrants who are deported, one citizen child is directly affected (Capps et al. 2007; Zayas 2015, 19). Using that formula, Zayas calculated that the deportation of 3,165,426 unauthorized immigrants between 2005 and 2013 has ultimately affected 1,582,711 children in mixed-status families (20).

Golash-Boza (2015, 6) argues that this wave of immigration enforcement constitutes a historical period of "mass deportation" because of the sheer numbers of individuals being removed. Obama deported more than two million people in the first five and a half years of his presidency (Golash-Boza 2015, 5). By the end of the decade, some four hundred thousand individuals were being deported annually—double the number at the beginning of the decade (Dreby 2015a, 22). Men of color, who are perceived to be expendable in the economy and unwanted in broader society, are disproportionately deported (Golash-Boza 2015, 5–6). This "gendered racial removal program" (Golash-Boza and Hondagneu-Sotelo 2013) has resulted in many "suddenly single mothers" struggling to be sole providers for their U.S.-born children (Dreby 2015a, 31). Deportation also has hit Mexicans particularly hard, given their overall share of the foreign-born and unauthorized population in the United States; in 2010, 83 percent of those detained, 73 percent of those forcibly removed, and 77 percent of voluntary departures were Mexican (Dreby 2015a, 22).

The raids and stepped-up deportations are evidence of the progressive and aggressive criminalization of unauthorized immigrants (Inda and Dowling 2013, 2). During the Obama era, undocumented immigrants were increasingly subject to a range of criminalizing practices (Coleman 2007, 56). Immigrant detention, the fastest growing form of incarceration, has expanded dramatically (Hernández 2008, 36). The DHS has developed "a vast complex of carceral spaces" for detaining immigrants pending removal, many of them managed by for-profit prison corporations (Inda and Dowling 2013, 16). Of this practice, Inda and Dowling note, "The delegation of immigrant confinement to organizations whose main purpose is to generate profits inevitably produces pressure to increase detentions: the more immigrants confined, the higher the profit. Immigrant bodies have thus become valuable commodities whose worth lies in being placed and kept behind bars" (16).

Another facet of the expanding criminalization of immigrants has been the collaboration between federal immigration and local law enforcement (Coleman 2007; Inda 2006a; Rosas 2006b). In 2006, the DHS initiated the Secure Communities enforcement program that linked the databases of local police agencies with the DHS and FBI, leading to the deportation of many individuals regardless of whether they had ever been charged with or convicted of a crime (Gomberg-Muñoz 2017, 33). In fact, the majority of immigrants detained through Secure

Communities were not dangerous criminals but rather individuals who were stopped by police for traffic-related violations (Guelespe 2015, 203). Some police departments have also made 287(g) agreements with the DHS (stemming from provisions within IIRIRA) that authorize local agencies to assist in federal immigration enforcement efforts (Massey and Sánchez 2010, 75). These linkages to state and local police forces have led to the massive expansion of immigrant detention and a surge in deportations (Menjívar and Kanstroom 2014, 16–17). It has also set the stage for unpredictable and stressful interactions with police and exacerbates the climate of fear in immigrant communities (Dreby 2015a, 25).

In the absence of federal reform, states and localities also started passing exclusionary policies in the mid-2000s (Inda and Dowling 2013, 13; Massey and Sánchez 2010, 76). The National Council of State Legislatures (NCSL) has chronicled the surge in activity in state legislatures spanning a range of policies related to immigration, including education, employment, identification/licenses, health, public benefits, law enforcement, and human trafficking (National Council of State Legislatures 2017). By 2005, there were already some two hundred bills related to immigration, which had tripled by two years later (Massey and Sánchez 2010, 76).

One of the most infamous and draconian state bills was Arizona's Senate Bill (S.B.) 1070 that passed in 2010. S.B. 1070 required state law enforcement to determine an individual's immigration status during a lawful stop, detention, or arrest. Critics argued that it sanctioned ethno-racial profiling (Schueths and Lawston 2015, 4). Though three out of four components of the bill were ultimately struck down by the U.S. Supreme Court and never went into effect, mere passage of the bill immediately impacted the health-seeking patterns and well-being of mixed-status families in the state (Hardy et al. 2012). Copycat bills modeled after S.B. 1070 emerged in Alabama, Georgia, Indiana, South Carolina, and Utah. Meanwhile, 130 different localities had passed or considered ordinances targeting undocumented immigrants between 2006 and 2011 (Varsanyi 2010), demonstrating unprecedented levels of local-level policymaking as well.

THE 2010S: THE DEPORTATION REGIME MATURES AND ENFORCEMENT EXPANDS

Into the beginning of the next decade, the deportation regime (DeGenova and Peutz 2010) had matured. President Obama continued with raids and also increased deportations overall to levels well beyond his predecessors (Zayas 2015, 18), earning him the infamous moniker "deporter in chief." In May 2011, Obama pledged not to target undocumented immigrants with strong family ties, as they did not pose a significant threat to public safety (Schueths and Lawston 2015). Yet in 2012, an all-time high of 643,474 immigrants were apprehended and 477,523 detained (Schueths and Lawston 2015, 6). About 67 percent of the two million undocumented immigrants deported since 2008 were picked up on minor traffic infractions or returning to the United States to join their families (Schueths and Lawston 2015, 7), underscoring the disconnect between official rhetoric and implementation of the policies.

Despite the major uptick in immigrant detention and deportations, Obama provided some relief for young adult DREAMers in the form of DACA, which he established through executive order in June 2012. DACA provides legal work authorization and deferral of deportation for undocumented young adults who arrived before their sixteenth birthday and prior to June 2007. DACA is a provisional status that must be renewed every two years; it is not a permanent pathway toward legalization, meaning that its recipients are still very much in a state of liminal legality (Menjívar 2006). At its four-year anniversary mark in 2016, 741,546 young adults nationwide had been able to benefit from the program (Wong et al. 2016), which has also allowed recipients to secure new jobs and higher wages, obtain driver's licenses, open bank accounts, and get credit cards.

In November 2014, Obama announced the expansion of DACA to increase the age cap and lengthen the renewal period from two to four years. He also announced the Deferred Action for Parental Accountability (DAPA) program, which would provide immigrants who are parents of U.S. citizens or LPRs work authorization for three years; eligibility criteria for DAPA included continuous presence in the United States for a minimum of five years and passing a background check. DAPA would have gone even further in improving the circumstances of mixed-status families, with some 3.7 million undocumented immigrants thought to be eligible (Migration Policy Institute 2015). However, DAPA faced a legal challenge when a federal judge in Texas issued an injunction on it in February 2015; in June 2016, the U.S. Supreme Court deadlocked on the case, leaving in place the lower court's injunction and ending the executive order that would have most comprehensively addressed the plight of mixed-status families, albeit not permanently.

As Donald Trump assumed the presidency in January 2017, he was on the record as opposing DACA and threatening to eliminate it. In his announcement about DACA on its five-year anniversary in June 2017, Trump announced the program would remain, though he simultaneously released a memo eliminating DAPA, leaving in limbo the millions of undocumented immigrants who might have been able to benefit from it. Changing course completely, on September 5, 2017, President Trump announced that he had decided to rescind DACA, leaving the fate of its nearly eight hundred thousand recipients uncertain. By rescinding the program, he is also undercutting the economic, social, and political contributions these young adults were making to U.S. society.

Beyond ending DACA, Trump has made mixed-status families ever more vulnerable. During the initial six months of Trump's presidency, he fulfilled his campaign promise to create a deportation force that would elevate removals to unprecedented levels. Specifically, he has expanded enforcement targets, sharpened enforcement tools, widened enforcement locations, and triggered pervasive fear of deportation and separation among families (Murray 2017). The biggest change is the elimination of the enforcement priorities from the Obama administration that focused on those with criminal backgrounds as a means of managing limited financial resources and logistical challenges; ICE is now instructed to arrest any individual they encounter (Murray 2017), which has made even those with no criminal records targets. Many individuals who have been ensnared are "collateral" victims, meaning that they were simply in the wrong place at the wrong time. Others are being detained and deported when they attend their regular immigration check-ins, a marked shift in practice from the Obama era. Beyond that, ICE is detaining people at "sensitive" locations—near schools, churches, and even courthouses. The Trump administration is also targeting LPRs more aggressively and even proposing to denaturalize (or revoke the citizenship) of naturalized citizens—an unprecedented move (Miroff 2018). Indeed, even native-born U.S. citizens of Mexican descent in the borderlands are also being targeted by the government for alleged "citizenship fraud" and denied passports (Sieff 2018).

Trump also quickly issued two executive orders related to enforcement once he took office: one focused on interior enforcement, calling for massive expansion of enforcement targets, encouraging states and localities to enforce federal laws, and reviving the controversial Secure Communities program (American Immigration Council 2017b); a second order on border security includes expensive plans to further militarize the border, curtail due process, expand detention and enforcement, and deny access to humanitarian protection (American Immigration Council 2017a). Trump has sought—and secured—major funding from Congress for his "super-sized" enforcement budget to pay for a border wall, additional detention beds, thousands of new enforcement agents, immigration judges, and U.S. attorneys to prosecute immigrants (Breisblatt 2017). Trump has also targeted "sanctuary cities" that fail to comply with information sharing between local police and immigration enforcement agencies, threatening to withhold federal funding from them. Yet interestingly, given that it was the birthplace of anti-immigrant policymaking in the 1990s, California has emerged as an important "state of resistance" (Pastor 2018), declaring itself a sanctuary state and passing other measures supportive of immigrants. Indeed, the state is now known as being one of the more progressive local contexts of reception nationwide.

In addition to his enforcement priorities, Trump has advocated for changes in the legal immigration system by calling for reducing levels of legal immigration by half by creating a "merit-based" system, ending the Diversity Immigration Visa Program, and curtailing family reunification, which has been a cornerstone of immigration policy since the 1965 INA. Indeed, he has converted the term "chain migration" (which had previously been a more neutral academic term describing migrant settlement processes) into a negative term undergirded by a threat narrative of extended family members easily accessing the legal immigration system despite this portrayal not being grounded in reality. He has proposed to restrict citizens and residents to sponsoring only spouses and minor children, removing pathways for siblings and adult children.

Collectively, President Trump's actions regarding immigration signal that he is aggressively targeting **all** immigrants (and, by proxy, their children and families) through an enforcement approach that builds on, and is ultimately the culmination of, thirty years of increasingly exclusionary immigration policymaking. His attacks against immigrants have resulted in a nonstop stream of stories about immigrants who have been harassed, detained, and deported, making it clear that no one is immune. Indeed, the culture of fear that these policies promote constitutes a grave public health concern, as Dreby (2015a, 9) noted, of U.S. enforcement approaches even before Trump assumed the presidency.

CONCLUSION

Over the last three decades, the "repressive power of the state" has been directed at immigrants of all statuses and their children; as Massey and Sánchez (2010, 76–78) have noted, "In a very real way . . . the United States now increasingly looks like a police state to immigrants, whatever their documentation." The heavy policing of immigrant communities has already had a tremendous and deleterious impact (Inda and Dowling 2013, 3), causing great harm and suffering among immigrants and their children alike (Schueths and Lawston 2015, xv; Zayas 2015, 17).

As comprehensive immigration reform has remained elusive and continues to be vociferously debated, children in mixed-status families are coming of age within a policy milieu that is antagonistic to them and their families and has consequences on their health and well-being. Scholars have been carefully documenting the effects of anti-immigrant policies on children within mixed-status families (Dreby 2012, 2015a; Schueths and Lawston 2015, xv; Zayas 2015, 17), and the popular media have started covering these stories with much greater frequency and sensitivity. Still, we know much less about how these policy developments have affected these children of immigrants as they have come of age and transitioned into adulthood.

My participants' experiences with immigration policies and enforcement practices provide these insights and are instructive in contextualizing the collective impact of thirty years of anti-immigrant policymaking at federal, state, and local levels. Border enforcement has formed the centerpiece of U.S. immigration policy for decades (Dunn 2010). However, as enforcement operations continue to expand to the U.S. interior, it is of growing importance to examine the effects of these activities on local populations—both immigrant and nonimmigrant. Because these enforcement efforts have been operating in border communities for two decades, they provide an important site from which to observe and theorize about the consequences of this immigration surveillance regime on local populations, including U.S. citizens.

In making sense of the legacies of Proposition 187 in California, Gonzales (2009, 37) refers to the "Proposition 187 generation" as a cohort of individuals whose consciousness was profoundly shaped by the policy context of the mid-1990s; García Bedolla (2005) similarly noted the imprint that Proposition 187 had on California youth's political engagement. Members of the Proposition 187 generation went on to play a role in organizing the mobilizations of 2006 as adults (Bloemraad, Voss, and Lee 2011, 16). Though my participants are younger, their lived experiences have been profoundly shaped by building anti-immigrant sentiment and the resulting policies that have framed their lives. In a similar vein, they might aptly be described as the "H.R. 4437 generation," whose political and social impact is still registering today.

As enforcement has become the cornerstone of U.S. immigration policy spanning both periods, my participants have been living under this repressive state power for literally as long as they remember. Thus I believe their generation could also aptly be characterized as the Gatekeeper generation. In the chapters to come, I consider the impact of the increasingly anti-immigrant political context on the lives of this H.R. 4437 and Gatekeeper generation. Foregrounding the experiences of these young adults, I highlight the negative effects of illegality, deportability, and racialized enforcement on their lives in both the United States and in Mexico. However, as I chronicle developments in their lives over time, I also highlight the critical roles that they have assumed in buffering the effects of these immigration policies and enforcement practices.

2

CONCEPTUALIZING CITIZENSHIP AND ILLEGALITY

I HAD BEEN conducting fieldwork at the center for nearly eight months when the first of the immigrant rights protests, the *mega marcha*, took place in Los Angeles on Saturday, March 25, 2006. Until they heard about the L.A. march, most of my participants were not aware of the impetus behind the protest—the passage of U.S. House of Representatives Bill 4437, which made "illegal U.S. presence" an aggravated felony and, among other provisions, made it a crime for anyone to assist an unauthorized immigrant in remaining in the United States. During the entire last week of March, thousands of teenagers throughout San Diego County—including many of my participants—joined the immigrant rights movement by participating in walkouts and protests that they helped to organize on social media and orchestrate locally, particularly in the large public park in their neighborhood. The week of protests culminated on Friday, March 31, which was fittingly César Chávez's birthday.

I was, needless to say, extremely eager to hear the teens' reflections on the protests. In the preceding months, I had been conducting a range of research activities in order to comprehend how they made sense of what it meant to

---

Parts of this chapter were first published in Christina M. Getrich, "Negotiating Boundaries of Social Belonging: Second-Generation Mexican Youth and the Immigrant Rights Protests of 2006," *American Behavioral Scientist* (vol. 54, no. 4), pp. 533–56. Copyright © 2008 by Sage Publications. Reprinted by permission of SAGE Publications (http://journals.sagepub.com/doi/abs/10.1177/0002764208324605).

FIGURE 5. A young protestor demonstrates his Mexican and American heritage and pride during the immigrant rights protests of 2006.

live in mixed-status families. Although these activities were informative, our discussions were fairly abstract, especially for younger participants who were just starting to fully understand the implications of immigration status. The immigrant rights protests brought the topics I had been researching to the fore and animated them, with the teens now framing the discussions from their own vantage points. Eager to express their perspectives on what had transpired, they held strong and complex opinions. Local newspapers called the immigrant rights protests a "teachable moment" for local school-aged youth; for me, they were turning out to be an immensely fortuitous "researchable moment."

When I arrived at the center on the Monday following the week of protests, they dominated conversation. I was particularly eager to talk to Paulina Santos, and I was glad to see that she was there since spring break at her school fell during that week. Paulina was one of the teenagers I knew best at that point; from the beginning of my fieldwork, she had been very friendly and engaging. She was not at all shy about asking me for help with whatever she was working on—or shy about anything else, for that matter. Paulina was extremely outspoken and confident in her opinions; she is extremely close with her mother, who nurtured these tendencies in her daughter. Based on previous conversations I'd had with Paulina about issues related to social justice, I was fairly certain she would have felt compelled to participate.

As I suspected, she had been active in protest activities the previous week. Hearing about the protests from friends on the main social media platform of that time, MySpace, she said, "I just knew that I wanted to go. What motivated me to go was *mi familia* [my family]. I have some, I guess you would say, illegal family members that work here. They don't have their papers, but I don't think they're criminals for being here. They're working and they're helping out the U.S. and I don't think that's right. That really hit me hard." Although Paulina's parents "had their papers"[1]—her mother was a citizen and her father a resident at that point—she identified strongly with members of her extended family who did not. Ironically, though she wanted to protest to represent her family, her mother "didn't want me to go. She said it was dangerous, and that she didn't want to see me arrested on TV. I told my mom, 'I understand your point,' but I still went." I asked what her mother said when she told her she had participated in the protests. She laughed and said, "Oh, she never found out."

Paulina was also concerned for her friends whose parents' status was less secure than hers, reflecting, "It got me thinking. My parents are Mexican, but

I'm lucky now because they have papers. I have friends at school who were born here and are American citizens, but their parents aren't. So what's going to happen to their parents? Is the government going to take them away? Are they going to kick them out? Are my friends going to be without parents?" Indeed, Paulina was working through the impact that the law would have had on her extended family and her friends' families. Paulina also realized that the law would impact her directly, though, saying, "I also heard something about how, if later on the laws do pass, that we will be considered criminals for hanging out with people who don't have papers, like if we're caught with them. And I'm not a criminal. I'm not gonna go around and be like, 'Hey, I need to check your papers before I'm your friend!' You don't do that!"

The question of who deserves to be present and claim membership in the United States emerged as a key topic in the nationwide immigrant rights protests in the spring of 2006. The protests highlighted conflicting systems for classifying immigrants' social belonging. Paulina's commentary on the protests indexed three such systems: (1) formal state categorizations, (2) social discourses about immigrants, and (3) second-generation young adults' cognitive maps of social membership. First, she contested the proposed bill and the shift in legal classifications that it would create (unauthorized immigrants and those who associated with them being felons). Second, Paulina critiqued dominant discourses about immigrant illegality and purported criminality that had been applied to her loved ones, even though, in her perception, they actually help the United States. Third, she revealed the teens' manner of distinguishing between those who have papers and those who do not.

The first two systems clashed with my teenaged participants' notions of social belonging, developed and developing in relation to the lived experiences of members of their families and friends. In this chapter, I scrutinize these different systems of immigrant classification to demonstrate how the teens situated belonging within the context of their mixed-status social worlds. To do so, I first examine the prevailing classification systems to which they are responding—what I have labeled as the *legal/formal* and *social/informal* classification systems (Getrich 2008), building on Coutin (2000) and Heyman (2001). This distinction also echoes DeGenova's (2002) elaboration of illegality as both a juridical status and a sociopolitical condition. I lay out the prevailing state categorizations produced by immigration law and then examine how these state categorizations also intersect with a set of less formalized—but nonetheless hegemonic—constructs of immigrant illegality predominant in U.S. society.

I then turn to participants' own classification system for reordering these categories. I show that they reinscribed state categorizations to better match the realities of their lives, drawing a more practical distinction between members of their social circles who have papers and don't have papers. The teens' boundaries of belonging were generally more inclusive and not limited to formal state categories. However, I also highlight how they simultaneously and paradoxically reproduced the illegality category at other points by defensively asserting their own "U.S. citizenship identity" (Ramos-Zayas 2003, 2004). I argue that they developed multiple—and, in some cases, competing—notions of inclusion and exclusion through which they teased out layers of similarity and "otherness" with regard to immigrants. The teens' subjectivities indeed bore the imprint of both of these positionings. I then return to the 2006 immigrant right protests specifically by examining the messages the teens sought to articulate about social belonging and the ways in which the protests shaped their burgeoning brokering skills in the process. This chapter is largely situated in the mid-2000s, during the immigrant rights protests and my fieldwork with participants when they were teenagers. Before tracing how these categories have constrained, followed, and targeted them and their family members over the ensuing decade and across borders, which I do in subsequent chapters, it is first necessary to understand their foundational conceptualizations of belonging.

Most examinations of citizenship have focused on adults. Inasmuch as they have been included in discussions of citizenship, youth have been portrayed as holding "an ill-defined partial membership" or "semi-citizenship" (Cohen 2005, 221) typically framed relative to their parents and characterized as a relation of legal and social dependency (Bulmer and Rees 1996; Cockburn 1998; Leiter, McDonald, and Jacobson 2006). Children are relegated to this position of partial membership because they are not yet seen as fully rational beings and are thought to be deficient in wisdom due to their lack of life experience (Roche 1999, 476–77). Cockburn (1998, 99) argues that children are thought to be "almost everything that the non-citizen is: they are irrational, incapable, undeveloped or dependent and are defined in terms of what they are not, that is, adult, responsible, rational, and autonomous."

Because they are perceived as "citizens-in-waiting rather than citizens in their own right" (Osler and Starkey 2003, 247), children lack independent representation or a voice in politics. Accordingly, "their interests fail to be understood because the adults who do represent them conflate, or substitute, their own views for those of the children" (Cohen 2005, 221). To remedy this omission, some scholars have called for the greater inclusion of children in examinations of citizenship. Cooks and Epstein (2000, 10) correctly point out that "there has been very little research on young peoples' understanding of citizenship" from their point of view. Roche (1999, 479) believes that including children in discussions of citizenship "is simply a request that children be seen as members of society too, with a legitimate and valuable voice and perspective."

Few scholars have investigated how citizenship is understood and experienced by immigrant or second-generation youth (Ong 2003; Maira 2009; Park 2005) and Latinx youth in particular (Aparicio 2006, 2007; Benmayor 2002). Scholars have also only started examining how children in immigrant families cultivate legal consciousness in a manner distinct from their parents (Abrego 2011) and understand the complex family structures in which they live (Abrego 2014, 2016; Boehm 2012; Dreby 2012, 2015a). This chapter furthers this discussion by considering influences that have shaped children in mixed-status families' understandings of citizenship and demonstrating how they articulated their own conceptualizations of belonging during the immigrant rights protests of 2006 and beyond.

PREDOMINANT SYSTEMS OF CLASSIFICATION

Given that categories such as *citizen* and *illegal immigrant* are socially, culturally, and politically constructed (Chavez 2008), it is important to interrogate their origin and application, which have come to feature so strongly in debates about immigration (Abrego 2011, 342; DeGenova 2002; Menjívar and Kanstroom 2014, 5). These categories were originally produced by the legal system (DeGenova 2002, 422; Ngai 2004; Rosas 2006a, 404) and encapsulate the relationship of individuals to the state. They are directly enacted by the state through formal processes and on-the-ground interactions with representatives of the state (e.g., immigration officials, judges, and lawyers) who "depict everyone as having an immigration status of one sort or another." The assignation of immigration status stems from a "nation-state model of citizenship, according to which an individual's relationship to a state confers rights and responsibilities" (Coutin 2000, 51).

It is important to "de-naturalize the reification" of these categories and deconstruct their taken-for-grantedness, as DeGenova (2002) and others (Boehm 2012; Chavez 2008; Coutin 2000; Willen 2007) have persuasively argued. It is therefore important to understand how those whose lives are profoundly shaped by these categories understand, interpret, reinscribe, and contest them. To do so, I start out by reviewing the first two classification systems Paulina indexed in her commentary on the protests, describing these predominant systems of classification as legal/formal and social/informal, merging distinctions elaborated by Coutin (2000) between *legal* and *social* and by Heyman (2001) between *formal* and *informal*; both sets of terminology capture important elements of classification.

LEGAL/FORMAL CLASSIFICATIONS

Current U.S. immigration law contains four major classification categories for individuals residing within the territorial borders of the U.S. nation-state: *citizens, lawful permanent residents, nonimmigrants,* and *unauthorized immigrants.* The first classification category encompasses individuals born in the United States or its outlying possessions, those whose U.S. citizen parents were abroad at the time of birth (and meet specific requirements), and those who naturalize (USCIS 2016c). All three have full access to all of the constitutional rights, duties, and obligations associated with nation-state citizenship, such as voting, jury duty, and paying taxes.

Lawful permanent residents (LPRs) are a second category of individuals to whom the state grants official authorization to live and work within the United States. Also referred to by USCIS as *permanent resident aliens*, LPRs are granted residence and work authorization and issued green cards (USCIS 2016b).[2] Legal immigration—as it is more commonly referred to in social/informal classification—operates through a system of quotas and preferences established by the Immigration Act of 1990 (Heyman 2001). Individuals apply for residency through qualified family members (per a system of preference categories), by falling under specific employment categories, or by being granted refugee status or asylum (USCIS 2014a). Other smaller mechanisms to gain residency exist, such as the Diversity Immigrant Visa and such humanitarian programs as the Battered Spouse or Child (through the Violence Against Women Act) and Victim of Trafficking programs (USCIS 2014a). Despite the common trope that immigrants should just "get in line" and "do it the right way" by immigrating "legally," pathways for adjusting one's status are limited.

The third formal category of classification—*nonimmigrants*—consists of individuals who are foreign nationals entering the United States temporarily and for a specific purpose, such as working in a specialty job, studying, or visiting; they are issued nonimmigrant visas, but their visas are more restricted and they are expected to leave at the end of a designated time period (USCIS 2016d). This category includes those who come under temporary guest worker programs, such as the H-2 visa program for "low-skilled" seasonal agricultural (H-2A) and nonagricultural (H-2B) workers. The category also encompasses nonimmigrant visitors who are granted permission to enter the United States for a range of purposes including business, tourism, medical treatment, international cultural exchange programs, academic studies and/or language training programs, or reunion with a fiancé (USCIS 2016d).

The fourth category of people produced by immigration law, *unauthorized immigrants*, reside within the United States without permission from the government by entering the country extralegally, overstaying their visas, or having their legal status revoked while in the United States (Coutin 2000). Unauthorized immigrants—also referred to by DHS as *illegal aliens*—pose a challenge to the nation-state model of citizenship because they are present within the territorial boundaries of the nation-state but not deemed official members of the national body. Illegality is a condition that is inseparable from citizenship (DeGenova 2002, 436; Menjívar and Kanstroom 2014, 9); as Coutin (2000, 50) argues, "Official law produces illegality by demarcating the legal." The enforcement wing of the DHS monitors unauthorized immigrants by forbidding them from entering the United States or, at their discretion, by arresting them, jailing them, trying them in court, and removing/deporting them. As immigration and criminal law have converged in the 2000s, removals can take different forms, including expedited removal (bypassing legal proceedings) and removal through judicial processes (Boehm 2016, 9). Removals take place at the border or within the U.S. interior, and deportations may take place with or without detention preceding them (9). Though these actions are taken against particular individuals, the chaos of removal is also felt by families and kinship networks that get unraveled (11).

Despite the existence of these categories, the history of immigration lawmaking is characterized by "constitutive restlessness and relative incoherence of state strategies, tactics, and compromises that nation-states implement at particular historical moments" (DeGenova 2002, 425). This incoherence is reflected in several categorizations that are "in-between" statuses whose holders exist in a state of "legal liminality" (Menjívar 2006; Menjívar and Kanstroom 2014, 9). One such categorization, Temporary Protected Status (TPS), is a form of administrative relief that allows otherwise undocumented immigrants to reside and work in the United States for eighteen-month intervals. The category came into being in 1990 in response to organizing by Salvadoran migrants, faith-based organizations, and immigrant rights groups. It is a temporary status without a path towards legalization, which leaves recipients perpetually anxious about the program's future (Abrego 2014, 15).

DACA is another more recent legally liminal category. DACA is a form of prosecutorial discretion established through an executive order issued by President Obama in 2012. DACA emerged in part in response to advocacy by immigrant youth and immigrant rights groups after the immigrant rights protests of 2006 (Nicholls 2013). DACA provides legal work authorization to its recipients and defers deportation for a period of two years. It likewise does not provide recipients with a more permanent path toward legalization or access to public health benefits or the ability to travel freely across international borders. Both TPS and DACA have been slated for termination by the Trump administration, meaning that recipients' futures are uncertain and they may find themselves undocumented again.

Coutin (2016, 49) argues that immigration status is often erroneously depicted as an aspect of person rather than a product of policies and histories, as changes to the TPS and DACA programs underscore. State immigration categorizations also shift as individuals gain or lose statuses and move between categories. IRCA, for instance, converted 2.7 million previously unauthorized immigrants—including the parents of many of my participants—into residents. This change of status had important implications for these individuals' social, economic, and political integration into U.S. society, and has, in fact, positively shaped their citizen children's lives, as the life trajectories of my participants whose parents have papers demonstrate.

These state categorizations are not merely legal distinctions; they also demarcate differential levels of social belonging in U.S. society. DeGenova (2002, 439) argues that "immigration law constructs, differentiates, and ranks various categories of 'aliens'"; indeed, the government's choice of terminology in using "alien" clearly reflects differential belonging. Aleinikoff (1997) likened this ranking process to the inscription of circles of membership, with citizens at the core and all other categories on the outside, and observed that this circle tightened in the anti-immigrant climate of the mid-1990s. Subsequent to the passage of the immigration and welfare reform laws in 1996, noncitizens experienced a deterioration in their protection from the law, an expansion of who is deemed to be potentially deportable, a decline in their ability to access social benefits, and an overall devaluation of their belonging to the nation-state. In the process, even LPRs' status has become less "permanent."

Increasingly, citizens are the only category whose membership is secure. Because of the hardening of the citizen boundary, eligible immigrants started naturalizing as a strategy to secure their legal status more broadly and to preserve their ability to remain in the United States, access benefits, and return to their home countries with ease (DeGenova 2006, 67; Menjívar 2006; Oboler 2006, 16). However, even the most protected form of status—birthright citizenship—is regularly contested for the children of immigrants in the political realm (Chavez 2008, 2017). Indeed, eliminating it would require changing the U.S. Constitution (Chavez 2017).

SOCIAL/INFORMAL CLASSIFICATIONS

Illegality is produced not only within the legal/formal realm of state categorizations but also in the social/informal realm (Chavez 2008; DeGenova 2006), where it has taken on a life of its own since the 1980s. As Kearney (2004, 134) notes, "Formal, legal identities coexist and interact in complex ways with informal popular patterns of sociocultural classification." These two realms are, in fact, deeply interconnected and mutually reinforcing (DeGenova 2002). The social/informal category of *illegal immigrants* may have its origin in the state's formal system of classification—as a foil to legal immigrants who are formally authorized to live and work in the United States. However, illegality has subsequently become redefined and reified via discourses circulating on the topic of immigration. Discourse, Nevins (2002, 162) argues, is "one of the most important ways in which social actors construct and reproduce social boundaries" by "establishing binary oppositions between 'us' and 'them'" (see also Chavez 2008).

Knowledge about immigration and the characteristics of immigrants is created, legitimized, and reproduced both from the state and within the realm of civil society, and it is reinforced through such entities as schools, churches, and the mass media (Rouse 1995, 362). Indeed, the media—through outlets such as newspapers (Coutin and Chock 1997; Nevins 2002), magazines (Chavez 2001, 2008), television programs (Tsuda 2003), the internet (Chavez 2008), and, increasingly, social media (Sunstein 2018)—are a primary site for locating such discourses. As Nevins (2002, 119) points out, the media are "a highly significant source of information about society and politics for the general population."

The media reflects the sentiments of the general population but also serves a role in creating knowledge about immigrant illegality that comes to be taken for granted as true (Chavez 2001, 2008; Foucault 1980; Gramsci 1971). Further, the media also serves a role in setting the agenda of the public debate (Nevins 2002, 119), as these discourses get produced in legislation at the federal, state, and local levels.

Contemporary discourses about immigration found in the media and public policies highlight social/informal categories of classification. The most predominant social/informal category is that of the illegal immigrant, which is widely deployed and "often used liberally and carelessly in an uncritical fashion" (Menjívar and Kanstroom 2014, 4). Nevins (2002, 96) points out that the "rise of the illegal as a discursive category is a relatively recent development," chronicling the rise of the use of the term after the 1950s. He concludes that the "illegal" label has been "increasingly employed" to describe unauthorized migrants "to the point where, today, it is almost exclusively the term of choice" (96). Despite its commonplace usage, Kearney (2004, 134) notes that the false application of the "illegal" folk category actually "defies the legal principle of a presumption of innocence prior to the proving of guilt." Thus the assignation of the "illegal" label actually falls outside U.S. notions of legal justice.

Chavez (2008) has compellingly articulated the "threat narratives" that animate illegality: invasion and reconquest, associations with criminality, a supposed unwillingness to learn English and assimilate, the purported theft of American jobs, and the overburdening of social services and health care. Nagengast (1998, 38) points out that immigrants have been demonized through "subtle and not-so-subtle forms of symbolic violence." In the post-9/11 social milieu, connections between national security and immigration have intensified (Oboler 2006, 15). Whatever the underlying logic or threat narrative, immigration has been characterized as a problem that ultimately needs to be solved. Hegemonic constructions of the "immigration problem" or, in even more alarmist terms, "the immigration crisis" (DeGenova 2005, 5) obscure the manifold economic and social contributions that immigrants make to U.S. society.

Another closely associated category is *illegal alien*, an individual who is beyond illicit and is unmistakably located squarely outside of the law and the U.S. imagined community (Chavez 2008). Ngai (2004, xix) points out that the term is a historical one used to refer to legal subjects, though today it carries other pejorative connotations. Chavez (2001, 90–91) examines the rise to prominence of the term *illegal alien* during the 1970s as reflected in magazine covers, highlighting how the "illegal alien" came to be constructed as "the morally questionable Other." Yet another related category, the *anchor baby*, highlights that stigmatization surrounding illegality extends beyond the immigrant generation. Chavez (2017, 3) examines the rise of the term *anchor baby*, finding that it first appeared in the 1980s in neutral academic prose that eventually took an alarmist turn in the early 2000s. The term is now regularly deployed in political rhetoric to refer disparagingly to a child born to a noncitizen mother in a country that grants birthright citizenship as a mechanism for improving the mother's or other relatives' chance of securing citizenship (Chavez 2017, 5).

These categories have become commonplace ways of referring to immigrants—even without specific knowledge about the legal status of the individuals in question. Thus, over time these categories stigmatize anyone who is (accurately or inaccurately) thought to be undocumented, including legally racialized ethnic groups like Asians and Latinxs (Chavez 2008, 24; Flores 1997). These categories preserve hegemonic views of "the nation" (Chavez 2008), which is implicitly white and English speaking. Within these formations, immigrants are not symbolically valued as members of U.S. society for reasons beyond their ostensible illegal behavior; indeed, they are viewed as "a threat to the social fabric of the United States" (Nevins 2002, 120). Accordingly, discourses in the popular media describe immigration with metaphors of war and natural disaster, viewing it as an "invasion" or a "flood" (Chavez 2001).

Predominant discourses frame the immigration debate between "us" (the lawful citizenry of the United States) and "them" (the immigrant interlopers). However, the deployment of the categories *illegal immigrant* and *illegal alien* takes the discussion about illegality out of the realm of the legal system, broadening and racializing boundaries of social exclusion. Through social/informal categories such as *illegal immigrant*, *illegal alien*, and *anchor baby*, boundaries of social membership have further excluded people of color more broadly and unquestionably people of Mexican descent in particular. As Ngai (2004, 2) points out, "Race and illegal status remain closely related." Within the social/informal classification scheme, even native-born U.S. citizens may be excluded because they do not conform to a unitary vision of the nation, ultimately rendering them "alien citizens" who, despite their birth in the United States, "are presumed to be foreign by the mainstream of American culture and, at times, by the state" (2; see also Flores-González 2017).

At the same time, however, these categories are regularly contested by people who are targeted by them. In fact, due to the ongoing efforts of immigrant rights groups and supporters, the *undocumented immigrant* has emerged as an increasingly used alternative to *illegal immigrant*, and one that is more sensitive to the circumstances of immigrants' lives. The term has gained currency to the degree that some media outlets are consciously and deliberately electing not to use the terms *illegal immigrant* or *illegal alien* in their reporting on immigration, a decision the Associated Press made in 2013. The DREAMer social movement has likewise taken the stigmatizing label of "alien minors" contained within the original DREAM Act acronym and converted the acronym into a symbol of hard work, dedication, and dreams for the future, using social media astutely to articulate these counterhegemonic messages.

ENGAGING WITH PREDOMINANT SYSTEMS OF CLASSIFICATION

Immigrant classification, then, has to do not merely with how belonging is formally structured by the nation-state and informally constructed in the social realm, but also with how people themselves understand their own and others' location within the social topography of the United States. Indeed, social membership is dialectically determined by the nation-state and its inhabitants (Espiritu 2003, 12–13; Ong 1996, 738), regardless of their formal legal status. People whose lives are profoundly shaped by both sets of categorizations have their own ways of making sense of them and categorizing their social worlds. These categorizations are much more grounded in everyday life experiences (Maira 2009, 15) and are relational, as people flesh out meaning in their mutual and daily interactions with people who are similar and different from them (Reiter 2013, xvii; Vila 2000, 2).

"A CITIZEN . . . SHOULD BE ANYONE WORKING HARD TO CONTRIBUTE TO THE COUNTRY": REINSCRIBING LEGAL/FORMAL CATEGORIES

As a first step in assessing how participants understood prevailing systems of classification during their teenage years in 2005–2006, I examined the accuracy with which they knew their family members' immigration statuses. To do so, I compared the answers they reported about the statuses of their family members in the youth survey with the statuses of those family members assessed in the household survey. In the youth survey, participants identified their own immigration status as well as that of their father, mother, and siblings. Similarly, the household survey asked the parents or guardian to identify the immigration status of each family member and provide further details about when each family member had received his or her residency and/or citizenship. Where discrepancies occurred, I assumed the parent or guardian in the household survey to be reporting his or her own status accurately.

When compared with their parents' answers, the teens' answers reflected some inaccurate perception of their parents' legal/formal classifications. Eleven teens (26 percent) in my sample of forty-two high school students incorrectly identified at least one of their parents' immigration statuses. I also asked the teens if their parents had changed their status during the teenager's lifetime. Even more teens were not sure if their parents had done so; sixteen teens (or 41 percent) could not accurately report if their father had changed his immigration status, while eighteen teens (43 percent) could not accurately report if their mother had.[3] The final question I asked was when any change in their parents' immigration status had occurred. Of the teens who noted a change in their parents' immigration status, extremely few could estimate when their parents had received their residency and/or citizenship—only two (11 percent) could pinpoint when their father had, and only four (22 percent) could pinpoint when their mother had.[4]

While the teens' lack of knowledge about the specific details of their parents' legal/formal statuses could be construed as reflecting a lack of awareness or indifference, I argue that their operating frame of reference was actually just different. Instead of drawing a sharp line of distinction between citizens and legal immigrants (as in the legal/formal classification scheme), the more salient distinction for them was between people who have papers and who don't have papers. Virtually all of my participants referred to a person's immigration status using this language. Having papers indicated that a person was here legally—whether they were citizens (native born or naturalized), residents, or possessed nonimmigrant visas. The lives of those who had papers were not subject to the same constraints as their counterparts who did not. Hence the teens' category for classifying themselves, family members, friends, and others reflected a reinscription of state categories of membership, collapsing the lines between citizens, residents, and nonimmigrants.

While they did not use the technical terminology associated with their parents' state-defined immigration statuses, the teens were acutely aware of who had papers or not. In fact, Beto identified high school as the time period when teenagers came to awareness about this contrast. High school was a difficult time for Beto as he came to understand the ramifications of his "situation."[5] His status came to the fore when his friends were able to get their driver's licenses at age sixteen and he could not. After that, Beto continued to become increasingly depressed as he started realizing that many more obstacles—like attending a four-year university without being able to apply for federal financial aid—lay ahead of him. This realization, in turn, caused him to put less effort into school. Beto admitted, "I didn't really push myself the way that I should have. I knew I had the potential; it was just other factors, like me not being able to go to college. I felt really discouraged."

In part because they were aware of the limitations placed on people who did not have papers, the teens clearly understood the advantages inherent in their own status as citizens. Sal, whose mother, other family members, and close friends did not have papers, reported that he felt privileged to be a U.S. citizen "all the time. *All* the time. I have the advantage of crossing the border, going to college. Doors open for me wherever I go. People sometimes see the citizenship more than they see the person." Esperanza, whose parents had papers but whose sister-in-law and friends did not, also felt that many opportunities available to her were reserved for citizens, saying, "Here [in the United States] everything is kind of set up for you on a silver platter. How can I not take advantage of it? It would be wrong on my part not to appreciate these great opportunities."

Though participants clearly understood the benefits of having papers, and the limitations of lacking them, many nevertheless felt that those who did not possess them should be allowed to be part of the "inner circle of membership" and included in the social body (Aleinikoff 1997; Chavez 2008; Heyman 2001). Consequently, they defined potential criteria for belonging to the U.S. nation-state in different terms. After spending a few months getting to know participants during daily programming activities, I conducted freelisting with four groups of the teenagers (twenty-eight total participants) in fall 2005 as one of my first formal data collection activities. I asked them to freelist their responses to concepts like *citizen* and *immigrant*. This exercise provided me a baseline for understanding how they understood these concepts. Many teens included noncitizens in their response to what a citizen should be. In this vein, fourteen-year-old Raquel argued, "In my opinion a citizen is a resident wherever they live even if they are illegal or not." When we discussed their answers as a group, the other six members of Raquel's group agreed with her that citizenship should have some basis in residence.

The teens almost unanimously asserted that citizens should be those who "contribute" to greater society. In the freelisting exercise, fifteen-year-old Blanca wrote that a citizen "is anyone who is living in the territories of the United States legally." She then continued, "What a citizen should be is anyone who lives in the U.S. It should not matter if you are legal or not, just that you are working hard to contribute to the country." Blanca's parents and siblings had their papers, though her aunts, uncles, and cousins who lived nearby did not. A cousin of Blanca's was unable to attend University of California, Los Angeles, because of being undocumented and not being able to pay for it—despite her stellar academic record and extensive community service—which really bothered Blanca.

The teens considered individuals such as Blanca's cousin to belong to the U.S. nation by virtue of their contributions. In an interview conducted in 2006 when she was eighteen, Paz referred to her undocumented uncle as a "good American," saying, "I know that there's a lot of people here who have really proven to be like good Americans—like my uncle, he has a family and all he has ever done here is work. He's the kind of dude that would never do drugs or crimes or any of the other things people think we do. He's been here for so long, but he's just never had the opportunity." Blanca's and Paz's statements highlight the sentiment that citizenship should be based on one's contribution to the country and individual deservingness rather than simply on one's status.

On the one hand, their statements expressed an inclusiveness for which the legal/formal classification system does not allow. On the other hand, though, their focus on contribution emphasizes that this inclusivity is not boundless; noncitizens have to earn their rightful place in U.S. society by becoming good neoliberal citizen-subjects who prove their worthiness through their economic performance and adherence to U.S. social norms of self-reliance and personal responsibility (Maira 2009; Ong 2003). Indeed, "deserving" is one of the principal terms the teens—and others—used to describe who should and should not be allowed to access citizenship and its accompanying rights and privileges during the immigrant rights protests. Baker-Cristales (2009, 79) noted that even proimmigrant protesters themselves internalized and reiterated these exclusionary discourses as they enacted citizenship. Indeed, I found that these discourses were deeply internalized and rearticulated by my teenaged participants.

"THE TERM *ALIEN* MAKES IT SEEM LIKE THEY'RE NOT EVEN HUMAN": ENGAGING WITH SOCIAL/INFORMAL CATEGORIES OF EXCLUSION

While the teens' boundaries of belonging were flexible in order to accommodate "deserving" immigrants in their lives, they were also quite attuned to the dominant social discourses that excluded immigrants in a general sense—and indeed incorporated those ideals into their notions of what citizenship should entail. Paz's comments also directly referenced common representations of Mexicans as drug users and criminals. Indeed, participants were quite aware of stigmatizing discourses that portrayed Mexican immigrants as job thieves, welfare cheats, tax evaders, and criminals (Chavez 2008).

The teens expressed great distaste for categories like *illegal alien* and *illegal immigrant*, used to describe their immigrant family and friends. This exchange derives from a focus group during which we discussed these categories:

CHRISTINA: So why exactly does this term—*illegal alien*—bother you?
VICTORIA: It makes it seem like . . . like they're not even human.
PAULINA: Yeah, that they're creatures—creatures you can step on.
IMELDA: Maybe since they don't really connect with them, they can just put them aside and call them aliens. You know, you don't really understand aliens.
CHRISTINA: So it's just a way of casting them aside?
IMELDA: Yeah, um-hmm.
CHRISTINA: What about the term *illegal immigrant*?
VICTORIA: I think they should just use another term when you're talking about people. I know the meaning, but they should still use another word.
WILSON: We're all immigrants. We all came from somewhere. I understand that there's laws by the government to keep us all in place. But we all deserve a chance to come and live in this place and go after the dream—the American dream.

Wilson's final comment revealed an inclusive identification with immigrants, but it was still tempered by a trope of deservingness. Though his parents had papers, which he was well aware of, his comment also hinted that the teens did not always envision themselves as belonging to the United States unconditionally. In an interview, Wilson more markedly underlined the strong negative association between Mexicans and illegality, saying, "I think when they hear 'illegal immigrant,' they automatically assume that it's a Mexican. They just think of Mexicans 'cuz that's all they see is just Mexicans trying to cross the border and get a job. But obviously the media or other people use this as a way to make us look bad." In these statements, Wilson recognized himself as a target of illegality even though he is a U.S. citizen.

In response to these negative categorizations, some of the teens adopted defensive discourses that highlighted the positive contributions of immigrants. Sal, who attended a multiethnic public high school, often found himself in the position of defending immigrants in classroom debates. One day after school, Sal recounted one such debate:

> We were talking about immigration and this kid said this stupid comment about how illegal immigrants clog up the highways and steal all of the welfare and then have kids here who we have to take care of. I was starting to get fired up and my teacher could see it, so he was like 'Sal, what do you have to say?' What I wanted to say was that my mom is illegal and she works hard cleaning people's houses. She doesn't have papers, so there are so many different jobs she can't get. But she doesn't complain about any of it. She's not getting in anyone's way. And the kids that he's talking about, that's me. So I was like 'bring it on' because I had a lot to say about that.

As teenagers, participants clearly recognized the perniciousness of the "illegal" label that had been leveled against them and their families. Furthermore, they recognized that attacks on "illegals" targeted them, highlighting their recognition that the social boundary of belonging was extended to include them, their family members, and their friends—people who should have been on the citizen side of the U.S. social membership boundary.

Given that the teens' statements revealed commonality with immigrants in some contexts, it was surprising that their ideas about what citizenship should be based on strongly reflected elements of dominant discourses in other contexts, in a sense erecting a boundary between them and immigrants. In talking about who deserved to stay in the United States, Federico asserted, "I think people that work for a living should stay and the lazy ones should go back to Mexico," indexing a stereotypical image. In his assessment of who should be entitled to citizenship, Wilson started out utilizing a rhetoric of inclusion—stating, "I think people should have an equal opportunity to get papers"—but amended his statement shortly thereafter, adding, "I mean, not everyone—not the criminals. There should be a security check and all, since that's a problem." The teens' absorption and reiteration of these dominant discourses underlined just how deeply ingrained these hegemonic messages had become, even for individuals like Wilson who recognized at some level that they were being targeted by them.

Another curious aspect of the teens' rearticulation of dominant discourses was that the ideals that they reinforced often did not reflect the realities of their lives. For instance, Isabel maligned immigrant use of social welfare programs, stating, "They shouldn't depend on welfare. If you come over here to work, to do something better with your life, you shouldn't get the money from the government. You're here to better your life, but not to depend on the country to give you the money 'cuz you had your kids here. If you're having kids here, it's like, you raise them, with your own money." At that point in time, Isabel and her younger siblings actually did have state-funded public health insurance, as I discovered through the household survey. Consequently, Isabel's statements about "them" not relying on the state's welfare system were inconsistent with the reality of her family's economic situation. Indeed, Isabel and others had internalized discourses predicated on neoliberal principles of personal responsibility and self-reliance (Ong 2003).

The teens' integration of these dominant discourses into their constructs of citizenship reflected what Pyke and Dang (2003, 152) refer to as "defensive othering"—a process by which coethnics deflect stigma from themselves by creating internal boundaries of distinction. Focusing specifically on legal status instead of ethnicity, Ramos-Zayas (2003, 2004) characterizes this distancing process as the assertion of a "U.S. citizenship identity" (see also DeGenova and Ramos-Zayas 2003). Ramos-Zayas described how Puerto Ricans living in Chicago deployed their identities as legal U.S. citizens to clearly differentiate themselves from Mexicans as a response to the racializing politics of citizenship that socially marginalized Latinxs of every national background and legal status. This citizenship identity entailed a "self-defensive re-racialization" of Mexicans as "others" and of illegality as a condition inextricably tied to being Mexican—but not Latinx more broadly (Ramos-Zayas 2003, 34).

In a completely different city and context, the teens similarly distanced themselves in a self-defensive manner from "illegal immigrants" who were lazy, engaged in criminal behavior, and overused social services. While the San Diego teens were not denying their Mexican-ness in this process of othering, they were nonetheless attempting to distance themselves from the socially stigmatized *illegal* category. While the regime of truth (Foucault 1980, 131) surrounding immigration has definitely infiltrated and shaped their collective consciousness, the teens did not buy into these formulations completely and uncritically. In discussing the inaccuracy of the "immigrants don't pay taxes" discourse specifically, Casandra noted, "But they do pay taxes. It's not like they can go up in the store and be like, 'Oh, I'm an immigrant, I'm not gonna pay taxes.'" In a similar vein, Isabel and Paulina—who had both reiterated the "immigrants should pay taxes" discourses earlier in a focus group—went on to talk about the complexity of the tax situation for immigrants:

> ISABEL: I agree that they have to pay taxes, you know, like anybody else—like any other American. But how do you want them to do that if they're immigrants? If they don't have that social security number or they don't have those papers that allow them to do that? If you think about it, how do you want them to pay taxes if they can't? I mean, if you would allow them, if they would have a way of doing it, they'd do it, you know?
> PAULINA: Yeah, I'm sure they would . . .
> ISABEL: Yeah, they would, because most Mexicans are honest people. They're not trying to steal over here or anything.

Isabel and Paulina recognized the unfairness in some of the hegemonic messages about immigrants, which they countered because of their intimate connections to undocumented immigrants, including, in Isabel's case, her own parents. Sal, who also had keen insight into what it was like to be undocumented by virtue of his mother's status, took it a step further and argued that some of his undocumented family members "act better than many citizens or residents. They don't break any laws and they give back to the community. They live as respectable citizens of the world, not just the United States."

"SOMEWHAT IMMIGRANT": NEGOTIATING BOUNDARIES OF INCLUSION/EXCLUSION

The teens' categories of belonging were unquestionably shaped by legal/formal and, more pronouncedly, social/informal categories of classification. Sometimes they aligned with dominant discourses about immigrants not belonging on the basis of their lack of contribution and deservingness, in those cases constructing immigrants as others. When the teens talked about citizenship in the abstract—that is, when it had no direct bearing on their family members and friends—it was clear that their ideas about social belonging had been partially filtered through the dominant discourses about immigrant illegality. Because of this influence, their conception of citizenship was not limitless, all-inclusive, and unabashedly proimmigrant. Not all immigrants were deemed to be "worthy" of belonging; however, that determination was made through an individual's own actions and demonstration of deservingness, echoing personal responsibility and economic contribution as crucial nodes of belonging.

It was clear, however, that, rallying around a U.S. citizenship identity was not the only way in which the teens framed belonging. Some of the teens identified more with their immigrant or Mexican side in alliance with their family members and friends who did not have papers. Because of the close relationships they had with these individuals, many teens argued that deserving immigrants should be able to be legitimate members of the United States, including those individuals who Sal argued "acted better than many citizens or residents." Hence they made clear claims that their family members and friends properly belonged because they did, indeed, contribute to the social good.

As teenagers, my participants did not have permanent social boundaries set up between themselves as citizens and undocumented and other immigrants. Instead, they developed multiple—and in some cases, competing—notions of exclusion and inclusion through which they teased out layers of otherness and similarity with regard to immigrants. During these complex and ongoing identity negotiations, the teens sometimes saw immigrants as being "them," while at other times they included themselves in the category of *immigrants* in alliance with their immigrant family members and friends. In fact, they also recognized that they were being treated and targeted as illegal themselves.

The teens' subjectivities (Ortner 2005) bear the imprint of both of these positionings. In fact, Isabel described herself as being "somewhat immigrant" by virtue of being a U.S.-born child of undocumented immigrants, suggesting that she had particular insight and sensitivity into the plight of immigrants that shaped her framing of belonging. Even though she was a citizen, the branding of illegality that surrounded her undocumented parents had intimately affected her and shaped how she viewed belonging. The teens' positionings on belonging was also illuminated by their orchestration of and participation in the immigrant rights protests, during which they advocated for the inclusion of their undocumented family members and friends.

ASSERTING BELONGING: THE IMMIGRANT RIGHTS PROTESTS OF 2006

The teens' commentary on citizenship and illegality from the freelisting, focus groups, and interviews prior to the protests was not just abstract or disconnected from the teens' everyday realities. In fact, they had already been negotiating competing legal/formal and social/informal constructions of belonging for some time throughout their childhoods and had commented on them in meaningful ways before the protests. However, the immigrant rights protests of spring 2006 prompted the teens to more completely formulate and articulate their own positions on belonging that reflected their complex subjectivities. As Paz succinctly stated, "Because of the protests, I had to develop an opinion. And of course I side with the people—with immigrants." The protests thus served as an important window into the claims they staked on belonging and their burgeoning legal consciousness (Abrego 2011).

The immigrant rights protests were an identity-making historical moment for this generation of California teenagers of Mexican descent, much in the way that Proposition 187 had been for teenagers more than a decade before. Exposure to policy and debate over legislation like Proposition 187 during their formative years can inform youth's opinions on immigration policy and immigrants over their lifetime (Abrajano and Lundgren 2015, 94). Gonzales (2009, 37) refers to the "Proposition 187 generation" as a cohort of individuals who came of age politically during this struggle, many of whom went on to play a role in organizing the mobilizations of 2006 as adults (Bloemraad, Voss, and Lee 2011, 16). In the interim, scholars had been documenting Latinx youth's growing political engagement in fighting for social inclusion for undocumented youth in California (Abrego 2006; García Bedolla 2000, 2005; Seif 2006).

The idea of a politically socialized generation became salient once again with the immigrant rights protests of 2006; indeed, one could easily describe the next generation of young Latinxs in California as the "H.R. 4437 generation." Nationwide, up to a million children and teenagers participated in the protests; many of them had never before engaged in any form of political activity (Bloemraad and Trost 2008; Bloemraad, Voss, and Lee 2011, 27; Getrich 2008; Zavella 2011, x). Through the protests, my participants expressed previously unconscious or tacit sentiments about their mixed-status families and social belonging (Getrich 2008). As a result, the immigration protests provided a richly informative lens for viewing the ways in which they asserted their cultural citizenship (Flores and Benmayor 1997; Ong 2003).

"IT'S MY RESPONSIBILITY TO STAND UP!": PROTEST EXPERIENCES

My participants were among the estimated 3.5 to 5.1 million people who participated in the largest mass mobilizations since the 1970s (Zavella 2011, ix). The key activities of the protests included the aforementioned high school student walkouts the week of Saturday, March 25 through Friday, March 31; the National Day of Action on April 10; and the Day Without an Immigrant events on May

FIGURE 6. Protesters at the May 1 "Day Without an Immigrant" protest at the U.S.-Mexico border.

Day (May 1). Some teens took part in all of the events, first with peers during the last week of March and then subsequently with their peers and/or families for the April 10 and May 1 events. In San Diego, the largest of the events was the April 10 protests, in which some fifty thousand people participated (Bloemraad, Voss, and Lee 2011, 8)

Based on their descriptions, the new legal/formal category of classification proposing to make both undocumented immigrants and those who assisted them criminals enraged the teens and prompted them into action. In this respect, the teens, like others, took counterhegemonic actions to contest the ways in which the state was constructing social belonging (Gonzales 2009). In discussing his distaste for H.R. 4437, Sal stated, "The bill makes illegal immigrants criminals and those that give them a ride, employ them, or whatever criminals. So that's a lot of people I know—my family members, friends, acquaintances. That's why I don't support it. It's not fair to them—or me." Sal had keen insight into how the legislation would make the conditions of these individuals' lives even more precarious; he reflected, "They have so much to contribute back to society. And they're not allowed to . . . That's why I feel for them and want to show them that I care."

Indeed, Sal was one of the few teens who was already knowledgeable about the bill, having completed several homework assignments on immigration even before the passage of H.R. 4437. Other teens reported researching the House bill online when the protests started in order to better understand its specific details. In this respect, the protests served as a knowledge-building experience for many of the teens. Paulina admitted that she did not know about the bill before the protests but subsequently knew "more than just what I heard. I actually did research on the internet and found out what the bill was."

The teens also commented on the use of informal/social classifications like *illegal* that stigmatized their undocumented family and friends—and even them. Miguel felt that the racialization of Mexicans was deeply embedded in the immigration debate, stating, "I feel like a lot of people use the immigration issue as an excuse to show their true colors or their racial views. And I mean, a lot of people just say immigration, what they really mean is Mexicans." During the protest period, Miguel felt this racist sentiment acutely at his university. Miguel was one of the few Mexicans with whom many of his peers had any contact; because of this, he felt the need to insert himself into debates about immigration out of a sense of duty. He explained, "When people are having political discussions about 'We should close the borders and kick all these immigrants out, all these Mexicans out' . . . in that scenario I have to voice my opinion. I know that a lot of these people—they might not understand, they might not like what I'm gonna say, but I feel like sometimes it's my duty, it's my responsibility to stand up just because that's a part of me."

The teens constructed advocating for family, friends, and Mexicans more generally as the "right" reasons for protesting; indeed, they often felt a sense of responsibility in doing so, as Miguel conveyed. They also maligned those who participated for the "wrong" reasons—like skipping school and getting into trouble. Such actions detracted from the messages of inclusion and affirmation that "those who actually knew what was happening" (as Casandra phrased it) were trying to convey. Further, they only served to reinforce notions of delinquency and criminality. The local San Diego media mostly highlighted people who participated for the "wrong" reasons, which irritated the teens. Frustrated at the takeaway message of the news reports, Sal related to me, "That's what the media chose to highlight—the *cholo*-type people throwing gang signs or waving Mexican flags or not knowing anything about the bill."[6]

The protests were also consciousness raising by forcing the teens to stake out their positions on immigration issues. Wilson chose not to participate initially, saying, "I had nothing to gain from it then, I wasn't informed yet. So I would've been like the others that just walked and didn't know what they were doing." In a focus group conducted two months after the student protests, he shared, "I saw something kind of disturbing on the news about the Minutemen. You know how most of them are white Americans? Well, some of them are Mexican, too! I just don't understand that." Wilson then went from not feeling knowledgeable about the issues to comfortably discussing them with his peers and actually reflecting on intraethnic differences of perspective on the topic of immigration. Hence the learning process for the teens extended beyond the period of the protests themselves.

In addition to being consciousness raising, the immigration protests were also identity affirming for the teens. Cármen recalled that before the protests, "I would be like, 'I'm Latina, Chicana, whatever you want to call me.' I didn't really pay much importance [to] it. But everything going on has changed my personal . . . way of seeing things. I know I'm lucky being who I am. I can't picture myself being ashamed of what I am. I grew up Mexican. I am Mexican." Cármen's comments reveal a transition in her sense of self—from being somewhat ambivalent about her Mexican heritage to proudly asserting it. Instead of feeling stigmatized by being Mexican, she came to see it as a source of pride, something that she would not choose to change.

Perhaps the teen who became most empowered by the immigration protests and who most strongly asserted messages of belonging was Sal. When the protests started, Sal deliberately chose not to participate, stating, "I thought I was doing a much better service by disproving the continuous stereotype that we just like to ditch school and that we're uninformed. I was pretty much trying to play the other role—of the actual informed person." Sal stayed behind at his public high school so that he could "make more of a contribution [by] talking about it with the people there at school." He continued, "I was like the only Mexican [who remained] at school. When I got to school I heard some people say stuff like, 'Oh, it's so clean around here today without all the Mexicans.' That pissed me off. But the whole day I was just talking, talking, talking, explaining everything. And people really seemed interested in what I was saying and I felt like I had things to back up what I was saying. I felt kind of honored—some people were like 'Wow, you know a lot about this stuff!'"

As the weeks went on and plans were being made for the next set of protests, Sal became increasingly frustrated at the school's lack of attention to the protests, which were very contentious among the students. He wrote a letter to his principal expressing disappointment that the school had not seized the opportunity to promote critical dialogue about immigration and suggesting that a forum should be held to tackle the issues. The principal called him into the office on the Friday afternoon before the planned May 1 "Day Without an Immigrant" protest and asked him to help her plan a forum, which he helped moderate. A few hours after the forum had taken place, Sal recounted to me what had happened:

> We had the forum in the auditorium. We didn't know if people were going to come or anything. At first, there weren't that many, but then tons of people came in. There were like six hundred or something! At first, I was a little nervous. But then I got warmed up. I would say something and then people would make their comments. Sometimes I would respond, sometimes others would jump right in and say something. And that was my goal—that's what I wanted. Not that we all agree about everything, but that we're open to each other. That we treat each other good instead of calling each other beaners and other names. And that wouldn't have happened if I was out on the streets—I would have just been another face in the crowd.

Beyond combating stereotypes about Mexicans and immigrants and encouraging critical dialogue among his peers, the forum was an immense boon to Sal's self-esteem. A few hours after the event, he reflected, "It was one of the best days of my life. I just couldn't believe that so many people came. And I got such a great response from the principal—she was like, 'Good job. This is great.' And some of my teachers, too. The whole thing is just so crazy. I still can't believe it happened. And the news even came and interviewed me. I'm just on such a high right now!" In fact, Sal was featured on the nightly news and in local newspapers. He eventually won an award from a local organization that heard about the forum he spearheaded. As May 2007 approached, Sal's principal asked him to come back and facilitate another forum, even though he had graduated the year before. Sal happily agreed, acknowledging that he felt extremely "honored" to do so when I saw him in July 2007.

The debate surrounding the immigration protests provided Sal the opportunity to cement his proimmigrant outlook and articulate it in a very public forum. Sal spent many years struggling to feel comfortable with his immigrant roots. For a long time, particularly when he attended a (predominantly Anglo) private high school on scholarship, Sal said that he felt "kind of strange or embarrassed" by his mother and just wanted to fit in with his peers. In talking about that time period, he said, "I was pretty much saying to my parents that I was embarrassed of their struggle, of what they put up with . . . I'll regret that for the rest of my life." After many years of working though this internal conflict, however, Sal came to the point where he stated, "You've gotta be proud of who you are and proud of what your parents have done for you to get you where you are."

Sal's comments highlight the embarrassment he felt at his parents being immigrants when he was younger. The protests, by contrast, provided him the space to embrace his parents' struggle and see it instead through a positive lens. Cármen also noted that the protests and accompanying classroom discussions helped her to see her parents in a new light, sharing:

> I never really paid so much importance that my dad crossed the border illegally, you know? Also that my mom worked the fields picking up melons and lettuce. I never really thought [about] that until a class when we were talking about all the hard work immigrants do. We were talking about how immigrants have to suffer crossing back and forth and [how] they risk their lives. I was like, "Oh my God—that's what my parents did!" And that's when it hit me because back then they didn't really talk about it. But I'm not ashamed of my parents getting here the way they did.

Cármen thus came to view her parents' undocumented status not as a stigmatizing marker but rather as a signal of pride for the tenacity they had displayed in crossing the border and working difficult jobs without papers.

Because they were relatively secure in their own status as citizens, some teens felt comfortable taking to the streets and asserting themselves to "represent" those who were being targeted by the legislation. In discussing her reasons for protesting, Blanca reported, "I participated 'cuz most of my family here right now are illegal immigrants, and they have no way to represent themselves. They can't really do much about anything." Blanca clearly drew on a rhetoric of fairness in critiquing the bill and advocating for her family members, including her cousin who was unable to attend college because of her status.

In addition to family members, other teens related that they participated in protests to advocate for their undocumented friends. Isabel shared a story about a classmate: "I have one friend who is really super close to me. She's like a straight-A student, she's involved in school, she's like a really great role model and everything. She also doesn't have papers. And she's like, 'You guys have that number—that number that can secure your future, the social security. I don't.' As she was telling us this, it hit us, you know? She's one of us, someone that we hang out with. And it was like, wow!" Isabel's statement that her friend was "one of us" unquestionably signals that she believed her friend—whom she also identified as a role model—deserved her rightful place in U.S. society. Isabel critiqued the state's distinction between her and her friend on the basis of immigration status and the practical consequences of this differential categorization. She also offered an implicit critique of dominant discourses suggesting that undocumented immigrants do not contribute to the social good in any meaningful way. Isabel's statement also highlights her recognition that she could put "that number" to practical use by advocating for friends.

CONTEXTUALIZING THE PROTESTS THROUGH A FAMILY FRAME

In analyzing the protests and their impact on the teens' development, it is clear that it was a knowledge-building, consciousness-raising, and identity-affirming period for teens like Paulina, Cármen, and Sal. But more than just the individual growth, their commentary also reveals that they took seriously the responsibility of representing their immigrant family members and friends who were being targeted. The 2006 immigrant rights protests, then, served as a mechanism for reinforcing family bonds (Bloemraad and Trost 2008, 518; Pulido 2007, 2) and cultivating broader Latinx solidarity across immigration statuses (Martínez 2008; Pantoja, Menjívar, and Magaña 2008, 500).

Indeed, nationwide, family-oriented frames were among the most dominant and successful ones used to mobilize protestors in 2006, in the process politicizing the family itself (Martínez 2008, 2013; Pallares 2015). This notion of family was not merely limited to the protestors' own family members but was also extended out to refer to the Latinx community in familial terms (Bloemraad, Voss, and Lee 2011, 27). The teenagers deployed *the family* as a political construction (Pallares 2015, 12); defense of the family played a central role in their formation as political subjects (Pallares and Flores-González 2011, 171). However, the family was not merely an abstraction that they deployed politically; in fact, they were well aware that representing their undocumented family members was instrumental in practical terms to keeping their family units in tact in light of the proposed legislation (Pallares and Flores-González 2011, 172).

The political engagement of youth in particular is not typically framed within this context of family participation (Bloemraad and Trost 2008, 508); in fact, children are generally viewed as politically apathetic or dismissed as unconventional political actors (Bloemraad, Voss, and Lee 2011; Pallares and Flores-González 2011, 170). To the extent that family dynamics are considered, the political socialization literature depicts children as learning from parents, with the transmission of knowledge being passed down through the generations (Bloemraad and Trost 2008, 509). Bloemraad and Trost argue for an alternative model of bidirectional political socialization in which "children with greater access to the English language and mainstream institutions provide political information to their parents and encourage them to participate" (509).

Indeed, this bidirectional model is much more applicable to my participants. Their English skills, inside knowledge of the system, and secure legal statuses provided them with greater protection and more tools for political participation than their parents possessed (Bloemraad and Trost 2008, 52). The teens were well aware of these advantages as they sought to represent their families and communities through these acts of collective brokering (Pallares and Flores-González 2011, 172). Indeed, being able to recognize individual problems as collective is an important point at which political consciousness develops in youth (García Bedolla 2005, 23). Looking beyond the security implicit in their U.S. citizen status, they assumed a collective identity in solidarity with their family members, friends, and other coethnics (Pallares and Flores-González 2011, 172). Thus they identified as immigrants in representing loved ones who did not officially belong (173). Through the protests, they were able to deploy and embrace their complex subjectivities, developed in the context of mixed-status social worlds.

What the teens took away from the protests is that they could take action to fight against forms of inequality directed at their families and friends and, by proxy, them. During a focus group discussion two months after the protests, the topic of birthright citizenship and how some legislators were fighting for its elimination cropped up. The issue, of course, hit home for the teens as they would have been the targets of this legislation had it been in effect when they were born. Paulina was quickly dismissive of the birthright citizenship measure, asserting, "It won't go through." I asked her why not, and she responded, "If you think about it, we'll start another march!" In a different focus group session, Guillermo had a similar response, stating, "We were born here, we're U.S. citizens. If they put the law in progress, everyone's gonna fight back, like in a good way, to make it stop." While their conclusions were perhaps overly optimistic (that protests alone were the best mechanism for changing policy), the sentiment behind it reflected that the teens had internalized a new way of responding to state policies and stigmatizing discourses that targeted their loved ones and them.

In the time since the protests, scholars have pondered whether the teens' activism in the realm of nonelectoral politics would translate into an increase in voter participation. There is some evidence that the energies animating the 2006 protests were, in fact, channeled into 2008 electoral participation (Bloemraad, Voss, and Lee 2011, 4). In the aftermath of the 2006 protests, youth have also taken on an even stronger role in the immigrant rights movement, leading the push for federal and state DREAMer legislation and an expansion of DACA to include undocumented parents of citizen children in mixed-status families. Beyond electoral participation and engagement with the immigrant rights movement through public forms of activism, though, I have found that the protests had enduring effects on my participants' political consciousness and their desire to represent their families and communities.

Among my participants, Paulina has really taken on the mantle of everyday activism and epitomizes the H.R. 4437 generation. After Paulina graduated from high school, she attended a California state university in greater Los Angeles. When she went to visit, she noticed the fields surrounding the campus and the immigrants working them. She reflected, "I saw the migrant workers picking strawberries and it reminded me of home, where my mom is from in Mexico. When you're entering campus, you see them. That was an important way of keeping me grounded." Paulina majored in political science and was involved in Latinx programs on campus that connected out to the local community and to international issues like water and food insecurity. During her senior year, Paulina was elected student body president—the first Latina to hold that position. Describing her time as president, she said, "I changed a lot of things! [Laughs] Before, there were a lot of social events. I was like, 'Where's all the political action?' Instead of using our money for pizza, I took a bus full of students to Sacramento to protest. We didn't have to spend $1,000 on pizza, you know?" After graduating and making the decision to return home to San Diego, Paulina became a youth organizer for a local chapter of a national nonprofit social justice organization, with immigrant rights as one of her major areas of focus. Her involvement in the immigrant rights protests in 2006, then, was just the beginning of her path working to promote social justice.

CONCLUSION

This chapter has examined taken-for-granted social categories like *citizen* and *illegal immigrant*, describing how they were constructed through both legal/formal and social/informal systems of classification (Coutin 2000; Heyman 2001). I laid out these classification systems as a backdrop for presenting the teens' own classification system that both reinforced and subverted these predominant systems of classification. I have argued that the teens' complex subjectivities have been shaped by both systems as they have sought to make sense of their mixed-status families and social worlds.

My participants' involvement in the immigrant rights protests of 2006 demonstrated that they were not partial or semicitizens at all but rather full citizens who were actively engaged in building their knowledge base, raising their legal consciousness, and growing into their roles as advocates for their families and communities—indeed, even transmitting their political knowledge to their adult family members. Instead of depending legally and socially on their parents, they served as advocates from their relatively privileged position as citizens on behalf and in defense of their family members and friends who did not have papers. In the process, they started to emerge as advocates within their families and communities, coming out strongly against enforcement of the strictly defined membership categories promulgated by the state. Electoral participation and public activism, though, are not the only important ways in which the legacies of the protests have lived on with this H.R. 4437 generation. I have also found that over time and as they have matured, my participants extended the brokering sensibilities that they cultivated during the protests by advocating for their families. In this respect, the protests helped lay the groundwork for the brokering activities they have continued to perform as they have matured into adults—the focus of chapters to come.

In chapter 3, I move beyond how the teens have engaged with illegality as a juridical category and sociopolitical condition to examine how it shapes their families' ways of being in the world (Willen 2007). In particular, I examine the effects of deportability—the constant fear of deportation (DeGenova 2002)—on members of mixed-status families, including the teens themselves. I examine the limitations imposed on those who don't have papers and how these shaped participants' childhoods in concrete ways, affecting their local mobility, transborder travel, and family well-being. I also highlight how they have buffered these impacts of illegality and deportability for their families in their adult lives.

3

CONTENDING WITH THE REPERCUSSIVE EFFECTS OF ILLEGALITY AND DEPORTABILITY

I MET UP with Isabel Clemente one morning in 2014 during San Diego's dreaded "June gloom," when a blanket of cool, moist air settles onshore to obscure the city's legendary sun and warmth. Greeting each other, we settled in to catch up at one of the trendy coffee shops that had just been built in the neighborhood. As we chatted about plans for the upcoming weekend, Isabel told me that she was going to Tijuana to commemorate the anniversary of her maternal grandfather's passing and was hoping that the weather would clear up before then. Isabel had faithfully participated in the important family ritual every year in the seven years since her grandfather had passed away, but lamented that her mother, Paloma, had been prevented from going to the funeral or subsequent gatherings because of her undocumented status. Isabel shared that it was "so hard for my mom not to be able to go because she lost her mom when she was ten, so my grandpa was her world." Though it was clear that Isabel's concern was with Paloma's emotional well-being, Isabel herself teared up as she talked about her mother's status-related limitations, signaling that they also deeply impacted her.

As the oldest child in the mixed-status Clemente family, Isabel started helping out her parents at a young age, especially because they had no extended family in San Diego as a resource from which to draw. As I asked Isabel to reflect back on her childhood later in our interview, she recalled, "I was probably like eight or nine years old when I knew that my parents didn't have papers. You learn it young. You learn it young because there's things like . . . not having a driver's license that matter. You bought something and you can't return it to the store because you don't have an ID. It's something as simple as that, as little as that, that makes you start realizing that your parents don't have papers."

Isabel continued to discover how important it was to "have papers" as she went about teenage rites of passage such as getting a driver's license and looking for her first job. When I had interviewed her as a sophomore in high school, she observed,

> I'm really seeing the difference having papers makes. I started applying for jobs and I had to put my social security, and at first I was like, "It's just my number, whatever." But then I started thinking about how much you actually need this number. I lost my social security [card] for a while. I had gone to driver's ed and wanted to get my permit. I didn't know my social security number, but I could just go down to the social security office and get it. Immigrants can't just do that, they can't just go, "Oh, I don't have one. Can I get one?" And for me, it was just easy.

In addition to realizing the importance and privilege of having papers, Isabel became acutely aware that *not* having papers was the reason her parents could not cross the nearby border to visit their extended family who lived just on the other side. During that same interview conducted when she was sixteen, Isabel exclaimed, "I wish my parents had their papers. I just see how much they want to go [to Tijuana] and they can't. When I cross the border I can just take my ID[1] because I was born in the United States. My parents can't do that. Not everyone has that option." Without the "option" of crossing available to them, her parents had to send her and her sisters along with her aunts and uncles who were able to cross as they passed through town on their way from Los Angeles to Tijuana.

Isabel's remembrances and realizations reveal her early and growing awareness of the limitations of her parents' undocumented status and, in turn, the benefits that having papers afforded her in doing mundane yet hugely significant tasks such as getting a driver's license. In one sense, the line between having papers and not having papers is clearly demarcated in the Clemente family, underscoring that legal status is a clear axis of stratification within mixed-status families (Abrego 2014; Menjívar 2010, 20).

Yet in another sense, illegality has impacted not only the options available to Isabel's undocumented parents but also those available to the Clemente girls. As Abrego (2016, 5) points out, "Illegality encompasses all members of a family even when only one person or a few people are categorized as undocumented." Indeed, illegality has clear ripple effects on citizen children in mixed-status families (Castañeda 2019; Castañeda and Melo 2014; Dreby 2015a; Ochoa O'Leary and Sanchez 2011; Zayas 2015), serving as a unique form of legal violence (Menjívar and Abrego 2012) and multigenerational punishment (Enríquez 2015).

In this chapter, I examine how illegality shaped my participants' childhoods and transition into adulthood within the context of their mixed-status families. Specifically, I examine how the "repercussive effects" (Comfort 2007) of immigration policies targeting undocumented members of their social networks shaped their childhoods and teenage years. As I will demonstrate, illegality and deportability have taken on particular prominence in mixed-status families in the border region (Heyman 2014). Given their proximity to the U.S.-Mexico border, participants' families felt the impact of immigrant enforcement particularly acutely as they went about their daily lives under Border Patrol surveillance. These enforcement activities have had mutually reinforcing practical and psychological effects (120; Szkupinski Quiroga, Medina, and Glock 2014). Participants have experienced these repercussive effects intersubjectively, underscoring the shared vulnerability of the family unit (Horton 2009). Yet as was clear from their burgeoning advocacy on behalf of their families, as highlighted in chapter 2, they have adeptly developed strategies for navigating around these limitations to protect their family members and friends.

THE REPERCUSSIVE EFFECTS OF ILLEGALITY AND DEPORTABILITY

ILLEGALITY AND DEPORTABILITY IN MIXED-STATUS FAMILIES

Though the scholarly examination of illegality grew out of the experiences of adult immigrants, increasing attention is being paid to how it extends beyond adults to shape the trajectories of the estimated 4.5 million citizen children living in mixed-status families (Abrego 2014, 2016; Dreby 2012, 2015a; Menjívar, Abrego, and Schmalzbauer 2016; Zayas 2015). Scholars have increasingly been documenting the linkages between exclusionary U.S. immigration policies and the intimacies of family life (Abrego 2016; Boehm 2012; Dreby 2015a, 9; Menjívar 2010, 7).

The effects of having "parents without papers" are apparent early and endure across individual life courses and generations (Bean, Brown, and Bachmeir 2015). As early as age two or three, parents' undocumented status has been demonstrated to affect children's cognitive and language skill development (Yoshikawa 2011, 2). Young children's development is adversely affected by their undocumented parents' poor working conditions, isolated social networks, and avoidance of programs and authorities. In fact, immigrants' unauthorized legal status plays a substantial role in stalling the social integration of not only immigrants and their children but even their grandchildren (Alba and Waters 2011; Bean, Brown, and Bachmeir 2015).

Immigration policies also intersect directly with family life to exacerbate these stalled pathways. Family separation has emerged as a common phenomenon under the deportation regime (DeGenova and Peutz 2010) that escalated in 2006 under Bush, intensified under Obama with stepped-up workplace and home raids, and flourished anew under Trump. In the immediate aftermath of these raids, children left behind experienced feelings of abandonment and exhibited symptoms of emotional trauma and psychological duress (Capps et al. 2007, 4). These forced separations have a profound direct and indirect influence on the health of not just the children but also immigrant communities more broadly (Lopez et al. 2017), including increasingly throughout the U.S. interior in the last decade. The expansion of enforcement activity that has already taken place under Trump is further exacerbating trauma and distress for members of mixed-status families, underscoring the feeling that no family is safe.

Deportations have also reshaped the structure of mixed-status families in marked ways. Since ICE primarily detains and deports fathers (Golash-Boza and Hondagneu-Sotelo 2013), children are more likely to remain in households with their mothers, who must deal with the aftermath of the deportation and face great economic uncertainty (Dreby 2012, 2015b). Beyond a decline in income, mixed-status families and households destabilized by deportation are characterized by prolonged housing instability and greater food insecurity (Capps et al. 2007; Chaudry et al. 2010; Zayas 2015). Mothers heading these now single-parent households fear that their own deportation would lead to the loss of custody of their U.S.-born children (Dreby 2012, 835), magnifying the profound levels of stress already present in the household.

THE EFFECTS OF ILLEGALITY AND DEPORTABILITY ON CHILDREN'S HEALTH AND MENTAL HEALTH

Additionally, immigration policies work in tandem with immigrant policies to stratify access to health care for mixed-status families. Per restrictions in the 1996 welfare reform law (PRWORA), undocumented immigrants are ineligible for public benefits, including Medicaid and CHIP, and are only eligible for emergency care, immunizations, and treatment for communicable diseases. PRWORA also imposed a five-year ban on legal permanent residents' access to benefits unless states passed overriding legislation (Horton 2014, 302). These eligibility restrictions were upheld by 2010's Affordable Care Act, despite its rhetoric of expanding health care to vulnerable populations. Due to these policies, members of mixed-status families have stratified access to health care and social services, not only between immigrant parents and their U.S.-born children but even among siblings with different birthplaces and/or immigration statuses (Castañeda and Melo 2014).

Moreover, scholars observed a chilling effect on access to public benefits among citizen children in mixed-status families in the aftermath of the punitive welfare and immigration reform laws of 1996 (Hagan et al. 2003). Many eligible children were "voluntarily" withdrawn from services due to their parents' avoidance of public institutions, fear of deportation, and apprehension that enrolling their eligible children in government programs would affect future chances at legalization. Latinx children in mixed-status families in particular have worse access to care and poorer physical health when compared with their U.S. citizen counterparts (Castañeda and Melo 2014; Hagan et al. 2003).

Illegality also concretely shapes the emotional well-being and mental health of children in mixed-status families (Abrego 2014, 98; Zayas 2015; Zayas and Bradlee 2014). Parental deportation has a detrimental impact on the emotional and behavioral functioning of children left behind (Allen, Cisneros, and Tellez 2015), effects that persist over an extended period (Dreby 2012). Postdeportation, children in mixed-status families also continue to face a multitude of barriers in accessing medical and mental health care (Allen, Cisneros, and Tellez 2015), exacerbated by their families' intensified vulnerabilities. Children in families that experience detention and deportation are often the "collateral damage of enforcement" (Zayas and Bradlee 2014, 167). With the expansion of enforcement taking place under Trump, family separation is becoming an even more pronounced phenomenon nationwide.

THE WIDE REACH OF DEPORTABILITY

Actual deportation episodes are not the only factor shaping mixed-status family members' insecurity, though; deportability penetrates everyday family life in marked ways as well (Boehm 2012; Dreby 2015a, 9; Menjívar 2010, 7; Zayas 2015). The mere threat of deportation provokes significant anxiety for children in mixed-status families, disrupting children's sense of stability while causing them to suffer from *nervios* (Dreby 2015a, 52–53). Psychological distress is even prominent among family and community members who are not the direct targets of enforcement (Szkupinski Quiroga, Medina, and Glock 2014). Deportability creates a culture of fear that Dreby (2015a, 9) contends constitutes a public health concern, given the millions of undocumented immigrants and their children who live under its threat.

To operationalize the effects of deportation, Dreby (2012) devised a deportation pyramid as a conceptual model to demonstrate its rippling effects on children in mixed-status families—both those who are directly affected by it and those who are potentially vulnerable to it. The top levels of the pyramid are focused on the former group and involve family dissolution and U.S. citizen children having to return to Mexico to live with family members. Moving down the pyramid, she highlights the long-term economic instability and emotional distress of separation as well as shorter-term economic instability, changes in daily routines, and emotional distress (831).

The bottom levels of the pyramid are focused on the larger group of children who are more indirectly affected by immigration policies that criminalize members of their social networks. She found that fears of deportation "were common among children regardless of their own legal status or that of their parents" (Dreby 2012, 839), underscoring the wide reach and pervasiveness of deportability within immigrant communities among individuals of all statuses. More perniciously, she found that young children began to associate immigrants with illegality regardless of their family members' actual immigration status, distancing themselves from their heritage and identity (830).

THE ROLE OF THE STATE AND REPERCUSSIVE EFFECTS OF ILLEGALITY AND DEPORTABILITY

Building on Dreby's analysis, Zayas (2015, 7) finds that through deportability, the citizen children of undocumented immigrant parents are denied the full benefits of their status, including protection from the state. Menjívar and Abrego (2012) also call explicit attention to the state, arguing that the effects of illegality and deportability not only are unintended consequences of immigration policies but also signal deliberate effects of state power. They describe the multipronged system of laws at federal, state, and local levels that promote a climate of insecurity and suffering for immigrants and their families as "legal violence" (Menjívar and Abrego 2012, 1387). These "cumulatively injurious effects of the law" include forms of material, emotional, and psychological suffering that obstruct and derail immigrants' paths of incorporation (1380, 1383). This suffering results from legal practices that are assumed to be fair and are naturalized, sanctioned, and legitimated through formal structures of power that are publicly accepted and respected (1413).

Unlike most punitive laws that target individuals and their behavior, Menjívar and Abrego (2012, 1388) highlight that "immigration laws and their implementation target an entire class of people mostly with noncriminal social characteristics, such as language spoken or physical appearance, that associate them with a particular immigration status." They also underscore that the application of these laws targets a wider range of documented immigrants and U.S.-born family members and that the violence that results from them is often subtle and damaging in both the short and long term (1400).

Extending Menjívar and Abrego's concept of legal violence, Enríquez (2015) argues that immigration laws and policies produce "multigenerational punishment," as legal sanctions intended for undocumented immigrants extend into the lives of U.S. citizens. As a distinct form of legal violence, Enríquez argues that multigenerational punishment leads to children witnessing and sharing in the risks, limitations, and punishment of their undocumented family members as well as the risk-management strategies they undertake to diffuse them (941). The family, she argues, is a particularly apt unit for interrogating multigenerational punishment because of the strong social ties, relationships of dependency, and shared day-to-day interactions (950). Castañeda and Melo (2014, 1892) also underscore that mixed-status families provide an instructive unit to examine the state's penetration at the household level.

Enríquez (2015, 951) concludes by noting that the concept of multigenerational punishment has applicability beyond immigrant families to other socially marginalized groups who are also the targets of legal violence, like racial minority men and their families. Indeed, Comfort (2007, 289) examines how punishment has repercussive effects that reverberate beyond the narrow target of the legal offender into the lives of kin, friends, and neighbors. She points out that the criminal justice system in the United States is narrowly focused on the accused as a freestanding actor and target for reprisal, but that in reality, "Legally innocent people are made to alter their behavior, reorient their expectations, suffer changes in their health, and otherwise experience the social and economic repercussions of punitive surveillance, confinement, and control" (272). Though *ripple effects* is the terminology most frequently used to describe how immigration policies impact mixed-status households (Castañeda and Melo 2014; Dreby 2015a; Fix and Zimmerman 2001; Ochoa O'Leary and Sanchez 2011; Zayas 2015), the term *repercussive effects* more directly implicates the state in prompting the punitive effects experienced by members of immigrants' social networks. *Repercussive effects* is also a particularly appropriate term for describing borderland neighborhoods where disciplinary forces constantly invade personal and communal space (Comfort 2007, 277).

Comfort highlights not only the material effects of punitive surveillance but also its more affective dimensions, including how people modify their behavior and reorient their expectations. Returning to mixed-status families, Zayas (2015, xiii) argues that the threat of their parents' deportation "colors . . . how [citizen children] view the world and how they move about in it, even how they perceive and judge themselves." As Zayas correctly points out, it is important to understand how children in mixed-status families come to terms with the implications of their parents' status since it has profound repercussive effects on their lives. Some attention has been paid to how young children make sense of deportation risk (Dreby 2015a; Horner et al. 2014). While they do develop an early awareness of their parents' status, younger children tend to see immigration status as a private family matter (Zayas 2015, 62). As they grow and mature, they may come to see that illegality is an issue that is more pervasive, public, and part of the broader legal system (63; Dreby 2012).

SUBJECTIVE UNDERSTANDINGS AND EVERYDAY REALITIES OF ILLEGALITY

It is crucial that we understand the subjective meanings of illegality (Menjívar and Kanstroom 2014, 6) for children in mixed-status families and how these meanings change as they mature. Beyond that, a comprehensive understanding of illegality and deportability necessitates that we examine how these processes shape mixed-status family members' ways of being in the world (Willen

2007)—individually and as a larger unit. There is also growing recognition that illegality is experienced differently by not only immigration status but also gender, generation, and life cycle stage (Abrego 2014; Menjívar and Kanstroom 2014, 7). These experiences vary for not only undocumented immigrants but also their children, and they affect them in different ways over time.

For my participants in the borderlands, illegality and deportability have dominated their families' lives since Operation Gatekeeper debuted in 1994, when they were young children. Indeed, as I will demonstrate, the effects on their lives are apparent upon examining the effects of immigration law on their quotidian practices (Menjívar and Abrego 2012, 1414). Illegality and deportability have influenced how they maneuver within their neighborhood and beyond, their abilities to get to know family members in the United States and Mexico, their responsibilities and obligations to their families over time, and ultimately their health and well-being. Indeed, their narratives demonstrate that they have experienced these repercussive effects intersubjectively (Horton 2009), sharing in their family members' status-related vulnerabilities. Yet I will demonstrate how as teenagers and now as adults, they contest these repercussive effects and do what they can to buffer the effects of illegality and deportability for their parents and other loved ones.

THE ENDURING REPERCUSSIVE EFFECTS OF ILLEGALITY

ARTICULATING THE LIMITATIONS OF NOT HAVING PAPERS

I originally undertook this research in the mid-2000s to better understand how teenagers made sense of differences within their mixed-status families and negotiated the limitations their parents' status placed on them and their families. As previously mentioned, I started out by conducting freelisting with four groups of teenagers in fall 2005 as a way of gauging how they conceptualized concepts like *immigrant* and *citizen*. After freelisting, I asked each group to respond to a set of follow-up questions prompting them to identify what citizens could do that undocumented immigrants specifically could not. They wrote down their responses to the questions independently of one another and then we discussed them as a group. They identified the following as benefits of citizenship: being able to cross the border (19; 68 percent), voting (18; 64

percent), securing a better job (16; 57 percent), having better access to education (6; 21 percent), driving legally (5; 18 percent), owning property (houses, cars, land; 5; 18 percent), and not facing deportation (4; 14 percent). Other perceptive answers that specific individuals identified included building credit, going places that require a valid ID, and having a voice in the government.

The responses they selected demonstrated a clear awareness of the benefits afforded to citizens and, by contrast, the range of limitations placed on those who did not possess citizenship. As I continued with my fieldwork, the interviews and casual conversations I had with the teens continued to illuminate the complexity of these limitations as they talked about all of the constraints their family members and friends faced in their daily lives. Over time, though, it became clearer and clearer that these limitations affected not only their undocumented family members and friends but also the teenagers themselves. The "weight of illegality" (Abrego 2014, 69) and the tangible presence of deportability factored profoundly into their childhood—and continues to reverberate in their adult lives.

I elaborate below upon the most salient limitations that they identified and continued to reflect on over time—local mobility, transborder engagement, and family dynamics—all of which produced embodied effects. To do so, I highlight their experiences and perceptions both from the vantage point of adolescence and now as adults reflecting back on their childhoods. As I demonstrated in chapter 2, instead of drawing sharp lines of distinction between the categories of citizens, LPRs, and undocumented immigrants, the more salient distinction for my participants was between people who have papers (citizens, residents, and those with temporary visas) and people who don't have papers (undocumented immigrants); thus, I default to their emic way of classifying the distinctions between themselves and their family members and friends instead of the formal state categorizations produced by immigration law.

"BECAUSE OF THE STATUS, WE REALLY CAN'T TRAVEL": CHALLENGES TO LOCAL MOBILITY

One of the principal limitations that repeatedly arose in interviews and casual conversation was im/mobility—how limited those without papers were in moving around the city, county, and beyond. Immigration laws limit immigrants' physical mobility in multiple respects (Enríquez 2015, 940). A primary constraint to mobility is that undocumented immigrants have historically been restricted from obtaining driver's licenses that would enable them to drive legally. Starting in 1993, some states began legislating undocumented immigrants' eligibility for driver's licenses, though the practice has become a political flashpoint and subject of great debate. California passed Assembly Bill 60 in October 2013 stipulating that undocumented immigrants could procure a license if they satisfactorily established California residency; however, the license could not be used for identification purposes and would have a recognizable feature to distinguish it (State of California Department of Motor Vehicles 2017).

For the bulk of my participants' lives, then, their undocumented family members and friends were not able to drive legally. This restriction made it difficult for their parents to drive to work, schools, and clinics; visit with family members; and run errands. Parents had to weigh the necessity of fulfilling their work, family, and other obligations with the risk that driving without a driver's license exposed them to (Guelespe 2015, 205). These restrictions also carried over to their children, who were also limited in their participation in after-school activities and jobs before they reached age sixteen. Beyond that, it also meant that when participants received their licenses as teenagers, they often became the most secure driver in their family, increasing demands and pressures on them.

As enforcement intensified in the 2000s, "driving while immigrant" became an increasingly risky activity, with increasing possibility that being stopped could trigger a deportation (Waslin 2013). When immigrants are stopped for any infraction (including the all-too-common "broken taillight"), they must admit that they are driving without a license. This admission is grounds for being taken into custody, which then triggers possible communication with ICE that could lead to deportation (Guelespe 2015). H.R. 4437 also proposed to make knowingly transporting an undocumented immigrant a crime. This provision hit home for the teenagers, as they were often involved in driving their parents around once they got their licenses. Sal critiqued this provision, querying, "What am I supposed to do—not take my mom to work?"

A second influence on undocumented immigrants' mobility is the entrapment that has accompanied the border enforcement strategies implemented in the mid-1990s (Núñez and Heyman 2007). Because of the disproportionate concentration of immigration law enforcement efforts at and near the border, undocumented border residents especially are impeded from free movement locally (354). Even public transportation like the bus and the trolley has become a site of surveillance, further compounding undocumented immigrants' immobility. Beyond potential encounters with immigration enforcement in and outside of their neighborhoods, immigrants also run up against fixed Border Patrol checkpoints that are located along major highways between twenty-five to one hundred miles into the U.S. interior (355) that preclude them from traveling to points beyond.

FIGURE 7. A uniformed Border Patrol officer stands guard by an apartment complex and shopping mall close to the border on the U.S. side.

Indeed, her parents' constrained mobility was one of the clues that first enabled Isabel to understand the implications of her parents' undocumented status. Though her father, Santos, had access to a vehicle, Isabel worried considerably about him driving, saying, "The cops are always around here. I always feared that he would get stopped or pulled over by the cops and have no license." With no other options for getting around when the girls were young, Paloma had to rely on public transportation. Over time, though, this practice became more risky as the Border Patrol would periodically board and conduct immigration sweeps. Consequently, the threat of deportability always clouded taking public transportation, provoking anxiety in Paloma and serving to confine her. Instead of venturing out, Isabel noted, "My mom would have to wait until somebody was home to drive her." Initially that person was her father, but over time Isabel, as the oldest child and first legal driver in the family, became her main ride. With some frustration, Isabel noted, "Once I got my license, everything laid on me. My [younger] siblings didn't drive, so there's no way [they] could help."

Though their neighborhood is already under heavy surveillance, the Clementes avoided going even further in the direction of the border whenever possible due to strong Border Patrol presence—even when Isabel was the one driving. This caution even extended into their shopping habits; as Isabel pointed out, "There's an outlet mall right by the border. We never went to the mall there because the Border Patrol is always there roaming the streets." Much of Isabel's father's extended family is in the L.A. area, but the Clementes were also not able to travel up to see them. There is a prominent Border Patrol checkpoint (San Clemente) on Interstate 5 en route to L.A., meaning they would not make it safely through. Thus, mobility challenges factored prominently into the Clementes' lives and left them increasingly anxious, homebound, and isolated.

Like Paloma, Tomás's mother, Luisa, has always avoided traveling outside of the neighborhood whenever possible. Like Isabel, Tomás is the eldest child in the Ramírez family, which consists of his parents and three younger siblings. His parents are originally from the same community in Michoacán; his father came to San Diego first and then returned to Michoacán to bring Luisa five years later. His father was able to acquire a green card but his mother has not been able to. When he was fifteen years old, Tomás reflected, "Because of the status, we just can't really travel. If we do—even just around here—we have to do it stealth." Note that Tomás includes himself as one of the family members who had to travel "stealth."

As an adult, Tomás moved to a different part of San Diego with his wife and their two children. Luisa sees them regularly, as she provides childcare for the children; however, she almost always watches them at her apartment in the neighborhood, per her preference. "She doesn't really like to go that far," Tomás explained, "because she doesn't know the area, so she doesn't feel comfortable. It takes so much for me to come in and say, 'Hey, Mom, do you want to come by? I'm having a barbeque.' I'm like, 'It's okay. You'll be in my car. I have a new car—we won't get stopped.'" Luisa's status and her anxiousness about it, then, have affected not only her children but also now her grandchildren.

Travel beyond the neighborhood is a source of anxiety for not just participants' parents but also their friends. Mateo's parents have had their papers since he was in elementary school and are able to travel freely, including his mother, whose job is in located in North County. But as a fifteen-year-old, Mateo noted a good friend's persistent hesitation about going to a nearby beach. He recounted, "We used to go to [the] beach a lot, and she never wanted to go. I was like, 'C'mon, why don't you wanna go?' and then it hit me like, 'Oh, I get it. It's because she doesn't have papers.'" Indeed, declining social engagements that took them outside of known (and relatively "safe") areas commonly signaled not having papers and served as a way for participants to index their friends' undocumented status without having to discuss it explicitly.

During childhood, being able to go to Disneyland was a particularly emblematic proxy for immigration status. The San Clemente checkpoint also prevented friends who did not have papers—or even those whose parents did not—from going to Disneyland. As Mateo observed, "[My undocumented friends] never wanted to go to Disneyland because of the checkpoint. There was always this constant struggle about what they couldn't do . . . It was on the down low, but it did limit their lives a lot." Beyond Disneyland, Mateo noted the cascade of limitations that accompanied the lack of status, saying, "It's tough for them. It's like, 'I can't drive because I can't get a license. I can't go to college because I don't have an ID and I can't get financial aid. And even if I do, somehow, I can't get a good job after.'"

Mateo's older sister Lisa similarly detected this pattern while growing up, saying, "Yeah, Disneyland and really just L.A. was how you knew [about people's status]. Especially with school when we had games and had to drive somewhere else, we knew who couldn't go and who could." Sometimes the whole group of friends would decide not to proceed with plans in light of their friends' inability to travel; as Tomás recalled, "One time we wanted to go to Disneyland as a group. But we couldn't. Well, we could but we don't want to leave my friend back behind. So we just decided not to go." Tomás and his friends also downplayed another San Diego teenage rite of passage—crossing the border into Tijuana, where the drinking age is eighteen, to party with friends—to make another friend feel better about his inability to cross the border. As Tomás shared, "We can't go to T.J.[2] So my friend's never been. We all say, 'Oh, yeah, it's not all that. You're not missing out on much.'"

"IF MY MOM HAD PAPERS . . . WE WOULD HAVE TAKEN MORE TRIPS TO MEXICO": RESTRICTIONS ON TRANSBORDER TRAVEL

As Tomás's story suggests, loved ones' undocumented status not only affects local mobility on the U.S. side but also shapes one's ability to travel to Mexico; indeed, the ability to cross the border was the first benefit of citizenship that participants identified in freelisting. (I more deeply investigate the implications of illegality for transborder life in chapter 6.) Tomás's mother has never returned to her hometown in Michoacán since she came to California; as a teenager, he clearly articulated that their lack of going back was not by choice: "My mom hasn't seen her mom since she left fifteen years ago. She's kind of used to it, but I think she really wants to go back. She'd definitely go back more if she could." At that time, when I asked him about his parents' hometown, Tomás commented, "I haven't visited yet, but I want to see how it's like and how they live—if everything's true what people say about it." Tomás's comments clearly indicated that there was a mystique about Mexico for him as a child, borne of the fact that he was not able to go. He mused, "If my mom had papers . . . I think that we would have taken more trips and met the rest of the family. Maybe we would have even stayed there for a few months or something when we were younger." There was a sense of longing in Tomás's voice as he talked about his parents' hometown—a sentiment echoed by other children of undocumented parents who felt that they were "missing out," as Sal phrased it.

Nearly a decade later, Tomás's family is still in the same position because of Luisa's status; no one from the family has been able to return to Michoacán yet. Over time, Tomás has lost a little enthusiasm about going to Mexico. As he reflected in 2014, "The status has always been the thing that's held us back from visiting. Now as I'm older, I just don't talk to my family there or have a connection with them. I don't know how they would feel about me going there. I don't know if they're, like, mad at me since it's because of me [that] she doesn't go." Clearly, Tomás bears emotional weight about his and his mother's lack of present-day connection to her hometown and extended family members there. Interestingly, though, instead of attributing her status limitations to larger structures of power, he has internalized the blame, even wondering if his family resents him and his siblings for the lack of visits. Tomás has mostly made his peace with his lack of connection to his parents' hometown, but he still has hope for his mother to be able to return. When prompted about the topic, he reflected, "I think [going back] is definitely something she dreams about. I'd like for her to be able to travel. She gave up a lot deciding to stay here after we were born and not going back where she has all her family. We don't have any family here, on either side. So we're lonely."

While Tomás's mother is from a farther-away Mexican state, the visiting patterns are more complicated for those who have family members in nearby Tijuana. As previously mentioned, Isabel's parents spent her entire childhood separated from her mother's extended family in Tijuana; Isabel's mother is one of twelve children. She describes the family as "super united," particularly given that Isabel's maternal grandmother died when her mother was ten and the siblings really came together for each other with her mother, the oldest, taking care of them. During all the years that Paloma has been unable to go home to Tijuana, "It was just something that she just lived with," as Isabel described it. Though she unquestionably missed her family, she at least sent her daughters with other family members who could cross to maintain that family connection in the hopes that something would change one day. So Isabel was able to get to know Mexico and her family there in a way that Tomás was not. However, as Isabel noted, her mother's desire to go back "became more imminent when my grandpa passed away and she couldn't go to the funeral. That's when it really hit us—she can't go, can't say good-bye to him. And then she lost my uncle and then she lost my cousin . . . and she just couldn't be there."

Not being able to go to the funerals weighed extremely heavily on Paloma and on her daughters, who felt some guilt about being able to go while their mother could not. Paloma was not the only one who was put in a quandary with ailing or dying parents; in fact, both Beto and Sal's undocumented mothers returned home to tend to their ailing parents despite the jeopardy it put them in for their return back across the border. As described in chapter 5, the trip back home to Jalisco resulted in disastrous consequences for Beto's mother, Estela, when she got caught while trying to return to San Diego and was detained. This episode serves as a mark on Estela's record and precludes her from trying to regularize her status. It has also ensured that she has not returned to Jalisco again and likewise does not cross locally into Mexico either—despite the fact that her eldest son, Luis, lives in Tijuana, unable to cross back without great risk. Thus, deportability is no mere abstraction for the Garcías but a daily reality that they must negotiate.

Family separations—both for those living undocumented in the United States and those deported in Mexico—means that family members who have a status that enables them to move freely must sometimes make tough decisions about which family members' needs to prioritize. Amada, for instance, talked about how her older sister was unable to return to Mexico—her birthplace— since she would not be able to cross back safely due to her lack of papers. She shared, "My sister wants to go to T.J., but she can't. She spent her childhood there and her whole life is there. She can't go to our house or visit her friends or her school. Her daughter is two years old, and she doesn't know it there at all. It's really sad . . . really emotional." Amada's family—her parents and three other siblings—spent many weekends at their family residence in Tijuana. The fact that her sister is unable to cross means that she misses out on special family occasions like Amada's *quinceñera* during the summer of 2005. Amada shared, "My *quinceñera* was in Tijuana and a lot of people couldn't come because it was there. We couldn't decide to have it here or there. If it was here, people there couldn't come; if it was there, the same thing."

"I HAD TO GROW UP REALLY, REALLY FAST": ILLEGALITY AND FAMILY DYNAMICS

Tomás's mother's inability to remain connected with her family and Amada's sister's missing out on important family activities highlight another dimension of mixed-status family life: social isolation. Many families with whom I worked were not part of large transnational communities with family members and neighbors from their hometowns who lived close by (see chapter 5). Even those who had those types of family connections were not necessarily able to travel around the region to see them much due their hesitation about undertaking nonessential travel. Tomás describes Luisa's life as being extremely isolated and constrained; he shared, "When I come back home, I'm like, 'Oh, how are you doing, Mom? What have you been up to?' She's like, 'Oh, nothing . . . I've just been in the house. No setbacks.' It's still just the same thing." Mateo similarly noted, "[My undocumented family members] are scared to go outside. They don't want to do things. So if there's a party or something going on, they'll miss out on it; they miss out on a lot of family stuff. Or if there's like a family problem, they're not able to keep up with it." It is clear, then, that status has played a role in limiting participation in everyday family life and social activities (Enríquez 2015, 940).

Tomás later reflected on the implications of this isolation on him and his three younger siblings, saying, "We were always kind of sheltered from the world because you can't go places because my parents can't go there, or they're afraid of going too far. You don't get to experience much." Tomás was determined to "expand his wings" beyond what the neighborhood had to offer from an early age. As he was approaching high school, he said, "I wanted to leave the area and go to a different school. I did my research and decided on [name of high school]—it was the cream of the crop. I woke up early every day to take the bus to school. I never played football before but I wanted to try it and I got involved in all these different sports. It was definitely cool to experience it because we live in such a bubble here in this area." Getting out of the bubble became increasingly important for Tomás. Despite being intrigued by the idea of going to college in Los Angeles or points beyond, he made the decision to stay close to home. However, he made sure that being local did not stop him from meeting new people from elsewhere. As he noted, "I wanted to go [to college] and meet new people and see what other people are all about. I'd make friends and then I'd ask them, 'Hey, can I go with you to see what it's like where you're from?'" He followed through on these requests, going with these friends to their homes throughout California. As he recounted, "Instead of staying in San Diego, I went up to Yucaipa with my friend for Thanksgiving. I also went up to San Francisco another time. I got to travel. I feel like I started to taste the world a little more."

Tomás has continued "tasting the world" as he and his wife and children have traveled out of state to visit her family. He talks about possibly wanting to move out of state but also worries about how that would affect his mother, saying, "I like San Diego, but one day I see myself moving somewhere else, and I would like for her to be able to see me. I mean, I would always come and see her. But it would be good for her to be able to take on something besides San Diego." Tomás's reflections demonstrate that he felt a tension between seeing the world and attending to his mother, who only felt comfortable in her neighborhood bubble because of her undocumented status, even after twenty-three years of living in the United States at that point. Indeed, as the oldest child of four by a few years, Tomás has shouldered significant responsibility for his family's well-being.

Some other oldest children also had to take on household responsibilities and authority due to their parents' status being less secure—a common phenomenon for children with immigrant parents (Menjívar 2000, 228; 2010; Orellana, Dorner, and Pulido 2003). For instance, Lisa and Mateo's older sister (by four and eight years, respectively) had a very different adolescence than they did. As Mateo pointed out, "My older sister had to help out the family and she didn't get to enjoy her life as much or really even plan her life. My parents didn't have papers, and she actually got a job when she was like sixteen and she was helping my family out. She didn't get the same opportunities I did because she had to have a job."

Isabel became a key member of her household when she was still quite young. Indeed, children of undocumented immigrants must cultivate a depth of insight and understanding far beyond their age (Zayas 2015, 15). As Isabel stated in 2014, "I had to grow up really, really fast. I always knew when there was no money or that my parents couldn't work because they didn't have the social." One of the primary ways in which the Clementes experienced illegality was as an economic barrier that limited her father's ability to provide for the family (Abrego 2016, 16). During her high school years, her family's circumstances were particularly precarious; as she recalled, "When the economy went down, construction went down really bad. It got so bad at home to the point where we almost had nowhere to live." At that point, her mother, who had not worked previously in part due to immigration-related fears, looked for a job. Paloma "knew some people that were working janitorial and they didn't have papers either," Isabel recalled, "so she started working there." Luckily, her family had lived in their house for long enough that the landlord was flexible with them as they reestablished their finances and made back payments.

Despite the stress of that period, Isabel gained admission to a local private university and paid for the costs with scholarships she had earned and with financial aid. She decided to "stay close to home. I knew I couldn't go away from home because I needed to be around to help out one way or the other." Her scholarship money and financial aid enabled her to live on campus during her first year, which was "really nice. It was easier to concentrate on school, and my GPA that year was really good." But her orientation was still very much back home; as she revealed, "For me, it was hard. I had $1,000 and I'm like, 'Okay, maybe I can pay the rent and help my mom. It was really different than some other students with different upbringings." Home life also continued to be challenging, as she recalled: "That time was really hard because my dad was working out of state and my mom doesn't drive. And since she doesn't have a license, she panics. So even though I was at school, I would have to go pick her up at work, come back to school, and then go pick her up again to bring her home before I went back to school. So sometimes I was studying for tests or doing homework. I always had to leave." Ultimately, Isabel lamented, "I just couldn't extract myself from home. I had to always be there in one way or another. I just moved back home after that because it was just easier. Sometimes I wasn't going to sleep until like two or three in the morning because of my mom's work." In some respects, Isabel sheltered her sisters from the worst periods and the stressors that she faced; as she said, "Things have been different for them. They haven't seen the struggle or what happened like I have." In fact, Isabel herself subsequently helped pay for her sisters' tuition and room and board so they could live on campus—even though it proved to be impossible for her to do so because of the precariousness of her family's circumstances. Abrego (2016, 17) has highlighted the tensions that emerge sometimes on the basis of difference in status; as the experiences of Isabel, Mateo's sister, and Tomás suggest, different siblings' levels of responsibility in buffering the effects of illegality on behalf of their parents can also serve as a source of tension among siblings in mixed-status families.

"WE LIVED THAT FEAR, TOO, EVEN THOUGH WE WERE CITIZENS": THE EMBODIED EFFECTS OF ILLEGALITY

Cumulatively, the previously articulated limitations have had clear mental health implications for my participants, resulting in embodied stress (Zayas 2015, 86). Children in mixed-status families like Isabel are anxious about their parents driving around or even taking public transportation; they fear that these activities might lead to deportation, and, over time, they learn to sensitively navigate their parents' and friends' limitations and take on more responsibility. Young adults like Tomás also reflect the pain of their parents not being able to return to Mexico; in his case, he suffered guilt over thinking that he and his siblings were what prevented his mother from maintaining connections with her family. As they transitioned into adulthood, young adults like Isabel also felt the weight of taking care of their parents to the degree that they knew they could not move away because of their increasingly prominent role within their families. These patterns suggest that children living with undocumented family members bear significant "somatic fallout" (97) that unquestionably shapes their broader well-being as well as their life paths as adults.

The roots of these repercussive emotional effects, however, extend far back into their childhoods, when they first learned about illegality and began to come to terms with what it meant. When they were young, participants held a more generalized fear about what might happen. Carlos was born in Mexico but crossed when he was young, and he was able to regularize his status as a child when his parents did. He reflected that "as a kid, I didn't really know 'I'm a resident' or anything specific. But there was always that fear of immigration taking you or something like that. I had that fear . . . with my other family that didn't have resident status or any documentation." Lisa described a generalized fear as well: "We didn't totally grasp the idea of what was gonna happen. You just had that fear without really knowing why or the consequences. It was just like, you get caught and game over. You get thrown to the other side. That was it."

As they got older, the fear became more specific and grounded in family members' experiences. Lisa derived insight into what would happen when a cousin without papers lived with them. When she was a teenager, she told a story about this cousin:

> When she went to work, my cousin would always be scared because she had to ride the bus. [The Border Patrol] would also go on the bus to take them off. The other day she told us a story about how she was about to get on a bus, like it was leaving and she was like, "No!" and she was running after it but couldn't make it. So she got on another bus and then she noticed that the bus she was going to go on was stopped by the Border Patrol and they took out people. And she was like, "Thank God!"

By that point, Lisa's own parents were squared away with their residency and had become more stable and secure. Yet Lisa recalled, "when my cousin lived with us for a while and she didn't have any papers. And we lived that fear, that same fear that she had about going to the bus, and going here and there. We lived it too, even though we were citizens. But we felt it, and we'd be like, 'Oh my gosh, there's a Border Patrol there.'"

Participants' statements underscore that they "lived that fear" of their family members, internalizing and embodying their vulnerabilities. Tomás similarly reflected, "It's kind of my fear too. I share in their fear." They "share" in this fear even when they knew full well that they themselves were safe by virtue of their status. Horton (2009, 23) observes that illegality "sets in motion a concatenation of shared vulnerabilities and intimate interdependencies between family members." A focus on intersubjectivity is important in understanding migration as a phenomenon that implicates more than just migrants themselves, illuminating "the ways in which subjectivity itself is deeply intersubjective in nature" (Desjarlais and Throop 2011, 91).

These shared family vulnerabilities also can produce physical scars for citizen children in mixed-status families. Such was the case with Isabel when she was in college. Eventually all of the pressure she was under came to a head. She was trying to be a successful college student while contributing financially to her household, making up for her dad's absence (while he was out of state working), shuttling her mother to her night-shift job, and taking care of her younger sisters. She experienced a major nervous-system health episode that forced her to drop out right before her senior year. Stress is thought to be one of the largest contributing factors to the condition. Isabel felt that its onset was unquestionably exacerbated by the stress she was under at that point; she literally embodied all of the immigration-related challenges her family faced.

With no health insurance in the United States, Isabel sought treatment for her condition in Tijuana, as many border residents do by necessity and preference (Castañeda and Melo 2014; Núñez and Heyman 2007). Luckily, Isabel had been spending time with her extended family throughout her childhood and had a good family support network in Tijuana to be with her while she went to appointments and to take care of her. She was able to recover, but once she did, she got a job to help support the family instead of returning to college. At that point, she became the most securely employed and highest-paid wage earner in her household and continued to take on an increasingly prominent role; as she noted, "My mom relies so much on me . . . for a lot of different things." Isabel's health episode clearly underscores the immigration-related vulnerabilities that citizen children in mixed-status families come to embody.

"IT'S JUST SOMETHING THAT WE'VE LONGED FOR FOR SO LONG": AMELIORATING ILLEGALITY

I have highlighted some of the more microlevel strategies my participants have deployed for maneuvering around illegality and deportability—taking over family driving duties once they got their driver's licenses, changing social plans with friends to be more inclusive, choosing to stay closer to home for college and beyond to be able to ensure family security, and taking on increasing financial and other responsibilities within the family. These strategies to buffer the effects of illegality have come at a mental and physical cost to participants. Yet over time, I have observed them taking more conscious steps to protect their undocumented family members and improve their collective family lot, often involving personal sacrifice.

As I examined in chapter 2, the immigrant rights protests provided a platform for developing brokering sensibilities (Bloemraad and Trost 2008; Getrich 2008), clearly contesting dominant ideas about immigrant illegality and policy proposals that sought to further criminalize and marginalize my participants and their family members and friends. As this chapter has revealed, as teenagers, they were simultaneously cultivating brokering roles within their families while actively maneuvering around the limitations that illegality and deportability imposed on their family members and friends. As participants matured, they also began to broker their family members' interactions with the state (Orellana, Dorner, and Pulido 2003, 519–20), more directly contesting their parents' illegality. Examining their words and actions as twenty-something adults, it is clear that participants are still very committed to their parents and involved in advocating on their behalf to improve their living circumstances.

Filing papers for one's parents as an adult is the ultimate way in which to eliminate the repercussive effects of illegality and deportability on their family's lives. Once a U.S. citizen turns twenty-one, she or he can file a "petition for alien relative," or I-130 form, for her or his family. Tomás heard about this option while he was a college student, saying, "My fraternity brother is really involved in this community. So he knows a few attorneys that do immigration workshops. You can ask them some questions and not have to pay them for answers. They teach you how to figure it out and start the process. I mean, I knew that you could do it when you turn twenty-one." Despite getting some information, though, Tomás felt a little awkward about seeking further information, saying, "I'm in college, so it's kind of weird to ask people about it. It's not like an open topic, like, 'Hey, how do I help my mom get papers?' You know?" Though he had not yet applied for her when I spoke with him in summer 2014, he noted, "That's something I really want to do, so she doesn't have to be afraid."

Isabel made filing for her parents a top priority once she started working after her health episode forced her to drop out of college; it was one of the few silver linings to emerge from that horrible period. She reported, "I filed for my parents when I stopped college and started working because it's a lot of money. So we applied, submitted all her paperwork. We were going to do them at the same time but when we met with the attorney, she felt that because my dad still crossed back and forth for a while with the passport, he could run a higher risk of deportation. So it was better if we filed my mom first and then my dad." Of course, after they had applied, there was a long stressful period while they waited for the determination. Isabel observed how the process affected her mother emotionally, saying, "As it was getting closer to the point when we knew we would find out, you could tell that she was dying, like spiritually inside . . . she just wasn't her. You would talk to her and things like that at home . . . something simple she would have usually not cared, she was mad or she would yell at us, something she never does. It was just that longing became time pressured, like it needs to happen . . . now!" Isabel's mother did, in fact, obtain her green card—"like the day before her birthday. She was just crying and crying as soon as she got it." Now that Paloma has her green card, she maneuvers freely throughout the region and has finally been able to see her family in Tijuana after twenty-four years—a homecoming I highlight in chapter 5 in examining transborder life.

After Paloma got her papers, there was a period of tempered enthusiasm as they waited to hear about Santos. Isabel recalled, "When my dad still didn't have anything, there was still that lingering fear. My mom's husband didn't have papers, so they could revoke her green card just like that." Isabel's father, Santos, did receive his papers a few months after her mother. When I saw her in summer 2014, Isabel proudly exclaimed, "My dad just got his license last Monday. He was really excited because he can finally drive and not have to worry about getting stopped or pulled over by the cops that are always all over here." In fact, she recounted a scenario that was mundane for many borderlanders but extraordinary in her own family's life: "My mom went down to T.J. by herself for the first time last week. My dad dropped her off at the border. She crossed over on her own and everything, because sometimes we [girls] can't go. She wants to go all the time now!" Reflecting on the significance of her parents' getting their papers, Isabel stated, "It's something that we've longed for for so long. It felt really good to do that for them. It's just such a sense of relief. We're more at peace." As Isabel stated this, her eyes once again filled with tears—this time happy tears.

Beto has also played an instrumental role in trying to improve his family's situation through his position as a citizen and the opportunities that affords him. Though he grew up undocumented, Beto married his high school girlfriend, a U.S. citizen, and was able to regularize his status through her in 2008, three years after he finished high school. He says, "She really helped me and helped my family in a huge way and I'll always be thankful for that." Getting his papers "gave me so many more options," Beto reports. Having better job opportunities was high on the list of benefits that he was able to access with his newfound status. Beto continued through the immigration process, ultimately gaining U.S. citizenship; however, he described it as "bittersweet. I was sitting there taking the oath and saying the whole allegiance to the flag . . . but I'm like, 'Why are there others—my family, students—who don't have this opportunity?'"

As soon as Beto was legally and financially able to, he hired an immigration attorney and filed an immigration application on behalf of both of his parents. His father's case was more straightforward, and they were able to successfully secure his papers without too much difficulty. Unfortunately, his mother's case is much more complicated due to her previous detainment. Thus, she continues to contend with the prolonged impact of illegality and the reality of not having any options—now or even in the future. Even though Beto and his father have made important gains in securing their own statuses, it has created new divisions within the family about who can drive, travel locally, and go to Mexico. It is thus with only a tempered enthusiasm that Beto talks about the changes to his life since he got papers.

CONCLUSION

I have examined how illegality and deportability shape the lives of children in borderland mixed-status families and their ways of "being in the world" (Willen 2007). Drawing from their own life experiences and reflections on them, I demonstrated the repercussive effects (Comfort 2007) of illegality and deportability on these young adults over time. Indeed, my participants bore the collective weight of negotiating their parents' and friends' inabilities to get around; the persistent insecurities implicit in traveling locally, regionally, and to Mexico; and the increased responsibilities they took on to make up for their family members' social isolation, economic insecurity, and inability to see one another. Though they have crafted these brokering skills over time and are well situated as citizens to carry them out, they have done so bearing the emotional and physical weight of these shared immigration-related vulnerabilities. They have also found themselves directly confronting the punitive power of the state in Beto's case.

In chapter 2, I described the blurring of boundaries between different classification systems that participants articulated as teens. This chapter builds on this notion of blurred boundaries, demonstrating that the repercussive effects of illegality extend well beyond those who are "illegal." Alba and Waters (2011, 11) argue that "there will be huge negative costs imposed on the next generation if a path to citizenship is not provided for the parental generation." I would argue that these costs are already being borne by the children of immigrants who have been subjected to the vulnerabilities implicit in their parents' status and lack of opportunities. While they may be citizens, they experience their parents' status emotionally and even physically, underscoring that they possess a form of diminished (Chavez 2017) or contingent citizenship (Boehm 2012).

In the next chapter, I consider another way in which second-generation Mexicans' rights as U.S. citizens are undermined through the border enforcement regime that has circumscribed their lives since they were young. The impact of illegality is not just something they experience in relation to their families but rather is a force that they contend with in their own lives as they walk around the neighborhood and cross the border. Just as they have found ways to contest the repercussive effects of illegality and deportability on behalf of their families, though, they have also cultivated mechanisms for maneuvering around border enforcement in their own lives.

4

EMBODYING AND CONTESTING THE EFFECTS OF RACIALIZED ENFORCEMENT

ESPERANZA MEDINA remembered clearly the story of when her mother crossed the U.S.-Mexico border without papers. As she told me when she was seventeen,

> My dad came over first and sort of laid the foundation and then had my mom come over. She originally didn't want to come . . . she had to leave my two brothers in Mexico with my grandmother. My mom described what the journey was like to me. It was at night, and they had to hide in the bushes. She was scared that the Border Patrol would find her. It was very cold and my mom was pregnant with me . . . there were no bathrooms and she really needed to go. She was with an uncle of mine and he was trying to bring her over safely to where my dad was waiting. They made it fine in the end, but it was really, really hard for her.

Even before she was born, then, Esperanza was already, in a sense, subject to Border Patrol policing and her mother's embodied fear about getting caught. Esperanza's mother also conveyed to her that fear predominated her family's

---

Parts of this chapter are reprinted by permission from Springer Nature: *Latino Studies* (vol. 11, no. 4, pp. 462–82), "'Too Bad I'm Not an Obvious Citizen': The Effects of Racialized U.S. Immigration Enforcement Practices on Second-Generation Mexican Youth," by Christina M. Getrich, copyright © 2013.

early years when they did not have papers, and that they "would have to stay undercover, really quiet . . . and not draw attention to themselves."

Unlike peers like Isabel, whose undocumented parents contended with illegality and deportability throughout her entire childhood, Esperanza's parents and two older brothers—who came to the United States to reunite with the family after a year or so of separation—were able to regularize their status. Esperanza did not remember precisely when her family members got their papers, though she knows it was when she and her younger U.S.-born sister, Victoria, were still little. By the time she was in high school, when I met her, her father and brothers had become citizens and her mother was a resident.

The fact that her parents and brothers had papers allowed Esperanza some measure of tranquility that she recognized very clearly some of her peers did not have. Very active in her church, she observed that many other children her age "had completely different life stories than I had. My circumstances were quite stable compared to a lot of friends I grew up with. Within my group, I was the one with the happy story with my family all together." She was easily able to imagine herself in their shoes, though, and reflected, "It makes me scared to think about if one of [my parents] didn't have their papers . . . there'd always be that chance that they could just be ripped apart from our family."

Despite possessing citizenship and her immediate family members' statuses protecting them from potential deportation and resulting family separation, Esperanza's description of her childhood in southeast San Diego is nonetheless peppered with remembrances of the Border Patrol and the fear they instilled in her from an early age. She felt this fear as she went about mundane activities such as walking from her house to her church, but even more prominently when she crossed the border to go to their sister parish in Tijuana or visit her older brother, who had moved there with his wife and young child while they applied for her papers. While crossing, she noted, "I get very nervous even though I know I'm a citizen. I'm dark . . . so you can classify me easily. That's what they do."

As citizens by birthright, second-generation Mexicans like Esperanza and Victoria should enjoy the full range of rights and benefits associated with U.S. citizenship, including that their membership go unquestioned.[1] However, in the borderland milieu, residents of all immigration statuses have come under the ever-intensifying gaze of various state enforcement agencies during the period of stepped-up border enforcement over the past two-plus decades (Dunn 2010; Inda 2006a, 2006b; Nevins 2002). Life in particular borderland neighborhoods like the one my participants grew up in is saturated with Border Patrol presence as agents roam around in their ubiquitous white-with-green-trim sport utility vehicles. Residents of a range of statuses have daily encounters with these vehicles and agents—unlike other neighborhoods in San Diego—underscoring that it is important to pay attention to locally based variations of how illegality is enacted (Heyman 2014; Menjívar and Kanstroom 2014).

The category of the *illegal immigrant* provides the justification for the surveillance of all individuals who are suspected of being potentially illegal (DeGenova 2002; Inda 2006b). But because *illegal immigrant* is a sociopolitical construction, its boundaries are not clear in practice, even to the immigration officials who are tasked with enforcement. Immigration enforcement activities, therefore, often extend beyond undocumented immigrants, targeting both residents and citizens of Mexican descent within a larger system of racialized governance that regards them as "presumptively illegal" (Menjívar and Kanstroom 2014, 13; see also Harrison and Lloyd 2012, 379). The production of these racialized boundaries serves to reinforce a biopolitics of otherness (Fassin 2011, 214; Sabo and Lee 2015) in the borderlands.

FIGURE 8. Approaching the San Ysidro Port of Entry from the U.S. side.

Both as teenagers and now as adults, Esperanza and her peers have recounted their frequent and generally unpleasant encounters with officials who repeatedly questioned their membership and required them to prove that they legitimately belonged in the United States. Such encounters made it clear that borders not only involve delineating and protecting state sovereignty but also are central in demarcating the social boundaries of citizenship and belonging (Behdad 2005). The lived experiences of these borderlanders, then, illuminate the biopolitics of citizenship and governmentality in operation (Gonzales and Chavez 2012). As Heyman (2014, 122) points out, these experiences of being monitored while crossing affect internal self-conceptions and have broader emotional and psychological impacts that can be cognitively scarring.

This chapter examines immigration enforcement in the San Diego–Tijuana region to establish how this system of surveillance has infiltrated the lives of second-generation young adults—an understudied segment of borderlanders (Aiken and Plows 2010; Bejarano 2005, 2010; Mendoza Inzunza and Fernández Huerta 2010). The previous chapter, chapter 3, documented how the children of immigrants "shared in the fear" of illegality alongside their family members, worrying about their well-being and avoiding risky places alongside them. The present chapter will demonstrate how these individuals more directly experience, understand, and negotiate their own encounters with immigration enforcement agents as racialized biosocial profiling becomes embodied as fear and distress in their everyday lives (Willen 2007, 2010).

The quotidian presence and practices of the state in the lives of borderlanders collectively contribute to the racialization of nonwhite residents in the border region (Goldsmith et al. 2009; Romero 2006; Rosas 2006a; Sabo and Lee 2015; Sabo et al. 2014). While the stated purpose of border policing is to monitor the international geopolitical border, these border enforcement policies and practices reinforce a racialized form of belonging that has negative implications on second-generation young adults. Thus we are also able to see the way in which it affects their embodied subjectivities as they navigate the biopolitics of citizenship and forge their identities (Gonzales and Chavez 2012). Yet these individuals, first as teenagers and now as adults, have also responded to these encounters by cultivating strategies of transformative resistance that allow them to contest the infringement of their rights.

THEORIZING RACIALIZED IMMIGRATION ENFORCEMENT

POLICEABILITY IN THE BORDERLANDS

As I have demonstrated in chapters 2 and 3, illegality is not merely a theoretical construct or an abstract condition but rather is a concrete state of being that has emerged as a result of the deliberate set of tactics the U.S. state has deployed to create and sustain the legally vulnerable condition of deportability (DeGenova 2005, 8). Though as Romero (2008, 28) points out, because immigration status is a social construction, it is "not complete without policing and surveillance." Rosas (2006a, 404) expands upon illegality and deportability through his concept of "policeability," which characterizes a system of racialized management through which both the undocumented and "those who resemble them" are subject to surveillance and state-mandated policing. Policeability more explicitly highlights normative notions of citizenship and whiteness operating in the borderlands (404).

These tactics of policeability result in a racialized law enforcement approach in which physical appearance serves as a way of controlling certain racial and ethnic groups (Romero 2008, 27). This form of racial governance (Rosas 2006b, 340) was codified in the 1975 Supreme Court decision in *United States v. Brignoni-Ponce*, which established that "Mexican appearance" was sufficient grounds for citizenship inspection (Goldsmith et al. 2009, 97; Romero 2006, 453). The decision in effect instituted that a person's appearance could serve as "reasonable suspicion" or "probable cause" and in so doing set up a system in which Mexicans and others are denied equal protection under the law (451). These repressive forms of violence are justified and legitimated in the name of fighting "illegal" immigration (Goldsmith et al. 2009, 117).

Romero (2006, 450) argues that immigration research has typically ignored the costs paid by Latinxs who are implicated by U.S. immigration policies. Indeed, the surveillance of citizenship is most highly concentrated in poor and working-class Latinx neighborhoods (453; Goldsmith et al. 2009, 96). The scale of impact of racialized immigration enforcement is elusive, since immigration agencies do not collect systematic data on citizens and residents who are stopped and searched (Romero 2006, 453). Human rights groups, however, have been documenting charges against immigration authorities of violence and harassment—perpetrated even against U.S. citizens—since the border operations were introduced in the 1990s (see, for example, Getrich 2000).

Scholars have also been documenting interactions between immigration officials and local border community residents. Romero examined a high-profile immigration raid in Chandler, Arizona, demonstrating how it functioned as a policing practice to reinforce the subordinated status of working-class U.S. citizens and residents of Mexican descent (Romero 2006, 450–51; 2008). Goldsmith, Romero, and their colleagues also found a systematic pattern of immigration officials' mistreatment of residents of all immigration statuses in their survey of households in South Tucson, Arizona (Goldsmith et al. 2009). In his examination of the longitudinal effects of Operation Blockade in El Paso, Texas, Dunn (2010, 182) demonstrates that the operation actually alleviated some of the aggressive enforcement practices that predated it in south El Paso and neighborhoods near the Rio Grande River initially, but that these racialized enforcement practices have more recently reemerged in force.

EMBODIED EFFECTS OF RACIALIZED ENFORCEMENT PRACTICES

An important dimension of these racialized enforcement practices that has drawn insufficient attention is the way in which fear and stress become embodied for border residents of Mexican descent of all immigration statuses. Willen (2007) builds on the two conventional ways in which illegality has been articulated (as a juridical status and a sociopolitical condition) by elaborating on an important third dimension: its effects on migrants' everyday, embodied experiences of being in the world. She demonstrates how African and Filipino migrants in Tel Aviv *experienced* their condition of illegality, which caused persistent, embodied tension and anxiety among migrants as they went about their daily lives. These embodied anxieties profoundly shaped migrants' subjective experiences of time (for example, perceived differences in risk between weekdays and weekends) and also how they maneuvered in both public and private spaces. In fact, the state's deportation campaign stripped undocumented migrants of the "possibility of experiencing the private space of home as a haven from the outside world" (Willen 2007, 26). Willen's third dimension of illegality provides a productive mechanism for linking the political and the phenomenal (Desjarlais and Throop 2011, 93).

Though the deportation regime (DeGenova and Peutz 2010) has deeply penetrated the U.S. interior to produce widespread vulnerabilities and embodied experiences of illegality nationwide (Harrison and Lloyd 2012), state violence and fear as a tactic of population control has long been the state's modus operandi in the borderlands. In fact, the normalization of state surveillance was an explicit component of the LIC doctrine undergirding border operations that debuted in the mid-1990s (Dunn 1996). Thus the borderlands provide a vantage point from which to understand the maturation of these dynamics of surveillance and the longer-term implications of living in—or, indeed, growing up in—a constant climate of fear. It is precisely in this context that my participants have come of age. This climate of fear has caused "persistent, embodied tension and anxiety" (Willen 2007, 16) for border residents of every immigration status. However, it is not merely deportability and the way it affects their family members by extension that shapes these young adults' lives in the borderlands; racialized border enforcement affects the way that they navigate mundane spaces under the ever-present gaze of the Border Patrol.

Thus, border enforcement must be understood as part of a broader project linking power, subjectivity, and embodied racialized practices (Correa and Thomas 2015, 250). Correa and Thomas elaborate a critical phenomenology of racial power through which power is inscribed not only through institutions and laws but also by the on-the-ground practices of those who exercise it— namely, political officials and law enforcers (241–42). They argue that the U.S.-Mexico borderlands must be understood as a racialized space of intersubjectivity through which local residents' bodies are managed, often paradoxically, by brown-bodied state agents (241). Their analysis adds another layer of intersubjectivity to border enforcement operations by considering how this system of racialized rule is also embodied and enacted by Latinx enforcement agents (240; see also Heyman 2002).

Sabo and Lee (2015) also call attention to the embodied effects of encounters with immigration enforcement agents that result in the othering of a population of U.S.-citizen and permanent-resident farmworkers of Mexican descent in the Arizona-Sonora borderlands. Drawing from a cross-sectional survey of 489 farmworkers, they found that both citizens and residents experienced significant levels of stress in anticipation of encounters with immigration officials (1). These "spillover" effects cause harm to farmworkers in multiple respects, including on a biopsychological level (2; see also Szkupinski Quiroga, Medina, and Glock

2014). Their findings underscore that even residents of Mexican descent felt vulnerable to being identified as "out of place," a vulnerability experienced not only at the port of entry but also in public spaces like worksites, neighborhoods, and local markets. They therefore refer to the "spillover" of such enforcement, experienced as profound stressors (Sabo and Lee 2015, 8). These spillover effects of enforcement also shape the embodied lived experiences of another segment of borderlanders: second-generation Mexican young adults.

NAVIGATING THE "EVERYDAYNESS" OF STATE POWER

Racialized enforcement activities strongly infiltrated the everyday lives of the borderland young adults with whom I have conducted research over the past decade. Heyman (1998, 166) uses the term *cotidianidad* (everydayness) to encapsulate this form of state power—the constant awareness of the presence of immigration officials in border communities and the accompanying wariness borderlanders have of them.[2] Part of this wariness stems from the fact that border enforcement practices operate on a principle of "presumed illegality" (Harrison and Lloyd 2012, 379; Menjívar and Kanstroom 2014, 13) under which all residents of Mexican descent are subject in their everyday lives. My participants' everyday encounters with immigration enforcement agents both at border inspection points at the international boundary and as they maneuver through daily life highlight not only how they make sense of these episodes but also how immigration policing becomes embodied among individuals who are not its nominal targets.

"WHEN I WAS YOUNGER, I'D ALWAYS GET TERRIBLE BUTTERFLIES IN MY STOMACH": IMMIGRATION INSPECTIONS AT BORDER CROSSINGS

When spending time in border neighborhoods in south San Diego, it is commonplace to hear people talk about "running down to T.J." for a variety of purposes that I explore further in the next chapter, chapter 5. Crossing the border, then, is a fairly ordinary activity for those who have an immigration status that permits them to do so.[3] Whether by themselves or with friends or family, participants return from a visit to T.J. by crossing the international U.S.-Mexico boundary through the San Ysidro or Otay Mesa Ports of Entry. Border crossings at the ports of entry are managed through inspection stations, where decisions are made about whether particular individuals may—or may not—enter the territorial boundaries of the nation-state. Border crossers pass through the international boundary (in both directions) either on foot or by car. Walkers are subject to an individual inspection; if a set of individuals are together in a car, the car as a unit is inspected. To reach this inspection point, the border crosser waits in a line until she or he reaches an agent, located inside a building (if crossing on foot) or in a booth (if crossing by car). Arriving at the front of the line, crossers encounter CBP agents, who evaluate would-be entrants through a process known as inspection (Heyman 2004, 307; Lugo 2000). Primary inspection involves an agent making a rapid determination (on average, within thirty seconds) about whether the individual being interviewed should be allowed to enter directly into the United States (Heyman 2004, 308). If border crossers do not pass the agent's initial examination, they may be sent to secondary inspection, also known colloquially as secondary (or *revisión* in Spanish). Here, definitive decisions are made about the attempted crossing, ultimately leading to a person's admission, rejection, or arrest (and possible prosecution; Heyman 2004, 308).

Typically, crossers must present documentation (such as a passport) to prove that they should be allowed to enter the United States. Regardless of documentation type, CBP agents make inferences about crossers based on visual cues, verbal cues, and responses to the agent's questions (Heyman 2004, 308). Agents ask crossers about their citizenship and visa status, activities in Mexico, and intended activities in the United States. The individual CBP agent wields substantial power to make determinations about the individual border crosser, though appraisals are not necessarily consistent and fairly applied (Heyman 2004, 314). These inspections can be aggressive, to the point of constituting a form of ritualized violence (Bejarano 2010). The risk and uncertainty renders the border-crossing experience quite stressful for many individuals—including those who have every legitimate right to cross the border.

My participants generally reported crossing the border to be a nerve-racking experience. Many, including Isabel, had early memories of embodied fear. As previously described, Isabel's parents often sent her and her sisters to Tijuana with family members to ensure that they would develop ties with their extensive Tijuana-based family. Isabel enjoyed her time with the family but always dreaded the return trip home. When she was sixteen, Isabel described the process, saying, "When I would cross when I was younger, I'd always get butterflies in my stomach, like terrible butterflies. And [my family] would be like, 'Why are you scared?' Before I crossed the border I always went to the store and bought gum. It's something I always did . . . because I was so nervous." Even though Isabel could not completely articulate her reasons for her nervousness when she was younger, she was acutely aware of the stressful nature of the inspection process, devising her own little ritual of comfort.

Years later, Isabel once again reflected on the crossing process, this time from the vantage point of adulthood. She noted that her childhood fear of crossing was related in part to the stressful nature of crossing itself: "You're so nervous because you've grown up with this fear of the Border Patrol. Sometimes they're just jerks to you when you cross. So you never know what kind of mood they're gonna be in or what's gonna happen when you talk to them." Thus the uncertainty of how she would be treated was one of the aspects of crossing that she dreaded. However, she then added that her larger concern was what might have happened to her family unit if something went wrong. As she stated, "When we crossed the border, honest to God, sometimes I felt like I had diarrhea. Even when we were minors, we knew that if they stopped us . . . even though we were with other family . . . if anything ever happened and they sent us to secondary . . . what if they needed our parents to come and get us, and they couldn't? It was just always that fear." She worried that visiting other family members in T.J. would set off a cascade of events that ultimately would result in her parents' deportation.

As Zayas (2015, xiii) points out, the constant fear of losing parents colors citizen children's view of the world and how they move within it. Dreby (2012) similarly highlights how parents' deportability causes citizen children to have to remain hypervigilant at all times for fear of destabilizing the family. Indeed, Zayas (2015, 97) argues there is a psychological and somatic fallout from having this monumental responsibility as a child. When I followed up with Isabel to see if she still felt that deep-seated fear—even though she is an adult and her parents have their papers now—Isabel stated, "It's a fear that's been there for so many years that it's hard to lose. I'll always have it."

Isabel's fear was not altogether unfounded, though in her case its concerns were never actualized. Paz, by contrast, recounted a dramatic event she experienced with her family once when they were trying to cross back into the United States. Paz's maternal grandmother lives in T.J. and partially raised her there during her first six years. Paz settled more into U.S. life as she got more deeply into her schooling, but she, her brother, their mother, and other extended family members still crossed regularly to visit her grandmother. They also went for other reasons as well; Paz explained that when her cousins got sick, her mother would often take them to Tijuana since the children did not have health insurance and their father (her maternal uncle) was undocumented. Paz recounted that one time as they attempted to cross back, "[The immigration officials] were like, 'I don't think this girl is a U.S. citizen' about my cousin. They were suspicious because the kids were my uncle's and he wasn't there. We were surprised. Normally we would just say like, 'Oh, we're U.S. citizens' and it's not usually a problem. But [this time] they ended up taking us away. I remember we were like all huddled in some office on the floor for hours and hours. It was really bad. We were all crying and crying and crying." While Paz's family was eventually released, the event was traumatic and perpetuated her fear of CBP agents.

During high school, Esperanza mostly crossed the border with her parents. Though all of them had their papers at that point, she likewise reported feeling a gnawing sense of nervousness whenever she crossed. During her second half of high school, Esperanza crossed several times a month to see her oldest brother, Adán, and his family. The following excerpt from an interview conducted when she was eighteen contains her description of what it was like to cross the border:

ESPERANZA: My dad always tells me to get my ID out probably every twenty minutes before we get to the actual border line. He always tells me what to say. He says, "Make sure you don't stumble, I don't want to end up in *revisión*." So we get there and the man takes our IDs and looks at them and then asks me more questions to make sure that I know San Diego.
CHRISTINA: What kinds of questions do they ask you?
ESPERANZA: They'll be like, "Where were you born? What's your address? What school do you go to? What classes are you taking in school?" Something that will give him a clue that, yes, I am a U.S. citizen. And he does the same to my dad, asking, "Where do you work? What language do you speak? When did you get naturalized?" So he has to have that all in mind.
CHRISTINA: So how do you feel during that questioning?
ESPERANZA: Well, I get very nervous because I know that even though I am a U.S. citizen, there's still that chance that they could hold me back and revise me and that will just take the whole night and I have school the next day.

Esperanza's account includes a very real fear for U.S. citizens crossing the border—that they will be detained in such a manner that it interferes with school, work, or other responsibilities. Esperanza's ongoing concern about getting stopped was rooted in the experiences of her family members who had actually been detained in this manner before. Esperanza recounted one such episode involving Adán:

> My brother is a U.S. citizen and he was crossing the border—he passes every day. One time this dog, for no reason, just came up to his car and started barking. He didn't have anything in his car—he was just going to work. The dog wouldn't stop barking. So the agents came in and they took him out of the car and they started checking his car for things. They handcuffed him and he was so embarrassed. He was tired so he didn't really put up a big fight, like, "Why are you guys checking me? Where are my rights?" They didn't find anything in his car, but still, I mean—he's a U.S. citizen. I don't know, I just felt that was unfair and unnecessary and made him late to his job, which he could've gotten fired from. I just don't think that was right.

FIGURE 9. Approaching the inspection booth at the San Ysidro Port of Entry from the Mexican side of the border crossing.

Esperanza recalled the embarrassment that her brother felt when he was stopped by the CBP agents and the injustice that he—and she on his behalf—felt for being falsely accused and having his citizenship questioned. She recognized that his rights as a U.S. citizen had been compromised. Even though Esperanza knew that her brother was not doing anything wrong, she still felt a sense of caution every time she got in the border line because of these past experiences of unpleasantness and humiliation.

Esperanza's experiences also highlight that she (as well as others) felt that the CBP agents often questioned and treated them too aggressively and intrusively. As a fifteen-year-old, Amada described herself as a "daily crosser." She was born in the United States but, like Paz, spent her early childhood in T.J. Amada's family maintained a T.J. residence that was, in fact, their preferred residence as the house was larger and located in what she described as a better neighborhood. The family went down to T.J. virtually every weekend as well as other times during the week. She expressed that she felt the agents scrutinized her excessively:

> I remember one time when I was coming with my dad they asked, "Who immigrated you?" What kind of question is that for a six-year-old? Another time they asked me, "Are you running away from home?" and I was like, "Why would I do that?" It's nonsense. And yeah, I know it's their job, but sometimes the questions are too much. They're like, "What were you doing there? What are you bringing back?" And sometimes it's really repetitive, especially since I cross every day. They'll be like, "I saw you yesterday—what were you doing in Mexico again?" And I'm like, "It's none of your business!"

While questioning individuals is within the realm of what CBP agents' jobs entail, ethno-racial profiling is not. However, in practice, those with darker skin are more likely to be treated unfairly during the border-crossing encounter (Bejarano 2010, 394; Lugo 2000, 360). In fact, Lugo argues that skin-color identification is actually the first component of border inspections (360). Though in its early days Border Patrol agents were predominantly white and had the explicit goal of policing the boundaries between whites and nonwhites in the region (Hernández 2010), the ethnic/racial composition of the Border Patrol force has subsequently shifted. By 2008, over half (51 percent) of agents were Latinx, 45 percent white, 1.2 percent African American, and 1 percent Asian (Pinkerton 2008). Heyman (2002) and Rosas (2006a) have described how even given the shifting demographics of the Border Patrol force, agents of all backgrounds rely not only on skin color but also on cues about supposed foreignness, adding another layer of complication to the system of racialized governance. Anecdotally, many teens expressed that agents of Mexican descent are indeed some of the harshest (this is echoed by Correa and Thomas 2015).

Paulina reflected that it was through the racialized border inspection process that she actually learned about race itself. Speaking when she was twenty-six, she stated, "When I was little, they didn't think I was my mom's child. We did secondary revision like all the time. It was really annoying! That's where I learned color. I didn't know color really existed until they told me that she couldn't be my mom because she was too dark." Paulina's discomfort with CBP agents has persisted into her monthly border crossings to her mother's family's rancho as an adult; she noted, "I can never say anything to them when they ask questions. It's like, I freeze." In fact, Paulina factored the CBP hassle factor into her decision about what type of vehicle to purchase, saying, "I drive a Mini Cooper now . . . champagne with black top and black rims. I was gonna get red, but you're more likely to get stopped [at the border] if you have a red car. So I was like, 'No thanks, I'll pass!'"

Like Paulina, Esperanza also reflected on the implications of skin color and perceived citizenship on one's border inspection experience in the following exchange:

CHRISTINA: So do the agents bother you a lot while you're crossing?
ESPERANZA: Yes. This one day when I forgot my ID, he was being really rude to me. I guess I can understand because I think it makes their jobs easier if you have an ID with you, but, I mean, there's always going to be those cases that you don't. I don't know . . . it's too bad I'm not an obvious citizen.
CHRISTINA: So what would you say is an obvious citizen?
ESPERANZA: I don't know. I think maybe if I was white and blond haired they'd let me go by faster. It's because of my skin color. I'm dark—you can totally tell I'm not like Caucasian or anything. So you can say, oh well, she's Hispanic. You can classify me easily. I think that's what they do.
CHRISTINA: Does that bother you?
ESPERANZA: Yes. I mean, as humans we categorize people and I know it's their job to make sure no illegal people cross. But it does bother me because it just makes me nervous when I really shouldn't feel nervous about it because I was born [in the United States].

Through her discussion of "obvious citizenship," Esperanza identifies skin color in particular as a "somatic mode of attention" (Willen 2007, 18) that indexes broader social membership. As teenagers, most participants were directly critical of the border-crossing process, in particular because it unfairly targeted them and their family members. Much of their discussion of this unfairness derived from a feeling that they were "legitimate" U.S. citizens or residents who deserved to cross without being hassled. Esperanza's younger sister Victoria, who likewise crossed frequently when she was in high school to see her brother and his family in Tijuana, mused, "You're always thinking, why isn't there a better way to do this? I guess there isn't, but, hopefully, they can come up with something because that's really a hassle, especially if you're U.S. citizens who are really U.S. citizens. We just want to come in and out and not be bothered."

"EVERY TIME I SEE A WHITE VAN I GET A LITTLE NERVOUS AND WALK A DIFFERENT ROUTE": THE SPILLOVER OF IMMIGRATION ENFORCEMENT INTO BORDER COMMUNITIES

Borderlanders' encounters with state power are not restricted to the ports of entry, as immigration officials have an "inescapable presence" (Lugo 2000, 354) throughout the region more broadly. The Border Patrol has powers of search and seizure beyond the boundary at fixed checkpoints (such as the aforementioned San Clemente checkpoint just north of San Diego County) and by surveilling areas "nearby areas and neighborhoods" in which undocumented immigrants "quickly fade into the general population" within 100 air miles of the border (U.S. Customs and Border Protection 2018). Border Patrol agents driving instantly recognizable white-with-green-trim sport utility vehicles frequently patrol neighborhoods that are close to the border or are heavily Mexican in composition. Indeed, residential segregation—the institutional practices responsible for the construction of many barrios—provides a mechanism for concentrating surveillance efforts (Goldsmith et al. 2009, 116). The relentless presence of immigration agents in these neighborhoods renders local residents a policed population (Heyman 1998, 159).

Latinx borderlanders of every immigration status are affected by the "spillover from border control" (Heyman 1998; Sabo and Lee 2015) because of the inherent difficulty of determining the legal status of individuals merely by looking at them. Nonetheless, Border Patrol agents rely on visual cues to identify would-be undocumented immigrants; they also fall back on tacit group stereotypes in making their assessments (Heyman 1998, 166). The reality is that undocumented immigrants, residents, and U.S. citizens of Mexican descent may all look similar, making the ability to distinguish between them visually in a snap judgment—or, really, at all—questionable. Nonetheless, all of these populations are subject to a "diffused form of racial governance" (Rosas 2006a, 338).

The mistreatment of people of Mexican descent spills over into seemingly "safe" places such as neighborhoods, workplaces, and schools. Border Patrol presence is strong in the neighborhood. As a teenager, Esperanza encapsulated the feeling of the Border Patrol always being around: "I don't know if they go undercover or what, or if they dress like normal people. But my mom would always tell me they're in white vans. So every time I see a white van I get a little nervous and just walk a different route." I then queried, "Even though you don't have anything to worry about?" to which Esperanza succinctly answered, "Yeah, I guess it's just ingrained in me." Again, Esperanza is a U.S.-born citizen, meaning that she should have nothing to fear of a potential encounter with Border Patrol agents. Nonetheless, she sustains a steady embodied fear of their power that actually shapes the way in which she maneuvers through her neighborhood. After she went away to college, she began to observe these dynamics when she returned home: "I started noticing that there are a lot more cops and Border Patrol [here]. Communities of color are full of them, at every corner." It is only with some maturity and distance that Esperanza came to realize that her childhood experiences filled with unpleasant encounters with uniformed officers were not the norm throughout greater San Diego.

Sal's childhood neighborhood memories were also tinged with Border Patrol encounters. He recalled one such notable time:

> Once we were playing freeze tag over there in the apartments when I was maybe like ten. I ran outside the complex and I was running like crazy. I didn't even notice that the Border Patrol was there. They thought that I was running because of them. They were like, "Hey, stop" in both languages. I was like, "Okay! I'm just playing freeze tag!" They didn't believe me at first. So they asked me a couple of questions. And then they were like, "Do you know it's against the law to run from the Border Patrol?" and I was like, "I didn't even know you guys were out here! We're just playing a game." And eventually they saw all of the kids coming out and what was going on with me and they were like, "Okay, we'll let you go." It was messed up.

Incidents such as Sal's inculcate in children both a hyperawareness and a deep-seated fear of the Border Patrol. That Esperanza and Sal were not able to freely maneuver within their neighborhood as children is evidence of the conspicuous fields of racialized surveillance within which they operate. Esperanza's sister Victoria characterized this feeling when she was fifteen as one of generalized paranoia, describing what life is like for people she knows: "My friend's cousin, I know him and he's always kind of paranoid. Like, when [we] were selling tamales [at] church, he saw the Border Patrol and he was like, 'Oh gosh, hide me!'"

Lisa's comments in 2014 echoed this sentiment of Border Patrol's ever-presence; she reflected, "I feel like the [Border Patrol] is everywhere. It's funny because I'm like, 'Oh my gosh, don't look at them' even though I have nothing to worry about. It's just that you're used to it. You just learn that fear and it sticks with you. I try not to but . . . I still do. It's always like, 'Why am I scared?' I should feel safe, but I still turn the other way." Even though Lisa possesses the rational knowledge that she should be able to remain calm during these encounters—particularly given that she is a citizen and now an adult—this embodied response to their mere presence still "sticks" with her. In reflecting on changes in Border Patrol's presence since he was younger, Tomás, who still goes back frequently to see his mother in the neighborhood, reported, "There's still a lot of fear of the Border Patrol. That's kind of like my fear too. I share in their fear of being kicked out of the USA or being deported."

Neighborhood streets, apartment complexes, and even church property are not necessarily spaces in which participants feel safe, as these accounts have demonstrated. Though one might think that school would be, Tomás shared that he had almost daily encounters with the Border Patrol as a child, saying, "When I was younger, you'd always see the officers hanging around by the school. From where I lived, I had to walk past the school and there was always someone stationed there. They stop you and ask, 'Hey, where are you going?'" In addition to this regular and sustained presence, Amada recounted an incident that took place in 2006 that punctuated the vulnerability of schools as sites of surveillance: "One day, the Border Patrol came to our school—like they were sitting there just outside of our school. And people were so scared. They were hiding in the bathrooms, literally. I think that's terrible. You had students—no matter what the citizenship—hiding in the bathroom. And it's just because of the Border Patrol. It's sad to me." Amada perceptively noted that even U.S. citizens ran into the bathroom, though they had no real reason to be scared.

Paz felt the power of the Border Patrol on her college campus in Pennsylvania, even though they were nowhere near her new residence. One day while in her dorm room on campus, she recounted, "I was talking to my mom on the phone—it was finals week. All the sudden, she was like, '*Ay, la migra!*'[4] and I was like, 'Where?' [Makes a ducking motion.] I got scared." I asked, "Even though you were all the way in Pennsylvania?" to which Paz responded, "Yeah, even though I was over there, I still got scared. And I'm not even illegal!" Paz's instinctive reaction to her mother's call that the Border Patrol was present was to duck out of fear. Thus, the sense of fear that Paz felt transcended the physical location of the U.S.-Mexico borderlands, ever-present in her habitus.

"YOU GET PUSHED AND YOU KIND OF PUSH BACK TOO": RESISTANCE TO STATE POWER

As all of these stories—set over the two-plus decades of the border enforcement campaign—have demonstrated, study participants internalize the everydayness of state power in an embodied manner. Their accounts of their everyday encounters with agents are peppered with feelings of fear, trauma, nervousness, unfairness, embarrassment, and even resignation. These feelings became embodied reality for them as they crossed the border and went about their daily lives within their neighborhood. Those who reported having negative encounters with immigration officials often felt indignant about being unfairly targeted, particularly because of their status as citizens and their feelings of legitimacy as such. Though border-control measures are unquestionably oppressive, as Kearney (1991, 58) long ago highlighted, the U.S. state has not achieved perfect control over sovereign and symbolic borders. For example, innumerable immigrants find ways to successfully cross the militarized border (Heyman 1998; Rosas 2006a, 2006b), engaging in "the art of undermining the state" (Rosas 2006a, 409).

Borderland young adults also found particularly creative strategies for manipulating this state power (Rosas 2006a), cultivating strategies of transformative resistance that allow them to contest the infringement of their rights and tap into their local knowledge bases (Bejarano 2010). These contestations represent performative "acts of citizenship" (Gonzales and Chavez 2012; Isin and Nielsen 2008). Some participants developed embryonic contestations of state power when they were teenagers. During my fieldwork, I accompanied two different groups of teens to a remote park that abuts the border fence. As a group of us approached the park for a community service project, we saw three

Border Patrol agents atop ATV vehicles. Fifteen-year-old Nancy jokingly said, "Aw, *la migra*. I don't have my papers. What are they gonna do to me?" Tomás, who was also fifteen at the time, laughingly asked, "What do you think they'd do if I just started running through that open part there? If they stopped me, I'd be like, 'Hey, I'm a citizen—I was born here. Why are you chasing after me?'" Their imagined reactions to the Border Patrol agents were not ones of fear; instead, they played with the possibility that they may have a measure of power because of their status as U.S. citizens.

A few months later, I accompanied sophomores Wilson and Marta as they took pictures in the park for the PhotoVoice project. They, too, joked about what would happen if they hopped the border fence and ran the other way into Mexico in plain sight of the Border Patrol agents. As they were shooting their pictures, Marta, who is quite thin, attempted to squeeze through the part of the border wall constructed of vertical metal slats, saying, "I just wanted to see if I could cross that way, too." In both of these examples, the teens' joking made light of the seriousness of crossing the border and having or not having papers. Their actions highlighted the ambiguity of their own sense of belonging—the realization they were "legitimate" even though it was entirely possible that the immigration officials would not perceive them as such. These jokes were a way for them to assert their belonging—imaginatively correcting the officers for assuming that they did not have the right to be in the United States. Secure in their immigration status, these four teens manipulated ideas about belonging in order to make a point, if only to themselves.

Paulina, who talked about "freezing" during Border Patrol encounters, also talked about not holding back in her (frequent) interactions with immigration officials, which is actually much more consistent with her assertive personality. Even as a teenager, she lamented, "It so pisses me off when we cross the border and they're like, 'Why were you in Mexico?' I'm like, 'Because I can be. Because I want to be. Because I have the right to come over here.' I tell my mom that it pisses me off because I was born here with a social security card in my hand." Sal similarly felt that regular encounters with agents forced him into defensive mode, relating when he was seventeen, "You get pushed and you kind of push back too."

Participants also described their own creative ways of maneuvering around state power beyond merely "pushing back" when pressed by agents. Isabel described the way in which her group of friends—of mixed immigration statuses—showed solidarity for one another when she was a sophomore:

I have some friends and a couple of them—like two or three—don't have papers. One of them got picked up by the patrol officers and they took him to T.J. So some of my friends, all the ones that could go, went down to T.J. and took money over to him. They made sure he had everything—that he was in a nice hotel and had food and all. And then later, the day after, they themselves crossed him. So they crossed and they're just speaking English, all of them. Nobody took IDs, nothing. So the [officers] asked them, and they were like, "Oh, we're citizens." So a bunch of teenagers went over to T.J. and crossed him back.

In this situation, Isabel's friends challenged the U.S. state's determination that their friend did not belong by successfully performing U.S. citizenship by speaking English and acting "American." Other scholars have documented similar "border security performances" (Bejarano 2010, 395) deployed by borderland youth by tapping into the language and clothing styles of U.S.-born Latinxs (Rosas 2006a).

As the performance of a U.S. citizen identity suggests, knowledge of how to navigate border crossings and encounters with immigration enforcement agents is an acquired skill. Once she was able to secure papers for her parents, Isabel then had to teach them how to navigate border crossings since they were not accustomed to crossing the border. Isabel recalled one of the first trips she took down to Tijuana with her mother to see her family once she got her papers. Her mother was understandably emotional, with which Isabel sympathized greatly. But Isabel also regarded the situation pragmatically, recalling, "When we were crossing, we're like, 'Mom, stop crying!' Now there's more inspection when you go into T.J.—it's not only when you cross into the U.S.—so we didn't want to get sent to secondary inspection. So we're like, 'Mom, calm down, it's gonna be prolonged if you don't calm down.' So she's over there like, 'Okay, okay,' trying to breathe and calm herself down while we're crossing." Isabel also noted that on the U.S. side, she's now taking her parents to new places that they never felt comfortable going to before because of their status, like the outlet mall right at the border crossing that they had so carefully avoided for all of Isabel's life. Having grown up in a transborder context and navigating the border crossing numerous times to spend time with the family, Isabel has highly attuned transborder knowledge and competencies (Bejarano 2010) that she is now imparting to her parents.

As she grew older, Lisa started playing up another component of her identity in these enforcement encounters: a college student. Lisa went to college in San Diego and lived at home for the duration. She rode the trolley to commute to school and periodically found herself in these types of charged border-enforcement scenarios. She shared, "I get really defensive when they [ask me for my papers]. One time when I was going to [college], it was like 11:00 a.m., a normal time. And they came up and were asking for IDs. I was like, 'I don't want to show you my ID.' They were like, 'What high school do you go to?' And I said, '[Name of university].' I still looked very young, but I was like, 'For what?' And he's like, 'We need to verify your age.' I was like, 'Leave me alone, I'm just trying to go to school.'" Despite having "learned that fear" that "sticks with you," Lisa got fed up with these regular encounters and played up her identity as a college student to get the agents to back off. In addition to being satisfying for participants in asserting their right to belong, these expressions of agency also serve to underscore the fragility of the system of power in the borderlands (Rosas 2006a).

Through college, several participants, like Esperanza, who went to a public university in San Diego, sought out programs of study that allowed them to critically understand Border Patrol surveillance and other forms of injustice in their communities. She had always been steered toward the sciences and thought she would become a doctor, participating in programs designed to support this path. During her first year, she discovered the field of ethnic studies and immediately gravitated toward it. What appealed to her about it was that she "was introduced to things that I already knew implicitly . . . but they explained how racism was sedimented in our daily infrastructure. Like my professor once said, 'Once you can see, it's impossible not to see anymore.' So even today with the things I do and the places I go to work . . . it's just so visible to me." After graduating from college, Esperanza decided to go to law school, also in Southern California. At the time of her follow-up interview, which took place after her second year of law school, she was still deciding in which area of the law she would like to specialize. It was clear from talking to her, however, that her regular encounters with agents of the state in her everyday life have fueled her desire to seek justice for members of her community.

CONCLUSION

Border enforcement has formed the centerpiece of U.S. immigration policy for decades (Dunn 2010) and is expanding under Trump, who has spent significant time obsessing about the wall and seeking to commit further resources to its fortification. These enforcement activities of the past two decades have taken a substantial human rights toll on border residents of all statuses (Dunn 2010), representing a clear form of violence that has been characterized through different labels. Sabo et al. (2014) describe these enforcement activities as a form of *everyday* violence that is experienced and normalized by citizens and permanent residents of Mexican descent in militarized borderland zones. Menjívar and Abrego (2012) connect the violence of the borderlands more directly to the legal realm in their elaboration of their concept of *legal* violence, which they describe as "the normalized but cumulatively injurious effects of the law" (1380). Though immigration enforcement may purportedly monitor the legal statuses of border crossers and local residents, it has been shown to really target ethnoracial characteristics, or Mexican-ness, which some have argued represents an institutional pattern of *structural* violence (DeLeón 2015; Goldsmith et al. 2009; Harrison and Lloyd 2012, 382).

As evidenced in this chapter, young adults are an important social category whose rights are compromised through the perpetuation of forms of everyday, legal, and structural violence. These young adults came of age during and continue to live in this period of intensified border control, which they have experienced firsthand through numerous charged encounters; indeed, they bear the scars of these encounters that have deeply affected their embodied subjectivities. It is because of the "presumed illegality" (Harrison and Lloyd 2012, 379; Menjívar and Kanstroom 2014) embedded within racialized enforcement practices that they came to realize, as fourteen-year-old Nadia phrased it, that they were not "welcome" in the United States. For children in particular, the racialization of citizenship is particularly dangerous as they are being sent the message that only "obvious" (read: white) citizens truly belong in the United States. The internalization of their feelings of second-class citizenship has the potential to negatively affect their sense of belonging and, ultimately, their incorporation processes.

Beyond their perceptions of belonging, as teenagers they easily recounted encounters at the border crossing and in public spaces that prompted embodied fear, tension, and stress. Some of these embodied responses unquestionably presented as they interfaced with naked state power directly, often without adults (or parents specifically) present to mediate its effects. Even as minors, though, some of these visceral reactions resulted from intersubjective relational fear about what might happen to their loved ones under these conditions of surveillance. Participants continue to be plagued by these embodied responses to interactions with the CBP and Border Patrol into adulthood; as Lisa astutely noted, "You just learn that fear and it sticks with you." Despite these enduring embodied effects, it is also clear that these young adults have actively engaged in everyday practices of resistance (Rosas 2006b, 341) to contest this system of racialized border enforcement. These practices of resistance are reactionary in that, when confronted at border crossings or in neighborhoods, these young adults not only assert their own legitimacy but also exhibit concerted efforts to protect family members and friends. Indeed, it is these sensibilities and intentional acts of resistance that allow them to serve effectively not only in their roles as brokers within their families but also on behalf of their communities, as Esperanza is hoping to accomplish in her career as a lawyer.

The previous three chapters have focused on participants' lives in the United States and in the border crossing zone between the United States and Mexico. Chapter 5 turns to their participation in transborder life, considering how family members' legal statuses have facilitated or impeded family life across borders. The chapter examines the role of the state in shaping their engagement in transborder life, demonstrating ways in which participants have emerged as linchpins for their families—as well as demonstrating the connections to Mexico that they have maintained and created outside of the reach of the state.

5

TRACING DIFFERENT TRAJECTORIES OF TRANSBORDER LIFE

CARLOS FRANCO and Beto García were both born in western Mexico within a year of each other and came to San Diego to join their extended families when they were toddlers. The Francos, though, were able to regularize their immigration statuses and started returning home to their beloved hometown, San Antonio, in Zacatecas every year starting when Carlos was in third grade. Since then, the Francos have taken a trip back to San Antonio every year in December for the holidays or in January to participate in the town's annual festival. When the four children were growing up, the Franco parents would load their family in the car and embark on the twenty-plus-hour journey to San Antonio, often driving through the night so they could get there faster, as Carlos fondly recalls.

Carlos and his three siblings have always embraced going back to San Antonio. As a teenager, he looked forward to going every year, telling me then, "I like everything about going—the environment there, the parties, the culture, my family, the food. Whenever we go, there are people just walking all over the place." In addition to regular visits, the Francos have chosen to hold important family events in San Antonio. During their annual trip back in December 2006, they held Carlos's younger sister, Ana's, *quinceñera* there so that all of their extended transborder family would be able to be present, which was possible since most of them have their papers and can therefore cross the border freely. Carlos served as a sponsor, renting the dance hall for the event.

As he transitioned into adulthood, Carlos's connection to San Antonio became even stronger; he met his eventual wife, Melissa, who also grew up in the United States, there during their annual visit during his senior year of high school. When Carlos and Meli were planning their wedding, they knew exactly where they wanted to hold it: San Antonio. He explains, "We decided to have the wedding where we met and where all of our families could come and stay with relatives." Now with three children of their own, Carlos and Meli continue to make the trek back to San Antonio so that their children will forge the same connections to culture, family, and place that they cultivated throughout their own childhoods.

Beto, by contrast, did not have the chance to go to his hometown in Jalisco when he was growing up because he and all of his family were undocumented. During his childhood, Beto felt that he was missing out on a tradition that many of his peers were able to engage in: going to Mexico. He was not even able to go to close-by Tijuana, unlike peers like Carlos, because of his status. As he reflected as a nineteen-year-old, "It's hard not having that option. I wish I could go back and see where I was born and just . . . see my family." Despite this, as a teenager Beto remained optimistic about the possibility of going to Jalisco, saying, "Hopefully one day I'll be able to go and experience life in Mexico, because I would just like to feel that life that my parents had."

As highlighted previously, Beto's older brother, Luis, was detained and ultimately deported to Tijuana when he was in his early twenties. Beto's first trip back to Mexico since he was three was to visit his brother in the aftermath of his deportation. He explained, "My brother was sent to Tijuana and [my wife] and I went over there to take him some stuff. I just felt like, 'Wow.' It made me a little more humble to be honest . . . I come from the barrio but driving through the streets of Tijuana . . . you have kids selling gum so they can get some food and seniors asking for money. The biggest slum here is still wealthier than the biggest slum in Mexico." This trip was certainly not the return to his Mexican hometown that Beto had idealized in his mind when I spoke with him about it as a teenager.

Carlos's and Beto's circumstances reveal very different engagements with transborder life. Because Carlos and his family members had papers, he was able to go frequently and participate actively in family and social life in Mexico; meanwhile, because Beto and his family members did not, he was unable to go and felt a void and sense of longing. Once he had papers, Beto's first trip back to Mexico was triggered by his brother's deportation, a very different type of family reunion than the Francos' annual trip to see their extended family. By examining the differences between Carlos and Beto and their families, it becomes clear that illegality shapes not only immigrants' and their children's lives in the United States but also the extent to and quality with which they are able to engage in transborder life in Mexico.

Transnationalism is both a widespread and commonly critiqued concept for describing how immigrants and their children maintain connections to their home countries. An initial wave of scholarship on the "new" second generation in the 2000s critiqued the notion that transnationalism was merely a first-generation immigrant phenomenon, describing second-generation engagement in transnational life (Fouron and Glick Schiller 2001; Glick Schiller and Fouron 2001; Levitt and Waters 2002; Smith 2002, 2006). Yet lingering questions remained about how transnationally engaged the second generation would continue to be as they became adults, in part because they were still too young at that point to be able to know the full scope of their involvement (Kasinitz et al. 2008; Portes and Rumbaut 2001; Smith et al. 2001). A life course approach (Levitt 2009; Smith 2002, 2006), then, is particularly useful for examining second-generation trajectories of involvement in transnational life, answering important questions about its durability (Kasinitz et al. 2008).

The new second generation's transborder engagements, however, are also very much shaped by the increasingly restrictive immigration policy context in which they came of age; not everyone *can* travel across international borders because of their or their parents' status. Scholars have documented how the state shapes transnational family life across borders and indeed have proposed a new term, *transborder*, to capture that movement (Stephen 2007). State categories of classification also make it so that some members of mixed-status families have restrictions on crossing the border and being with family members on either side (Boehm 2012). The San Diego–Tijuana region provides an especially productive site for examining transborder life, as inequalities of immigration status prominently shape the mobility of different family members, as Beto's family exemplifies. For those who can cross, like Carlos's family, living in a border zone offers a rich range of opportunities for engaging in transborder life.

After reviewing relevant scholarly discussions of transnationalism, I demonstrate that second-generation Mexican borderlanders are, indeed, continuing to engage in transborder life into adulthood. I describe three forms of second-generation engagement in transborder life—(1) "hometown," (2) local/"everyday," and (3) state-prompted transborder life—and demonstrate these forms by highlighting the trajectories of six individuals as they have navigated transborder life through their individual and family life courses. Incorporating a longitudinal view, it becomes clear that these second-generation Mexicans' engagements in transborder life are not merely extensions of their parents' involvement in their ancestral homes but rather represent a complex set of practices of their own (Levitt 2009, 1239). In fact, as I will demonstrate, their grounding in transborder life and their unique transborder competencies allow them to serve effectively as brokers for those whose families are divided by the border.

TRANSNATIONALISM SCHOLARSHIP: WAVES, FLOWS, AND BARRIERS

FIRST-WAVE TRANSNATIONALISM: CORE CONCEPTS AND UNITS OF ANALYSIS

The concept of transnationalism has become a "mainstay" (Smith 2006, 279) of immigration research since the early 1990s as scholars grappled with the experiences of immigrants who were settling in the United States but also maintaining varied connections to their home countries in Mexico and the Caribbean (Basch, Glick Schiller, and Szanton Blanc 1993; Glick Schiller, Basch, and Szanton Blanc 1992, 1995; Kearney 1991, 1995, 2004; Kearney and Nagengast 1989; Rouse 1991, 1995). These scholars argued that the prevailing model of immigrant settlement did not take into account the complexities of immigrants' movements—or agency—within the changing conditions of the global capitalist system (Glick Schiller, Basch, and Szanton Blanc 1992).

Scholars proffered a plethora of concepts to better characterize the connections immigrants actively forged in multiple geographic locales, including *transnational community* (Kearney 1991, 1995, 2004; Kearney and Nagengast 1989), *transnational migrant circuit* (Rouse 1991, 1995), and *transnational village* (Levitt 2001). As a means of moving "beyond the container of the nation-state" (Stephen 2007, 21), scholars also theorized about more abstract units not tied to specific communities as such, including *transnational social spaces* (DeGenova 2005; Smith and Guarnizo 1998) and *transnational social fields* (Basch, Glick Schiller, and Szanton Blanc 1993; Glick Schiller, Basch, and Szanton Blanc 1992; Levitt and Glick Schiller 2004).

Smith (2006, 6) eschewed these labels, instead describing participation in *transnational life*, which he characterized as regular and meaningful practices and relationships with the home country. He also pointed out that transnational life is not merely constituted by practices of engagement but also "is embodied in identities and social structures that help form the life world of immigrants and their children" (Smith 2006, 7). Stephen (2007, 5) similarly wrote of the *transborder lives* of Oaxacans in Mexico, California, and Oregon, arguing that they possessed "the ability to construct space, time, and social relations in more than one place simultaneously." She advocated for the descriptor *transborder* instead, arguing that migrants crossed multiple borders simultaneously: ethnic, class, cultural, colonial, and state borders within Mexico, the U.S.-Mexico borderlands, and different regions within the United States (6).

SECOND-WAVE TRANSNATIONALISM: THE SECOND GENERATION AND TRANSNATIONAL FAMILIES

In the early 2000s, a second wave of scholarship (Glick Schiller 2003) extended debates about transnationalism to the children of immigrants (Fouron and Glick Schiller 2001; Glick Schiller and Fouron 2001; Levitt and Waters 2002; Smith 2002, 2006). From the beginning, sociologists focused on U.S. assimilation predicted that that transnationalism would fade with the second generation (Portes and Rumbaut 2001), rendering it "mainly a first-generation issue" (Smith, Cordero-Guzmán, and Grosfoguel 2001, 20). Critics suggested that it was not a forgone conclusion that parents' transnational lifestyles would necessarily translate into active engagement among their children (Alba and Nee 2003; Kasinitz et al. 2008; Portes, Escobar, and Arana 2009).

Some of the critique of the concept was methodologically driven, privileging larger-scale surveys over ethnographic case studies, which sociologists felt did not capture the true prevalence of transnationalism or contribute to theory building (Glick Schiller 2003, 109). Kasinitz and his colleagues (2008, 264) examined the transnational behaviors of six different second-generation groups in New York through a telephone survey and concluded that across groups, sustained transnationalism was "unlikely to persist into later generations." Indicators of this generational decline included not intending to live in their ancestral homes and dwindling language fluency (Alba and Nee 2003; Kasinitz et al. 2008; Portes 2001; Portes and Rumbaut 2001).

Despite these negative prognostications, Levitt (2009, 1239) asserted that some members of the second generation were "more deeply and intensely embedded in transnational social fields" and did "not simply choose between the home and the host-land. Instead they strike a balance." Indeed, a second generation that is deeply engaged in transnational life calls into question the utility of the generation model, in which the children of immigrants are envisioned as moving along a stepwise, irreversible process of assimilation to U.S. society (Glick Schiller and Fouron 2001, 157). Glick Schiller and Fouron contended that in opposition to this process, the children of immigrants "develop multiple, shifting, and simultaneous identities, deploying them in relationship to events they experience at home, school, and work, and in the country of their birth as well as that of their ancestry" (173). They suggest that the children of immigrants instead be conceptualized as "the generation of identity" (Fouron and Glick Schiller 2001, 58).

Scholars have ethnographically documented the complexity of second-generation identity and involvement in transnational life through multi-sited and long-term ethnographies. Smith (2006) chronicled Mexican families who divide their time between the state of Puebla and New York City over fifteen years. He argues that "in contrast to a classic 'immigrant adolescence'—caught statically between 'Americanization' and preservation of Mexican customs—a set of more complex and interesting transnational adolescent practices, both positive and negative, has emerged" (282). On the positive end, he found that youth drew on rituals and their community being a "safe space" to help them forge a positive Mexican identity in adolescence; however, he also found that such phenomena as transnational gangs emerged because of negative forces youth confront in both locales (202, 240).

Also drawing on fifteen years of multi-sited ethnographic fieldwork, Boehm (2012) focused on transnational Mexican families living in San Luis Potosí and New Mexico. She found that youth are prominent actors in transnational migration flows, yet that these processes are quite gendered; while boys' migration is encouraged and serves as a rite of passage, girls' migration is much more constrained and controlled (123, 125). She posits that, based on her participants' understanding of their own identities, the children of immigrants might more accurately be referred to as the "transnational generation/*generación transnacional*" and suggests that rather than a generational unit, they be recognized as having "a spectrum of different life experiences" (114–15).

TRANSNATIONALISM ACROSS THE LIFE COURSE

Smith and Boehm both draw attention to the importance of observing transnational life over an extended time frame. As Smith (2006, 205) notes, "Forms of transnational involvement change with the life course, attenuating and intensifying at different stages." He found that some children who resisted transnational life when they were younger embraced going to Mexico as adults, whereas others who cherished going when they were younger were less able to because of their adult responsibilities—despite their desire to (186). Indeed, Smith (2002, 2006) provides a valuable contribution to a broader call for research that considers transnational trajectories and transitions as individuals move through life stages (Levitt 2009; Pries 2004).

It is also important to extend the scope beyond individuals since youth are part of larger family units that also change over the life course (Levitt 2009, 1228; Levitt and Jaworksy 2007, 137). As Pries (2004, 29) points out, stemming from one family or household's original "migration event," distinct subgroups of families may subsequently end up exhibiting different patterns of incorporation, return migration, or participation in transnational life. Boehm (2012) also underscores that "transnational families are, without question, *dynamic*. Migrants, whose lives are characterized by frequent movement, continuously maintain, reassert, reconfigure, and transform family" (33; italics added). Though part of this dynamism results from family members "changing desires" (Pries 2004) and "taking advantage of resources" (Levitt 2009, 1226) in an affirmative sense, the configuration of family units and patterns of transnational life is also heavily constrained and controlled by the state.

THE ROLE OF THE STATE IN CREATING DISPARITIES IN TRANSNATIONAL FAMILIES

Indeed, state power and restrictive immigration policies shape the context of migration and affect how Mexican families are constituted in transnational space (Boehm 2012, 54, 56; Dreby 2010, 2015a). Increased enforcement activities over the last two decades have resulted in quicker and longer-term settlement and an accompanying decline in circular migration (Massey, Durand, and Malone 2002; Massey and Sánchez 2010; Smith 2006). Simultaneously, the large-scale deportations that started with Bush, became a hallmark of the Obama administration, and have accelerated under Trump also contribute to the extended, painful family separations that are a feature of contemporary mixed-status and transnational families (Abrego 2014; Dreby 2010; Menjívar and Abrego 2009).

Family members participate in transnational life differently depending on their immigration statuses as designated by the state; undocumented and "DACAmented" (Gonzales, Terriquez, and Ruszczyk 2014) immigrants cannot cross international borders by land or air, unlike family members who are citizens or residents. Importantly, transnational family members' immigration statuses shift over time, causing the family to be reconfigured as these shifts disable, complicate, or enable movement across borders (Boehm 2012, 19). However, as I will demonstrate, these disparities within families can also *necessitate* participation in transnational life for those members who are able to cross the border. Indeed, as U.S. citizens, second-generation young adults may logically serve as the linchpins between family members who cannot traverse the border.

Disparities in family members' movements across borders are especially pronounced in border communities. As Levitt and Jaworsky (2007, 144) point out, "Spatial scales, the cultural-historical particularity of places, and the global nature of what flows through them produce different kinds of transnational social fields, or arenas with different clusters of transnational activities." Indeed, place is an important factor shaping distinct migration experiences (Brettell 2006; Levitt and Jaworksy 2007, 143). Much theorizing about transnationalism and the second generation has been rooted in New York (Fouron and Glick Schiller 2001; Glick Schiller and Fouron 2001; Levitt and Waters 2002; Smith 2002, 2006). New York has traditionally been "an important site of transnational action and a node in the global economy," which renders it "a historically important site of home country and diasporic politics" (Smith, Cordero-Guzmán, and Grosfoguel 2001, 2, 11).

However, some predictions about the transnational lives of the second generation—including its durability—play out quite differently in borderland communities, which have historical, dynamic, and ever-evolving transborder connections (Alvarez 1991; Heyman 1991; Vélez-Ibañez 1996). The state also has a particularly pronounced role in shaping transborder life across generations in the U.S.-Mexico borderlands. I follow Stephen (2007) in using the term *transborder life* to capture the extensive boundary crossing that second-generation Mexicans perform in both Mexico and the borderlands, and to underscore the range of transborder practices that have emerged as a result of state policies that produce divisions within families.

SECOND-GENERATION MEXICANS' ENGAGEMENT IN TRANSBORDER LIFE

Second-generation Mexicans living in San Diego participate actively in transborder life, which is greatly facilitated by the proximity of Tijuana and access to the Mexican interior via the Tijuana airport. To understand their participation in transborder life, it is important to know more about their immigrant parents' Mexican states of origin and engagement with transborder life. I provide this background and then turn to the distinct patterns of transborder life that have emerged throughout their teenage and early adult years. Specifically, I elaborate three forms of second-generation engagement in transborder life: (1) hometown, (2) local/"everyday," and (3) state-prompted transborder life. To describe these forms, I present the transborder trajectories of six individuals and their families, also describing others who exhibit the same forms and sentiments.

PARENTS' REGIONS OF ORIGIN AND ENGAGEMENT IN TRANSBORDER LIFE

Though my focus is more on the children in mixed-status families, it is important to first examine their parents' engagement with transborder life. In the survey I conducted with a household representative in 2005–2006, I asked them to identify from which Mexican state each child's parent hailed; I gathered data on a total of sixty-eight parents.[1] I then grouped the states into regions according to the typology set forth by Mexico's National Population Council (CONAPO), which divides the thirty-one Mexican states and the federal district (Mexico City) into four general regions: West, North, Southeast, and Central (Alarcón 2005, 111).[2] The distribution of the parents' home states is fairly representative of trends for San Diego County overall. The majority (thirty; 44 percent) of parents are from states in the West, including those that were part of the original bracero flow (Runsten 2005, 4). Thirteen parents (19 percent) are originally from the North, including next-door Baja California Norte, while another twelve (18 percent) are from the Southeast, part of a more recent flow stemming from some of the poorest Mexican states. The smallest segment (nine; 13 percent) are from Central states, a more recent sending area for San Diego–bound migrants (38).

In part because of their diverse origins, most families were not part of an archetypal transnational community. Many of the women, for instance, did not come to the United States with or in order to reunite with husbands from their hometowns; rather, they joined other family members like older siblings and parents. When they married,[3] their husbands were not necessarily from their hometown or even their home state. Overall, only about half of the couples (sixteen; 47 percent) were from the same Mexican state, and of those, only half were from the same hometown. In fact, nearly half of the sample of mothers (sixteen) married men whom they first met in the United States. Thus many of the couples are part of "mixed-state" marriages, decreasing the likelihood that they would be part of a cohesive transnational community.

Despite not being part of transnational communities, though, many still participate actively in transborder life on two different stages—their hometowns and nearby Tijuana / Baja California Norte.[4] Most parents who "have papers" (i.e., citizens or residents) continue to visit their hometowns in the Mexican interior, though with variable frequency, ability, and commitment. As Luisa noted, though, making the trip can get harder for families over time, stating, "When we were younger, we would go every Christmas. But as we got older, it just got a lot harder because of school and all of that." For others like Wilson, most of the extended family lives in the United States, making the trip to Mexico less likely. As he commented, "I don't have any family there anymore. My only family tie is my *tío* (uncle) who lives in the capital, and that's it. Everyone else is on the East Coast [of the United States]."

Parents who have papers also make local visits to Tijuana and participate in a variety of activities like obtaining familiar goods and services (going to the doctor and buying medications), engaging in leisure activities (going to concerts and the movies), and spending time with family and friends (eating out or taking day trips). Some families needed to live in Tijuana on a shorter- or longer-term basis as shifts in family members' immigration statuses or family finances necessitated or allowed for it. Not surprisingly, the segment of parents least likely to participate in transborder life on either stage are those who are or were undocumented and are entrapped (Núñez and Heyman 2007) in San Diego.

My second-generation participants' involvement in transborder life has unquestionably been shaped by their parents' choices and decisions (Boehm 2012, 117). However, even as teenagers, some started participating in transborder life on their own terms as they started driving, gaining new freedoms, and crossing by themselves, including in the absence of family members who were unable to cross. Indeed, from the vantage point of their adult lives, it is clear that although the state and their families play significant roles in shaping their participation in transborder life, they are active agents in shaping their own transnational destinies in all three forms elaborated here: hometown, everyday/local, and state-prompted transborder life.

1. HOMETOWN TRANSBORDER LIFE

Hometown transborder life for second-generation young adults consists of trips back to their parents' hometowns—the majority of which were farther into the Mexican interior, given that three-quarters of the parents (fifty-one of sixty-eight) hailed from West, Southeast, or Central Mexico. Visits to these regions are by necessity less frequent, take more advance planning, and can end up costing much more money compared to hometown visits involving parents from closer-by states. Nonetheless, many participants still engaged regularly in hometown transborder life with their families as teenagers. Some families took an annual trip back to one or both parents' hometowns for the holidays or in the summer, while others returned for life-cycle rituals like *quinceñeras* or weddings. Annual trips home are typical for Mexicans who are citizens or permanent residents and are able to do so (Durand, Massey, and Zenteno 2001, 122–23). For children in these families, these return trips to Mexico served as "a key ritual in second-generation adolescence" (Smith 2006, 127), as revealed in the trajectories of Carlos and Esperanza.

"YOU JUST GET THIS FEELING BEING OVER THERE": CARLOS AND THE FRANCO FAMILY. Carlos's family exemplifies one of the more "traditional" patterns of transborder engagement, characteristic of the most-established migration pattern in San Diego from the Western states. Carlos's parents, Luis and Camila, are both from the same rancho of San Antonio in Zacatecas, though they met each other in San Diego after each had migrated separately to join family members already there. In the early years, they migrated back and forth, and their children's countries of birth reflects that movement: Carlos and another sibling were born in San Antonio, while the other two were born in San Diego. Migration is a community norm in San Antonio; Carlos estimates that only 25 percent of the town stays during the year, saying, "Usually there are more women and kids because, you know, the men come and work and send the money back. It's quiet when everyone's gone." Though some family members from San Antonio live in San Diego, the larger node of their transborder community is in Central Texas. In many ways, the Francos' trajectory of transborder life is more typical of Mexicans who do not live in a border zone.

Of the thirty-four families in my sample, thirteen (38 percent) of parents reported making an annual family trip home, though the trips did not always take place at the holidays. Other parents reported making it home on a less frequent basis, with ten families (29 percent) saying that they went home every few years. Camila's extended family showcases several reasons why families go less frequently. Her two younger sisters also live in San Diego, but their husbands are not from Zacatecas; they are from Tlaxcala and México, respectively. One family rotates between Zacatecas and Tlaxcala and does not necessarily even take their trip every year depending on finances; the other visits only every few years, splitting time between Zacatecas and México. While some mixed-state couples end up favoring one parent's hometown, others seem to split the family's time and travel budget. Camila's extended family also reveals that very different levels of engagement with transborder life can exist within a given family. As a teenager, Carlos noticed the differences between himself and his cousins who went back less frequently, saying, "Sometimes it takes them two years to go back. They go and they don't really know how to interact with the people and everything, so I think that kind of keeps them away."

Unlike his cousins, Carlos feels extremely comfortable and has nothing but positive associations with San Antonio. As he relates, "You just get this *feeling* being over there." During his senior year of high school, Carlos visited San Antonio as he did every winter break. In San Antonio, he describes,

> There's a little courtyard in the middle of town in front of the church. Every Sunday, everyone goes and walks around. The tradition is that the older boys and girls go there to basically find someone. I had just arrived and I was crossing the street and I saw this girl getting some fruit. As soon as I saw her walking around, I went after her and we started talking, exchanging names and everything. I got back home and I told my mom, "Mom, I met this girl. She's really pretty and this is her name." And it turns out she was the daughter of my mom's best friend from high school. I pressured my mom to go see her . . . I was like, "Let's go! Let's go! I need to see that girl again!"

Meli, the girl Carlos met, grew up in the San Antonio satellite community in Central Texas, but like Carlos, returned every year for the holidays. Carlos and Meli kept in touch after they met during his senior year of high school and he even went down to Texas to visit her a few times. Though they briefly lost track of each other for a year when he was in college, they would always see each other in Mexico every Christmas. Eventually, they decided to be together as a couple. As Carlos reflects, "My dad always told me since I was little, 'You need to find someone from San Antonio, somebody that knows your culture and has the same beliefs, someone that you can relate to.' So I told my Dad, 'This is her; she's it!'"

Carlos describes their engagement as being very traditional; as he shares, "My whole family went driving to Texas and did it the traditional Mexican way of asking for somebody's hand." Once they decided to have the wedding in San Antonio, Carlos and Meli's extended family members helped extensively in wedding planning; as Carlos shared, "My family all stepped up and were like, 'We'll help you with this and that.' My aunt over there basically handled food and all that. My uncle—my grandpa's brother—got the permits for the hall. It was a lot of help from everybody." Carlos emphasized that it was important to him and Meli that after they finished the relatively more intimate ceremony and dinner, the reception was open to everyone in the town who wanted to come. It was a large affair, and most of their U.S.-based families made the trek back home for the wedding.

Since they got married, Carlos and Meli have had three children and lived in both San Diego and Texas, where their respective families reside. Going to San Antonio is still very important to them both as adults; as Carlos says, "We still embrace it . . . and I want my kids to embrace it like I did growing up as well. I always wanted to go. I bought my son his boots and sombrero. I try to get him to sing traditional Mexican music and he'll sing to his grandparents. That way he knows his culture." Even though it is important to Carlos to keep going back, they are finding it difficult to make the annual trip back; as he laments, "We've been wanting to go, but every year something happens where we just can't. I'm paying back my student loans, which are not small. Last year my son had surgery. Expenses like that happen all of a sudden and take away our savings." Smith (2006) similarly found that many of his New York–based second-generation Mexicans found it increasingly challenging to make it back as family and financial responsibilities increased in their twenties. In January 2016, right after the birth of their third child, though, Carlos and Meli were excited to be able to take the annual trip back to San Antonio with their children and his parents.

"I WOULDN'T MISS [GOING TO MEXICO] FOR ANYTHING": ESPERANZA AND THE MEDINA FAMILY

Another individual who takes an annual trip to her mother's hometown—both growing up and now as an adult—is Esperanza. Esperanza's parents are originally from different states—her mother from Michoacán and her father from Tabasco. Her parents met in Michoacán, where her two older brothers were born. The Medinas return to Morelia every August to participate in an annual week-long service with their international evangelical Christian church. In the case of the Medina children, religion has served as a powerful motivator of second-generation transborder engagement (Levitt 2009, 1239). As a seventeen-year-old, Esperanza likened the experience of going to Morelia to being among family, saying, "It's full of people that look and dress similar to me, so it feels very special. It's like family, really close—like you can go into anyone's house. You just feel like you know everyone because you share that common bond with them. It's really cool." Esperanza felt that sense of belonging not only because her actual extended family lives there but also because an extended community of parishioners from her church lives in her mother's neighborhood, whereas in San Diego many neighbors and schoolmates do not share her faith.

Despite these affirmative feelings, though, as a teenager Esperanza sometimes felt like she stood out, sharing, "It's obvious that you're not totally Mexican because you have an accent in your voice; they can distinguish that. Sometimes when I'm over there I wish I could talk just like them so I could fit in more." She also felt that there were visual cues that set the Medina children apart, saying, "They can tell right away you're American because of the flashy glasses, the heels, the purse . . . they know you're American just by looking at you." Her feeling of being on the outside extends beyond these outward markers, too; she related that even now as an adult, "When I'm in Mexico, it's like you're not Mexican sometimes. You don't know what this is or you don't know what that cartoon is. You know, *real* Mexican things." Smith (2006) likewise found that his second-generation teenagers reported feeling "not Mexican enough" at times, despite their desire to fit in (147). In fact some participants cited these feelings of exclusion as diminishing their desire to be engaged in transborder life.

Esperanza still looks forward to her annual trip back to Michoacán, a tradition she kept up even through college and law school; her sister, Victoria, has likewise made the trip every year. As she strongly asserted when I asked her in 2014 if she still goes, "I have never missed an August. I wouldn't miss [going back to Mexico] for anything." During one of her August trips back, she met her now-husband, José, a Mexican national from Nuevo León in the North who also made annual treks for the church gathering. As she was preparing for her last year of law school in 2014, they were still figuring out where they were going to live and how they were going to negotiate transborder life. Still based in Nuevo León, he worked in agriculture and had traveled to the U.S. Midwest for business, which was one possible place to settle. At that point, Esperanza thought that they would live in Mexico initially after she finished law school. She noted how complex her decision-making process was, saying,

> The decision of going to Mexico was very difficult to make for me, because my parents came here so that their kids have a better future, you know, the whole American dream. When I first told her, my mom stayed quiet. My dad feels like I'm making it too complicated for myself because he wants me to find someone from [the U.S.] that has a degree here and that can help me stay here. But for me . . . my value set is really embedded in my religion. I needed someone with that same kind of love for my church.

Victoria, who is younger than Esperanza by three years, also married someone from the church who came to the United States as a child and maintains connections to his hometown in Jalisco. The girls' oldest brother, Adán, also married a woman from the church from Baja California Norte when Esperanza was in high school. Because his wife did not initially have papers, they made transborder living arrangements, residing in an apartment in Tijuana while her paperwork was processing. Adán continued to cross the border every day to work in San Diego.

During high school, Esperanza would go to Tijuana about monthly to convene for family and church gatherings. Both then and now, she does not have the same affinity for Tijuana as Morelia, though, saying, "It's not a city I've been particularly in love with, especially the crossing part." In fact, both parents and teenagers cited the long border wait as a deterrent to going to Tijuana more. Despite this, Esperanza continues to spend time there with her church and also visiting with her sister-in-law, who now does a reverse commute, living in San Diego but working and attending to extended family obligations in Tijuana. Esperanza envisions living her future life as a transborder one, setting up residences in either or both the United States and Mexico, depending on employment opportunities for both her and her husband.

Carlos and Esperanza's trajectories have some important similarities. Both of their parents are from farther-away Mexican states and both grew up taking annual trips to their parents' hometowns deeper in the Mexican interior. Both had positive associations with these trips, which allowed them to stay connected to their family members, community, and church. Yet Esperanza also alluded to the exclusion she has felt over the years; thus for her, as with many of the second generation, feelings of belonging and alienation can end up coexisting when in Mexico (Smith 2006, 159). Both Carlos and Esperanza continue to be involved in and committed to this hometown transborder life into adulthood. Both met their spouses—neither of whom are from San Diego—within this context of transborder life. Though Carlos envisions his future life either in San Diego or Texas to be close to their respective families, Esperanza is open to living in San Diego, elsewhere in the United States, or somewhere in Mexico, depending on opportunities for her and her husband. Carlos' and Esperanza's stories demonstrate that engagement in hometown transborder life can and does extend into the next generation—and perhaps even beyond, for Carlos and Meli's three children—for those who have papers and are able to freely come and go.

2. LOCAL TRANSBORDER LIFE

Much of the literature has focused on hometown transnational life and the types of experiences and engagements that Carlos and Esperanza describe. In the borderlands, though, it is possible to engage in local transborder life as well. In fact, in the youth survey taken as teens, participants revealed that they spent more time visiting Tijuana or Baja California Norte than their parents' hometowns or home states. Tijuana is unquestionably the more predominant node of transborder life because of its proximity and accessibility. As teenagers, eighteen (43 percent) reported going on a monthly basis, while another seventeen (40 percent) said that they went at least every few months. None of them indicated that they never went. Though Waldinger (2013, 762) has argued that most transnational engagements with home country collectivities are "episodic and asymmetric," that is not necessarily the case in the borderlands, as Paulina and Sal's stories reveal.

"HALF OF WHO I AM IS THERE": PAULINA AND THE SANTOS FAMILY

Paulina and her family—her parents and two younger siblings—are among the most engaged in local transborder life. Paulina grew up frequently shuttling back and forth between her home in south San Diego and her mother's family's rancho, Las Palomas, in Baja California Norte relatively close to the border on the Mexican side. Her mother, Mari, was born and raised in Las Palomas but by age eighteen had followed the path of her older sisters to San Diego. Most of Paulina's ten maternal aunts and uncles also live on the U.S.

side of the border but closer to Las Palomas than San Diego. Even though they are U.S.-based, she noted, "Every weekend and during all vacations, they're all in Mexico." Paulina and her family join in the family gatherings as frequently as possible.

As a teenager, Paulina liked to go to Las Palomas frequently, saying, "We have to go at least once a month or else I'm not satisfied. I just have to go. If they don't take me, it's like something is missing." Indeed, it was often Paulina and her siblings who really pushed the issue of going. As a sixteen-year-old, Paulina revealed, "It's all me. I'm like, 'Let's go, let's go!' And then we'll all be like, 'Come on, *papi*, we want to go. Come on, *mami*.' And then my mom always tells us, 'Okay, let's vote.' So we always vote, and us three girls always vote to go." Paulina described that she felt something was missing if she was not able to go frequently; Viruell-Fuentes (2006, 349) has similarly described members of the second generation's "longing for a place and people that made them feel 'whole.'"

One aspect of going to Las Palomas that Paulina enjoyed as an adolescent was the connection to nature; as she described it in 2006, "There's a lot of pigs and cows and horses. I'm a horse lover—I have a horse there . . . once I'm on it, I don't get off. There's a lot of cropland areas all around. We go to the water that's supposed to feed the croplands, but there's a little hole where you can go in and swim. Like about twenty people fit in it, and it's really fun." As teenagers, many spoke of how they relished the opportunity to enjoy small-town or rural life—very different from the lifestyle in their urban San Diego barrio. Carlos similarly described how he explored areas surrounding San Antonio as they got older, saying, "We would to go where there were waterfalls, rivers, really nice places we never thought could be there. It was like Hawaii in the middle of nowhere—really green and crystal clear water. We enjoyed it a lot."

Going to their parents' hometowns, then, provides an alternative lifestyle that has many appealing aspects, including more freedom to explore. Indeed, Paulina also started flexing her autonomy as she got older; when she got her driver's license in fall 2005, she started going to Las Palomas even more frequently— including by herself. In June 2006, she recounted, "This weekend, I went by myself. I told my mom, 'Bye, I'm leaving.' And she goes, 'No you're not!' And so then I was like, 'All right, but if I tell you I'm going to the store and you don't see me come back in a couple of hours, chances are I'm over there already.'" While Paulina went to the rancho on a monthly basis during the school year, she spent even more time there in the summer.

Even though she cherishes her time at Las Palomas, Paulina was less thrilled when her family had to live in T.J. for a year when she was around ten years old. She explained, "We had to live in T.J. because my dad didn't have his papers then and he got caught and we had to go there while they fixed the papers. We had to show monthly house bills, water bills, proof of where my dad was working and all of that so they wouldn't think that he jumped the border again. That was really hard. We had to move everything from here to there. So a lot of stress came to our family."

During that time, Paulina and her mother commuted across the border to San Diego every day for school and work. Paulina remembered, "We had to wake up at five in the morning to get there on time. I hated it so much!" Similar to Paulina, Cármen, Paz, and Amada spent segments of their childhoods living in Tijuana because of their parents' immigration statuses or precarious finances. For all of them, the time that they spent crossing the border and contending with border enforcement diminished their positive feelings about going to Mexico.

Overall, though, Paulina cherishes her time in Mexico. As a teenager, Paulina chose to hold her *quinceñera* in Mari's hometown in November 2005, musing, "Where else would I have it?" She went shopping for her dress with her mother over a long weekend in Mexico City. Several of the girls went shopping for dresses or even held their *quinces* (as they refer to them) in Mexico, such as Amada, whose *quince* I attended in Tijuana was a lavish affair. These families spend quite a bit of money on the *quinces*; in fact, they can serve as status indicators for families that may otherwise live in modest circumstances in the United States. Significantly, Paulina's immediate family members all have papers now and therefore could cross the border to attend. In addition, Paulina received a very generous gift from her parents: "For one of my presents, my parents bought me a piece of land about one-half block from my grandma's house. One day I'm going to retire on my piece of land. I'm going to build a big house on it one day and live there for good!"

Paulina decided to attend college in the L.A. area, which she decided to do in part so she could move out of her family home in San Diego and live on her own. Though she enjoyed her college experience, she felt like "it was hard because I missed out on a lot of family events in Mexico—family reunions, a couple of weddings, baby showers." After she graduated, she moved back to San Diego and started going to Las Palomas more, stating, "Now that I'm back in San Diego, I go minimum at least once a month. It's very important to me. Half of who I am is there." Sometimes she goes just to be there; as she revealed, "I'll go for the whole weekend and I'll just go and sit—not necessarily for a party, but just to go."

"I ALWAYS FELT LIKE I WAS MISSING OUT": SAL AND THE DÍAZ-MONTOYA FAMILY. Sal is another individual who became increasingly involved in local transborder life as he got older. Paulina connected with her mother's nearby hometown because she spent significant time there as a child. Sal, however, did not gain that same familiarity with Mexico, largely because his mother and primary parent, Elena, was undocumented for his entire childhood, meaning that they were not able to cross the border. As he related as a seventeen-year-old, "When I was younger, I always felt like I was missing out on something. All of those other people got to go back to their parents' towns, but I never did."

As the Díaz-Montoya case highlights, first-generation parents' immigration statuses not only affect their own ability to engage in transnational life but also influence the extent to which their second-generation children may cultivate relationships with Mexico (Foner 2001, 50; Suárez-Orozco and Suárez-Orozco 2001). Indeed, in my sample, the children of undocumented immigrants were the ones least likely to have participated in hometown or local transborder life. While conventional wisdom would suggest that whether or not individuals forge or maintain cross-border connections depends on the extent to which they are brought up in transnational spaces (Levitt 2009, 1228), Sal's trajectory in transborder life highlights that that is not necessarily the case in the context of the borderlands.

Since she arrived in the United States in 1982, Sal's mother, Elena, only returned to her home state of Guanajuato once, to visit her sick father. Of that trip, she recalled, "I just needed to go. I didn't know how I was going to get back or if it would hurt my [immigration] application, but I didn't care. He died when I was there, so it was a good thing I went when I did." In fact, funerals and family crises are sometimes the only times when many undocumented individuals like Señora Montoya even attempt to return home. However, it is a risky endeavor, as they have to cross through the ever more militarized border in order to ultimately return.

Sal has never been to his father's home state of Michoacán and has only gone to his mother's hometown in Guanajuato twice, once for a wedding and the other time to visit. Relatives on his mother's side escorted him there since his mother could not take him. Members of several other families have also served in this "fostering" role in lieu of parents who were unable to cross due to their immigration statuses or other travel restrictions. Teenagers from three families (the Hidalgos, Duartes, and Valencias; see Appendix B) all spent summers in their parents' hometowns in Mexico, transported by relatives who could cross. Though some of the impetus behind these trips was practical—parents needing childcare assistance for the long summer—these extended visits also served as a way for children to learn about Mexican culture (Smith 2006, 200) since their parents could not take them. In discussing whether he would like to go back to his mother's hometown more when he was a teenager, Sal replied, "my *tío* (uncle) has a big house and always asks me if I want to go. I said to [my sister] Luz once, '*Vámanos* (let's go),' and she was all like, 'Nah, I don't want to.' So then I just said to myself, 'Screw it for now.' I get bored there anyway; there aren't enough young people. The cousins are all older. So it's not that great."

Even though he is glad to have visited his mother's hometown, T.J. has emerged as the place where Sal has forged his connection to transborder life. As a sixteen-year-old, Sal started going to T.J. on at least a monthly basis, even though he was never accompanied by his parents. Sal's primary purpose for going to T.J. was social: he liked to go to hang out with friends and eat out. Sal also admitted that he liked to go visit museums, "get to know more about my culture," and "get a feel for the place," indicating it was a way for him to stay in touch with his Mexican roots. In discussing why he liked going to T.J., he shared, "Whenever you wanna get rid of that American atmosphere, T.J.'s the best escape for it. As soon as you cross that border, it's a whole new world. If ever I'm tired of this rushed, organized, always-running-by-clocks-and-schedules type of lifestyle, just crossing the border, it's like freedom." Indeed, "freedom" was a common descriptor that many participants used to describe life in Mexico.

In fact, it is during the teenage years that many participants started exercising this "freedom" by going to T.J. on their own. Some of these activities were sports-related, such as with Noe, who started training for *lucha libre* (a form of wrestling popular in Mexico in which fighters wear colorful masks to conceal their identities) a few nights a week during his senior year. Hernando and Manuel participated in soccer leagues in T.J. and trained with a semiprofessional team (which Hernando did in summer 2004 and Manuel did in summer 2005). Lucía also went down to T.J. three times a week with her sister to take dance classes at a studio there, as did Amada and members of her *quinceñera* court, who learned the traditional dances they would be performing at the event. Certainly it was easier for older teens to participate in these types of activities without their parents since they can drive and have more freedom of movement—especially male children (Boehm 2012).

After he finished high school, Sal spent progressively more of his time in T.J. After a few years, he decided to move to T.J. full-time and commute across the border to his job in San Diego. He wanted to pursue that sense of freedom and also became frustrated with the extremely high cost of living in San Diego. In the meantime, his father had also moved to T.J. because of immigration-related troubles. He helped his father financially, sometimes as his roommate. He also met a Mexican-national woman and eventually moved in with her. When he first moved to T.J., Sal's commute was atrocious; his office was located an hour away from the border and he had to leave extremely early in the morning. He was eventually approved for a Secure Electronic Network for Travelers Rapid Inspection (SENTRI) pass, which provides expedited processing for preapproved low-risk travelers. He subsequently switched jobs to a workplace located a little closer to the border, though he still has to contend with a long and unpredictable border commute.

As an adult, Sal also likes to take his vacations in Mexico, having now visited multiple Mexican states. Unlike the three previous families, neither of his parents goes to their hometown with any regularity these days, and he does not independently participate in his parents' hometown transborder life. But Sal is glad that he's had the chance to become more deeply engaged in Mexican social life, even making his membership in Mexico official by getting dual nationality. Even as a teenager, Sal admitted, "I've always wanted to be a Mexican citizen. I know it sounds kind of weird, but I've always wanted to belong to both places. I know you can't do that. But in a way, I kind of feel like I wanna be a part of that, too." Just recently, he purchased a home in Tijuana, which, he notes, he would have been extremely challenged to do in the United States.

Sal's pattern of local transborder life—both then and now—is quite different from Paulina. Paulina had intensive exposure to life in her mother's nearby hometown and lived in T.J. when she was young. Like many families from close-by areas, hers has always spent significant time shuttling back and forth over the border. Paulina also spends holidays and ritual occasions at the family rancho, going by herself as she started getting older. Though she is still principally based in San Diego now, Paulina is as engaged in transborder life as she ever has been with a new sense of commitment. However, because of his mother's immigration status, Sal missed out on the type of transborder life that Paulina so deeply embraced. But instead of shying away from transborder life as many of his peers who also had undocumented parents have ended up doing, he took it upon himself to cultivate activities there as a teenager and ultimately chose to live there as an adult, despite the complications inherent in doing so. He has actually shifted his primary locus to T.J., where he spends virtually all of his free time outside of his San Diego–based job. Sal is someone whose choices in transborder life exhibit great simultaneity (Levitt and Jaworksy 2007; Tsuda 2012); indeed, he participates and belongs in both nation-states—tipping the scale in favor of Mexico as time goes by.

As these families' experiences underscore, moving households back and forth across the border depending on family members' immigration and financial circumstances is not uncommon over an individual's and family's life course. Paulina's and Sal's reverse commutes across the border from T.J. to the United States also highlight bidirectional movement in transborder families borne out of both necessity and preference. Indeed, movement from San Diego southward is not the only way in which local residents engage in transborder life. Their families' experiences also underscore the importance of examining more sharply the role of the state and family members' statuses in shaping transborder life across the life course.

3. STATE-MEDIATED TRANSBORDER LIFE

All transborder life is, at some level, state mediated, as some individuals possess a status that enables them to cross while others do not. In the 1990s, when some parents like Paulina's father were caught out of status, the whole family temporarily took up residence in Mexico. Other parents, like Sal's mother, did not get caught, but her undocumented status shaped her children's (limited) trips to Mexico as children. Sal's story, however, demonstrates that he became significantly more engaged in transborder life during his teenage years and into adulthood, which was by choice—and was possible, in his case, due to being a U.S. citizen. In examining the shifting immigration statues and family situations of other families over time—like Beto's and Isabel's—the continued, and even attenuated, role of the state in creating divided transnational families in this latest immigration policy chapter becomes clearer.

"I HAVEN'T REALLY BEEN TO MEXICO": BETO AND THE GARCÍA FAMILY

Although Carlos, Esperanza, Paulina, and Sal are all citizens and, as such, all have the ability to cross the border freely, Beto grew up undocumented and was therefore unable to participate in any form of transborder life. As he told the story of when he came when he was nineteen, "I don't really remember anything. My mom just told me that I guess how I came here with my grandpa, he was crossing the San Ysidro border and my mom just put me down on the ground and was like '*Córrele, córrele* (run, run). Follow your grandpa!'" Beto's grandfather was a bracero and helped Beto's father get established when he went up to San Diego two years before Beto came. Most of Beto's family settled in the largest node of their hometown's transnational community in an agricultural community in Northern California, though some clustered in San Diego. Beto visited Northern California, where many extended family members lived, when he was a child, even though going there with his aunt presented dangers if they had been stopped at a checkpoint or along the way. Beto grew increasingly frustrated with his family's uncertain circumstances in the United States when he was a teenager, recalling, "When I was younger, I would tell my mom, 'You know what, Mom? I just want to go back.' I didn't feel like I could be here, like I was wanted here."

Beto's mother, Estela, is the only family member who returned to Jalisco when he was a child; like Sal's mother, she went back to attend to a parent, in this case her extremely sick mother when Beto was ten. As Beto stated, "She didn't think twice; she just went." Estela got caught when she tried to come back to the United States, though, and was sent to a detention facility for several weeks. Beto remembered, "She would call and cry on the phone. I would see my dad talk to her, and I would cry too because I missed my mom and didn't want anything to happen to her. Once she came back, she had this big bruise on her leg. She went through a lot." He also recalled the impact that it had on their household, saying, "My mom always took care of us. When she was gone, he had to cook for us and the house got dirty. We were trying to help my dad, but we just missed our mom." Estela ultimately made it back to San Diego to rejoin her family and has not undertaken a trip to Mexico since.

Their family's complications with immigration continued once Beto's brother Luis was deported to Mexico and became separated from the rest of the family. At that point, Beto became the only link between his brother and the rest of the family in the United States who could not travel to Mexico. Luis is actually thriving in Tijuana and is enrolled as a university student, but the family separation is still hard. As mentioned in chapter 3, once he became a citizen and was financially able to, Beto filed an immigration application for both of his parents. While his father has since secured his green card, his mother's case is much more complicated due to her previous detainment. As soon as his dad got his papers, though, Beto took him to see Luis in Tijuana, sharing, "I wasn't gonna miss it for the world. I recorded their encounter after six years. It was hard, you know—hard to see my dad cry. And it was bittersweet." Beto then showed his mother and younger brother the partial family reunion. Beto and his father spend more time in Tijuana these days, not only visiting his brother but also going to the doctor and the dentist, as many border residents do. In December 2015, Beto dropped his father off at the T.J. airport so that he could return to Jalisco for the first time in two-plus decades, though his wife was not able to join him for the trip back home.

By virtue of his position as a citizen, Beto is the connector between all of his family members of different immigration statuses—his deported older brother who cannot cross back into the United States, his resident father who only recently is able to cross, his in-legal-limbo mother who cannot, and his DACA-recipient youngest brother, who cannot easily travel outside of the United States. In the case of the García family, the U.S.-Mexico border serves as a prominent physical barrier to family unity (Boehm 2012, 63). Beto's engagement in transborder life is less about the positive associations some of his peers have described or the dimensions he envisioned when he was younger—getting to know his hometown and extended family—and is more about the practicalities of keeping his family connected. Indeed, the ripple effects of state enforcement policies have necessitated that Beto become involved in local transborder life. Beto's story demonstrates clearly that strategies are "always made in the context of, and in response to, membership in a household and its changing needs" (Pries 2004, 5).

Beto still feels, in some ways, that "I haven't *really* been to Mexico. I've been to the border towns and I visit my brother, but like they say, border Mexico is not 'real' Mexico." Financial and family obligations have been the main reasons he has not been able to go back to Jalisco. Nonetheless, he says, "It is in my future plans to go back where I was born one day. I've only lived it through my parents' eyes the way it was twenty years ago. I talk to my aunts and uncles and they tell me it's not the same thing as it was then. I pulled up the town on YouTube and have done some research on it to see what it's like now. But it's not the same."

"IT WAS NICE TO HAVE THE FAMILY TOGETHER FOR SOMETHING HAPPY, FOR ONCE": ISABEL AND THE CLEMENTE FAMILY

Like Beto, Isabel's family life has always been circumscribed by family members' statuses and restrictions in crossing the border. The Clementes are both from the same neighborhood in nearby Tijuana; as Isabel describes it, "They lived right next to each other. My mom's family is on a hill, and my dad's family is right under the hill." The Clementes came to San Diego as teenagers to join her father's, Santos's, family members; despite living mere miles from their neighborhood, they were unable to return for more than two decades. Not being able to go was quite unbearable at times for her mother, Paloma, in particular; as Isabel stated, "We're so close to the border here. If we ever got super close and my mom would see the Mexican flag on the other side, she would cry. That flag was her country, and she couldn't go but she could see it. So close, so far. It was really hard."

Even though the Clementes could not cross themselves, it was important for them that their daughters remained connected with family members and life in Mexico. So the other adult family members who could cross the border would take Isabel and her two younger sisters across to Tijuana when they would go. As with Sal, this "fostering" by other family members has emerged as an important mechanism by which undocumented parents are to connect their children to family and social life in Mexico. As a fifteen-year-old, Isabel described the process: "My uncle and his wife, they come from L.A. So they call us and ask, 'Hey, do you wanna go?' They pick us up, and we go to my uncle's house. Then they drop us off on their way back home. That's just how it works for us."

Isabel enjoyed certain aspects of her regular visits to Tijuana growing up, including the independence. She said, "It's much more liberal there. When I was eleven or twelve, I went to see my aunt, and it was just me by myself. She told me, 'You know where the store is, right?' and I was like, 'Yeah.' She said, 'Can you go bring me tortillas? You can go by yourself.'" Indeed, Isabel was granted a higher level of freedom when in Tijuana. Smith (2006, 176) found that for second-generation youth, going to parents' hometowns can be "like temporarily moving to a better neighborhood: it allows parents to ease up on their teens and teens, especially girls, to experience themselves as competent and autonomous, a very different experiences of adolescence." Isabel's life in San Diego was also more constrained because of the immigration-related restrictions she faced alongside her parents (see chapter 3).

While Isabel liked going to the large family reunions on Paloma's side, she felt guilty about the times that she did not want to go. As a fifteen-year-old, she reflected, "I can go and sometimes I don't want to. One time, I didn't really want to go and my mom was like, 'You're gonna go!' Now I look back and it makes me feel bad because she wants to go so badly and I was crying because

I didn't want to." Some of Isabel's reason for not wanting to go as a child was simply that her mother was not there too; as she noted now, "I didn't like going that much because it just didn't feel right without my mom. We liked going but we didn't like spending the night over there without her."

Unlike Beto's family, Isabel's family's lot improved as she transitioned into adulthood. As chronicled in chapter 3, Isabel also filed for her parents' immigration papers at age twenty-two, as soon as she saved up enough money from her first adult job to be able to do so. Once she finally got her papers, Paloma's first trip back home in two-plus decades was a family affair. Isabel's middle sister came back home from college in Northern California since, as Isabel noted, "We all wanted to be there for my mom when she crossed because it's something that she's longed for for so long. By some miracle, we were able to get the money for her to afford the flight for just one weekend." The only downside to the weekend was that Santos was not able to go yet because his papers were in process.

Isabel and her siblings planned the reunion with an aunt in T.J. so that her mother's return would be a surprise for the rest of the extended family. Isabel recalled the day they went:

> It was probably midnight when we crossed. We went to my aunt's house, which we went to because we didn't want her to have a panic attack or something. So we went there first. They started crying when they saw each other. I knew she wasn't going to sleep and she was just crying and happy . . . so much emotion. I had bought Zzz-Quil for her to sleep for a few hours because she was going to go through so much emotional distress and I was worried because she hadn't been eating well because she was just so excited. I think she slept for like two or three hours. We got up early that next morning and left to the cemetery and stayed pretty much all day. It was just her time to mourn. It was the point of closure for my mom to finally say good-bye to her dad.

After the day at the cemetery, they continued on to the large family house Señora Clemente grew up in, which Isabel affectionately calls "the house." She remembers,

> One of my mom's friends from her childhood played like he was having a party at his house next door so my uncle didn't even think about it. We get there and my aunt didn't recognize my mom. She thought it was just a friend of mine or something. She finally realized it was my mom, and they hugged and started crying

and my other uncle was like, "What's going on?" Then he realized it was my mom and started hugging her and crying. Even some of the guys that you would have never thought would cry cried. Everyone started getting there and they started calling everyone else to come. We were all just really excited. It was nice to have the family together for something happy, for once.

Participating in transborder life has greatly enhanced Paloma's life. As Isabel reflects, "Now we look at pictures. I see how she looked a year ago and now she looks all different because . . . she's complete now. She's seen her family that she hadn't seen in twenty-two years." Isabel's father got his papers a few months later, and the girls similarly accompanied him for his maiden voyage back to Tijuana. The interesting generational inversion is that Isabel is the one who is taking care of her parents and teaching them how to navigate transborder life. Isabel also noted that on the U.S. side, she's now taking her parents to places that they never felt comfortable going to before because of their status, like the outlet mall right at the border crossing. Having grown up navigating the border crossing, Isabel has developed highly attuned transborder knowledge and competencies (Bejarano 2010).

Beto's and Isabel's stories of their transborder families' lives and limitations are much more painful than the regular and celebratory visits to their parents' hometowns that Carlos, Esperanza, and Paulina describe. After he finally was able to cross back to Mexico after nearly two decades in the United States, Beto's unceremonious homecoming was to bring his deported brother some essential items from home in the United States. Though Isabel went to her parents' neighborhood in T.J. regularly, it never quite felt right without her parents. Beyond that, the fear that she felt returning from these trips to her parents' neighborhood in T.J. also colored the experience for her.

As adults, Beto and Isabel have both taken on strong roles in their families, serving as connectors between U.S.- and Tijuana-based family members as their immigration situations have changed. They both submitted immigration applications for their parents to increase their stability in the United States and to enable them to return to Mexico. As their parents have gotten their papers, they are showing them the ropes of transborder life, with which their parents are unfamiliar since they spent decades avoiding detection. Though the Clementes' circumstances have improved and all of them can now go to Mexico together, the Garcías' situation has become even more complicated and challenging as each family member has different crossing capabilities. Yet in both scenarios, the now grown-up children are playing important roles in keeping their families connected—and will likely continue to do so.

CONCLUSION

Despite predictions that second-generation youth would become less involved in transborder life as they matured into adults, a very different pattern has emerged among second-generation borderlanders. Some individuals like Carlos, Esperanza, and Paulina grew up visiting their parents' hometowns and continue to do so on a regular basis, as much as the constraints of adulthood allow them to. Living in the borderlands also enables second-generation Mexicans like Paulina, Sal, and Isabel to participate in local transborder life through both family-oriented visits and activities outside of the family as teenagers and now as adults. In fact, four of the six individuals described in this chapter—Esperanza, Sal, Beto, and Isabel—are actually *more* engaged in transborder life than they were as teenagers. Though assimilation theorists might suggest that as these second-generation youth grew up and became involved in U.S.-based relationships that interfered with maintaining transborder practices, many second-generation adults are actually meeting their partners or spouses through their transborder networks. When participation in transborder life is not brokered by parents any longer, adult concerns can serve as detractors to transborder life.

Yet one of the biggest detractors of participation in transborder life remains individuals' and family members' restrictions on movement because of their immigration status. Examining the transition to adulthood, some individuals have taken a more active role in bridging the border and divisions between transborder family units. Beto and Isabel both fought hard for their parents to be able to go back to Mexico, filing paperwork and paying significant fees to apply for status for their parents. While Beto's connector role is more by necessity, as his family continues to face barriers to being reunited, Isabel's is to help her parents develop the transborder competencies they now need to navigate the borderlands.

Indeed, as lifelong transborder specialists, second-generation Mexicans have developed extensive local knowledge bases (Bejarano 2010). Further, their abilities to manage multiple cultural repertoires have allowed them to cultivate coexisting identities (Smith 2006, 12) that situate them well for navigating their transborder lives, which I explore in chapter 6. In addition, as Levitt and Jaworksy (2007, 134) note, these skills and connections serve them well to "become transnational activists if and when they choose to do so during a particular life-cycle stage." In chapter 6, I highlight how second-generation Mexicans have become activists and advocates for mixed-status families as adults in both in their private lives and their chosen careers.

6

BROKERING BELONGING IN THE SHADOW OF THE STATE

I GREETED ISABEL in July 2015 with a huge hug, extending my congratulations on her recent college graduation. The event was the culmination of a long ordeal, with intertwined family and health challenges forcing her to leave college during her senior year four years earlier. Once she recovered from her illness, Isabel took a full-time job at a residential retirement community in order to help her family stabilize economically. As she noted, "I had to stop with only fifteen units left to graduate—knowing that was tough. I could have already finished. But at that point in my life I just couldn't. I had to help my family out." Following two years' work at the retirement community, Isabel had finally been able to return to school part-time (on top of her full-time job) to finish the outstanding credits for her bachelor's degree.

Following graduation, Isabel hoped she would be able to negotiate a pay increase at work. As she said, "I love what I do and I love going to work. But I haven't been able to demand a raise since I didn't have my degree yet." Her boss's response to her petition was lukewarm, and she was told any pay increase would only be minimal. Isabel was frustrated, especially because she believed she was already performing a lot of "extra" work. Her colleagues frequently called on her to translate for clients in reviewing care options and to help direct them and their family members to additional resources. Though she found it personally satisfying to perform these tasks—providing her a good opportunity to use her

Spanish to help Mexican families with the daunting process of putting their elders in a long-term residential facility—it was not one of her official job duties, and she was also not properly compensated for her services. She also accommodated clients' needs during the off-hours, indicating, "I'm not salary, but I'm taking calls at home. I don't mind it because I like what I do, but I do want to get paid more."

Isabel decided that she was going to look around for a new job and started updating her resume. She asked if I could help her polish it, which I was happy to do. When I opened the document, I noticed right away that Isabel downplayed her skills—underrating her Spanish fluency, not featuring her full range of health system skills (including negotiating insurance policies and authorization processes) as prominently, and not highlighting her numerous customer service awards. Once we polished her resume, foregrounding more of her skills as strengths, Isabel started looking around for jobs, targeting her search to social work. She found a few jobs that were promising but not quite the right match. After about a month or so, though, she called me and was excited to share that she had found "*the* perfect position," working at a multiservice family center in an area of San Diego that was demographically similar to her community. She asked me if I would be willing to serve as a reference for her, to which I responded with an enthusiastic yes. I realized at that time that I had known Isabel for nearly half of her life and would be well situated to speak to her character, life experiences, and work history.

The interviewer from the center promptly called me and asked me a fairly typical set of reference questions about how long I had known Isabel, in what capacity I had known her, and so forth. She then stated, "A lot of our families are in really difficult circumstances. They're really low-income, and many of them are immigrants who don't really know the system here. How do you think Isabel would handle working with these kinds of families?" I paused for a moment and replied, "Isabel is the oldest child in 'this kind of family.' Her parents struggled quite a bit throughout her childhood in finding secure jobs, keeping up with bills, being isolated from their extended families, and navigating life in the United States. Isabel has been translating for them and helping them with all of these things since she was young. She would be perfect for this job, because she understands these families' struggles intimately and has been honing these problem-solving skills her whole life." The interviewer concurred, echoing that she had been impressed with Isabel's maturity and astuteness in answering their questions about how she would approach different scenarios. It was clear to me by the end of the call that Isabel would definitely be offered the job, which she was the next day. She happily accepted and got the raise and valuation of her skills that she deserved.

As I thought about Isabel's new job, I realized it was perfect for her not only because she would be able to benefit from her newly minted degree and the skills gained at the retirement community, but also because she would be able to draw from life experiences in helping her own immigrant parents navigate life in the United States. Indeed, scholars have chronicled the important contributions that the children of immigrants often make to the smooth functioning of the family unit (Dreby 2015a; Katz 2014, 3; Menjívar 2000, 2010; Orellana 2009; Orellana, Dorner, and Pulido 2003). These contributions often start with translating and interpreting (Dorner, Orellana, and Jiménez 2008; Foner 2009), as they did with Isabel; as she noted, "Since I was little—like seven—I had to learn how to translate because my mom didn't understand English that well. But you become aware of things pretty quickly."

As Isabel's comment suggests, in the process of translating and interpreting, children develop a deeper awareness of the adult world around them. Children's "everyday work" (Orellana 2001, 366) can serve to connect their families to this outside world and open their access to resources, knowledge, and information (Orellana, Dorner, and Pulido 2003, 505). Children often serve as intermediaries between their families and local institutions (Menjívar 2000, 229), such as health care, social services, and school (Bloemraad and Trost 2008, 511; Katz 2014, 17; Kibria 1993; Menjívar 2010; Orellana, Dorner, and Pulido 2003; Orellana 2001, 2009). Employees in these settings are also quite reliant on children in immigrant families, particularly in low-resource areas.

Much of the literature on children's brokering activities is focused on childhood, considering the impact of brokering on children's development and educational progress. Even though some studies examine multiple time points (Dorner, Orellana, and Jiménez 2008), the analyses are still squarely situated within childhood; in fact, Katz (2014, 18) identifies the age range of eleven to nineteen as the most intensive time frame for child brokering. Most studies do not follow these child brokers as they transition into adulthood; thus, it remains to be seen how they continue to engage in these activities as adults. In Isabel's case, she remains committed to contributing to her household into her twenties; in fact, during her early twenties, circumstances necessitated that she effectively become head of the household. The literature also fails to capture the ways in which children who perform this everyday work growing up may naturally transition into careers utilizing these brokering skills, as Isabel does in her job as a social worker.

Less attention has also been paid to children's work in helping their families negotiate the immigration bureaucracy or the role that children's legal status plays in their brokering activities (Dreby 2015a). Orellana (2009) and her colleagues (Orellana, Dorner, and Pulido 2003, 519–20) have described children's brokering interactions with the state, such as translating important documents and negotiating encounters with authority figures in welfare, social security, and immigration offices. However, beyond knowing English better and having a keener sense of the functioning of U.S. institutions, many children of immigrants also possess an important resource and form of security that their parents do not: U.S. citizenship. Being a citizen provides them leverage their parents may lack and can add value to their brokering roles. This advantage is important not only during childhood but also as U.S. citizen children mature and take on increasing responsibilities in their families and communities, including navigating the immigration bureaucracy to try to regularize their parents' immigration statuses, which Isabel ultimately did.

In the preceding chapters, I demonstrated that my participants were cultivating these brokering roles—and activities specifically focused on immigration—as they came of age in a time period and place of increasing insecurity for their mixed-status families. In chapter 2, I highlighted how the immigrant rights protests served as a vehicle for participants' burgeoning legal and political consciousness (Abrego 2011; Blomeraad and Trost 2008). Participants like Paulina reflected on their duty to "represent" those who had a less secure immigration status—a commitment she carried forward as her university's student body president and in her job as a youth organizer with an activist organization. In chapter 3, I highlighted how individuals like Isabel ameliorated their parents' undocumented status vulnerabilities by filing paperwork on their behalf to regularize their status. In doing so, Isabel sought to end the lifetime of insecurity and fear that her parents had endured, an experience that she and her siblings had suffered from as well.

In chapter 4, I demonstrated that although my participants embodied the fear and distress of the constant surveillance, they also cultivated strategies of resistance to navigate immigration enforcement. I showed how participants like Esperanza found a way to couple their intensifying political consciousness with life experiences to embark on careers advocating for immigrants, in her case by being an attorney. And in chapter 5, I highlighted how the state promotes, constrains, and even necessitates the movement of members of mixed-status families across the U.S.-Mexico border. I demonstrated how individuals like Beto serve as the linchpin between their family members divided by the border.

The children of immigrants living in mixed-status families in the U.S.-Mexico borderlands are adversely affected by the U.S. immigration policies and enforcement practices that have framed their childhoods. They undoubtedly bear the scars of these policies and practices and the collective trauma they have wrought upon their families. However, it would not be accurate to characterize them as simply stuck "in the middle" (Katz 2014) of these larger structures constraining their lives; rather, they are active strategists and brokers—border crossers par excellence—who advocate for themselves, their family members, and their community and who possess a unique skill set that enables them to do so effectively. Their brokering sensibilities began to emerge in the context of the 2006 protests. However, as the previous chapters have been demonstrating, they also refined navigation and problem-solving skills within their mixed-status families as they became adults.

In this chapter, I turn more comprehensively to brokering roles the children of immigrants from mixed-status families continue to play as twenty-somethings. After reviewing the literature on the children of immigrants as brokers, I highlight the ways in which they have carried forward—and even intensified—their brokering activities into adulthood. For some, these activities are more private, performed on behalf of family members out of a commitment to advancing their family unit and giving back to their parents and community. Indeed, in the follow-up interviews I conducted in 2014, "giving back" was a common refrain among my participants, underscoring that their commitments have continued forward into adulthood. As will become clear, however, their brokering skills are also translatable job skills that have situated them well for service-oriented careers in the public sphere such as social workers, organizers, and lawyers. As adults now, these second-generation young adults broker boundaries (Massey and Sánchez 2010) for their families and beyond. Because many of the boundaries they must broker are constructed by the state—in the form of state categorizations that demarcate different vulnerabilities between them and related border enforcement tactics that render all of them subject to surveillance—I refer to these boundaries as borders.

THE WORK OF CHILDREN IN IMMIGRANT FAMILIES AS TRANSLATORS AND BROKERS

CHILDREN'S WORK IN TRANSLATING AND INTERPRETING

Scholars focused on the developmental and educational trajectories of the children of immigrants have chronicled the important contributions that they often make to the smooth functioning of their family units (Katz 2014, 3; Orellana 2009; Orellana, Dorner, and Pulido 2003). Children's contributions often start early in childhood with translating and interpreting, since parents who do not speak English often depend on their children, whose English language skills acquired in U.S. schools quickly surpass those of their parents (Dorner, Orellana, and Jiménez 2008; Foner 2009). Many contributions consist of invisible activities that take place within the home, such as answering the phone, reading and interpreting mail, and performing other tasks for their families (Orellana 2009, 4). These contributions are variously referred to as natural translation, family interpreting, language brokering, and paraphrasing (Orellana 2009, 1).

Beyond just language, though, children also become more familiar with U.S. social and cultural norms in school, positioning them well to explain them to their parents (Katz 2014, 6). Children's "everyday work" as helpers (Orellana 2001, 366) opens families' access to resources, knowledge, and information in a range of different domains, including educational, medical/health, commercial, legal/state, financial/employment, housing/residential, and cultural/entertainment (Orellana, Dorner, and Pulido 2003, 505). For many children, doing this work is such a normal, everyday activity that they do not consciously realize that they are even doing it (Dorner, Orellana, and Jiménez 2008; Orellana, Dorner, and Pulido 2003). However, acknowledging the concrete work that children perform dispels the notion that children's activities exist solely within the realm of "help," "learning," or "development" (Orellana 2001, 367). In working-class communities in both the United States and their parents' countries of origin, children's labor can be essential for household survival (377). Indeed, as Orellana (2009, 2) argues, children's work "should be considered as part of the labor cost equation in this current era of global economic restructuring in which many nations increasingly rely on an immigrant work force."

In practical terms, children's work often involves serving as intermediaries between their families and local institutions (Menjívar 2000, 229), including in health care, social service, and school settings (Bloemraad and Trost 2008, 511; Katz 2014, 17; Kibria 1993; Menjívar 2010; Orellana 2001, 2009; Orellana, Dorner, and Pulido 2003; Portes and Rumbaut 2001). Their regular "acts of brokering" connect their families to the outside world (Orellana 2001, 366). In underserved communities, immigrant families may face serious structural difficulties in securing linguistically and culturally appropriate local resources (Katz 2014, 12). Thus, children perform essential work in bridging resource gaps for their families. But it is not only parents who are reliant on children in immigrant families. Teachers, doctors, salespeople, social workers, and others employed in a range of institutional settings also depend heavily on these children's contributions, often out of sheer necessity (Orellana 2009, 2).

In these encounters outside the home, children emerge as the "experts" who are ultimately in charge of negotiating their families' well-being and integration into U.S. society (Orellana 2001, 378). Several ethnographic studies have highlighted the critical importance of children's contributions to Mexican and Central American immigrant households in the metropolitan areas of greater L.A. (Katz 2014; Orellana 2001; Orellana, Dorner, and Pulido 2003) and Chicago (Dorner, Orellana, and Jiménez 2008; Orellana, Dorner, and Pulido 2003). In immigrant communities, having immigrant parents who need assistance navigating interactions outside of the home "may be the norm, rather than the exception" (Katz 2014, 2), underscoring children's critical role in household functioning. In fact, as they get older, many youth step up their contributions by taking on additional income-earning and household responsibilities, including taking care of siblings (Menjívar, Abrego, and Schmalzbauer 2016, 117–18; Orellana 2001).

CHILDREN AS ACTIVE BROKERS

In the process of translating and interpreting, children gain deeper insight into how the adult world functions. As they gain these insights, they come to play more active roles in brokering encounters, making decisions, and actively managing the dynamics of these encounters (Bloemraad and Trost 2008, 511). The view of children as active decision makers inverts the conventional perception of the child as occupying a position of social and legal dependency relative to adults (Leiter, McDonald, and Jacobson 2006). This perception of dependency does not adequately encapsulate the critical individual and familial roles children may play in decision making (Heidbrink 2014, 14).

Instead, children should be recognized as cultivating both individual and collective strategies for assisting their families (Katz 2014, 3). As they get older, they often develop additional linguistic and cultural competencies and take on even greater responsibility and authority within the family (Menjívar 2000, 228; 2010; Orellana, Dorner, and Pulido 2003). This pattern runs counter to popular and traditional developmental theories that posit that adolescence is a time during which children break away from the family as they develop an independent, autonomous self (Dorner, Orellana, and Jiménez 2008, 516; Katz 2014, 5). Such a vision of adolescence reflects assumptions about adolescent development centered on white, middle-class Americans as opposed to being grounded in the particular experiences of minority and/or immigrant families (Dorner, Orellana, and Jiménez 2008, 519).

Within immigrant families, parents often rely most strongly on the eldest child to broker for them (Dreby 2015a, 88; Katz 2014, 32). This disproportionate reliance on the eldest can actually serve as a source of tension with their younger siblings who do not wish to acknowledge them in this role of authority. Beyond age order, females more often end up assuming greater responsibility as family brokers than male children (Dreby 2015a, 94; Katz 2014, 32; Orellana 2001, 382), also potentially aggravating sibling conflict. Indeed, the complex relationships of siblings within immigrant families is an area that has not received much scholarly attention (Menjívar, Abrego, and Schmalzbauer 2016, 109–10).

There are other potential downsides to children's brokering, including that brokering responsibilities may adversely impact schooling and children's developmental processes (Dorner, Orellana, and Jiménez 2008, 520; Dreby 2015a). Children taking on these positions of authority and asserting their autonomy can also potentially introduce intergenerational strain and conflict (Foner 2009, 3). Indeed, the role reversal inherent in these acts of brokering can give children power over their parents and exacerbate preexisting conflicts (Foner 2009; Pallares and Flores-González 2011, 167). Further, the undermining of parental leadership and authority is another potential negative repercussion of children being forced into taking on these adult decision-making roles (Bloemraad and Trost 2008, 525; Dreby 2015a, 89). In their classic segmented assimilation framework, Rumbaut and Portes (2001, 308) describe the process of dissonant acculturation, through which the children's learning of English and American cultural outlooks "so exceeds their parents' as to leave the latter hopelessly behind." Dissonant acculturation is thought to place the children of immigrants on a disadvantaged path, along which ties to the family and ethnic community are severed (Portes and Rumbaut 2001, 52–53). Immigrant parents' lack of legal immigration status can also serve as a mechanism for further exacerbating the inversion of power relations between parents and their U.S.-born children (Dreby 2015a, 179).

A more optimistic interpretation of what children gain by being brokers is that their work can serve to "strengthen their loyalty, commitment to, and responsibility for their family and community" (Menjívar, Abrego, and Schmalzbauer 2016, 118; Pallares and Flores-González 2011, 172). Despite concerns about potential detrimental effects on children's development, their brokering work may actually serve to be a positive force in their maturation process (172). Some children's sense of self is deeply rooted in their identity as being the family helper (Katz 2014, 11). For U.S.-born children in immigrant families, brokering work may allow them to honor the "immigrant bargain" their parents have made, through which the parents' migration-related sacrifices are redeemed by the successes of their children in the new country (12; Smith 2006, 125–26). Although children are seen to be honoring this immigrant bargain during their childhood, it is less clear how their brokering activities and commitment to upholding the immigrant bargain continue on into adulthood. Further, their parents' status-related vulnerabilities may necessitate that they continue to be involved in ensuring family well-being.

CHILDREN BROKERING THE STATE

The literature on the brokering work of children in immigrant families most commonly situates their work as taking place at home or in educational, health care / social service, and commercial settings. Orellana (2009) and her colleagues (Orellana, Dorner, and Pulido 2003, 519–20), however, have also called attention to the work that children have performed specifically in relation to the state, documenting a limited set of tasks performed under these auspices. Children's brokering work vis-à-vis the state includes more everyday, passive activities, such as translating official letters received in the mail, as well as more specialized, heightened encounters with authority figures in welfare, social security, and immigration offices (519).

In these more episodic heightened encounters, children come to feel the gaze of state surveillance quite acutely (Orellana 2009, 74). They potentially witness punitive interactions with social workers in which their parents are humiliated, infantilized, and mistreated (Orellana, Dorner, and Pulido 2003,

519). Due to this negative treatment, children may develop more protective stances, guarding the family from excessive incursions from the outer sphere into their homes and personal lives (521). Unlike paid professional adult translators, though, children are not neutral parties in these exchanges; rather, they are well aware that their words could be used against their parents and therefore translate strategically and in support of their families (Orellana 2009, 74).

Children also bear witness to the ways in which their family members (of any status) are mistreated in encounters with the Border Patrol and CBP officials. These encounters also provide children a window into how state institutions and the agents who staff them perceive immigrants, including in stressful encounters in which their social legitimacy is called into question. Children whose parents are undocumented eventually realize that such encounters are to be avoided at all cost. From these range of different encounters with state actors, they also come to understand that citizens and LPRs have better access to resources for navigating them (Menjívar, Abrego, and Schmalzbauer 2016, 128). Indeed, brokering state power may not fall to the eldest or female children within the family but instead to citizens within them who can drive legally and engage verbally with agents from a more secure position. Even children who have a lighter skin tone may be identified as the family representative for these encounters (Romero 2006, 2008). Dreby (2015a, 93) has found that legal status shapes children's differential contributions to their families, although she found that it was actually U.S.-born children with unauthorized parents who helped out less, suggesting potential power and hierarchical conflicts within mixed-status families.

Children's interactions with agents of the state and the familiarity they gain with the political structures that constrain their families may also contribute to their burgeoning political consciousness. As Bloemraad and Trost (2008, 520) argue, children's translation and interpretation in a range of institutional settings "naturally spills over into political translation." Indeed, they observed that during the 2006 immigrant rights protests, children had access to English language skills but were able to leverage their knowledge of political information to help inform and mobilize parents (Bloemraad and Trost 2008, 507). Even beyond the 2006 protests, children in immigrant families can also influence the political socialization processes of their families more broadly (Bloemraad and Trost 2008; Katz 2014; Wong and Tseng 2008).

BROKERING BORDERS IN FAMILY, COMMUNITY, AND PROFESSIONAL LIFE

While the scholarship on the brokering work of the children of immigrants has compellingly established the phenomenon and the ways in which it affects children's development and family life during childhood, there are still lingering questions about how these brokering activities continue over time as children mature, leave their childhood homes, and even start families of their own. Further, more needs to be established about the brokering activities they perform as adults and how their brokering is shaped by their engagements with the state, the ultimate arbiter of their parents' exclusion. It is also crucial to contextualize their continuing brokering work as adults temporally (a period in which no comprehensive immigration reform has passed and more punitive measures have been implemented) as well as geographically (borderland communities where illegality, deportability, and policeability are experienced particularly acutely).

I seek to answer these questions by highlighting the brokering experiences of my participants as they have matured into adulthood. I will examine two facets of their brokering work: work performed for family and community in the private sphere and work performed in the public sphere through formal employment. While I separate them analytically, the sets of brokering activities they perform are most definitely intertwined; for instance, the private sphere brokering work Isabel has performed for her family since she was young unquestionably shaped the path that led her to become a social worker specializing in work with vulnerable immigrant families like her own. Ultimately, the competencies they have cultivated in brokering for their families have also equipped them with very particular skills sets that are professionally valuable.

"I GO AND HANDLE IT!": BROKERING FOR FAMILIES WITHIN THE PRIVATE SPHERE

I had been struck more than a decade ago by the very adult roles that some of my teenaged participants were playing in their families—particularly among those, like Isabel, who had undocumented parents. Though she was only a high school sophomore during my intensive fieldwork, Isabel was already deeply involved in dealing with the challenges her family faced. On numerous occasions, she came to me or other adults at the center to seek advice on how to help her family with challenges related to employment, housing, and even food. Although Isabel's parents had really struggled most of her life, their circumstances worsened when she was in high school as her father had difficulty finding steady work when the economy took a downturn. As she recalled of that time, "It got to the point that it was so bad at home that we almost had nowhere to live. We were so many months behind in rent and we didn't have any way to solve that." Note that Isabel included herself as one of the individuals who had to strategize about how to address their financial woes and housing insecurity.

Many of the adult Clementes' challenges were directly related to their undocumented status. Despite living in California for nearly two decades by then, the Clementes still had not found a suitable niche in the local labor market and had very little safety net. As the oldest child, Isabel bore the weight of these adult issues more than her younger siblings. In fact, she tried very hard to shield them from their insecure circumstances and was largely successful in this respect. Yet it was hard at times for Isabel to witness how different her siblings' experiences and attitudes were. When talking about them, she sighed and said, "They've, in many ways, had it much easier than I have. Sometimes they take things for granted and just don't see the work we have to do. Sometimes I feel like they're ungrateful." In this statement, Isabel sounds notably like a parent; she has included herself in the "we" putting the work into the household, existing essentially in a parental role in relationship to her sisters.

As she continued through high school, Isabel had some aspirations of going away to college elsewhere in California; she knew, however, that would not be possible. She ultimately chose to go to a private college nearby, having received scholarships and considerable financial aid due to their low household income. During her first year of college, while she lived on campus, Isabel continued to be a strong presence in the household, sometimes contributing her financial aid money to help with expenses and always running back home to shuttle her mother to work or put out some kind of fire. She moved back home after a year, in part because her dad could only find work out of state, which only intensified the rest of the family's reliance upon her, as she effectively became the head of the household.

As described in chapter 3, all of this pressure ultimately culminated with Isabel being struck with a health episode that necessitated her leaving school and seeking care for several months. Once Isabel got better, though, she started working full-time to help support the family; their economic situation finally stabilized, opening the door of opportunity for her sisters. Isabel's sisters had more opportunities precisely because of Isabel's sacrifices and contributions. Whereas leaving San Diego had not been an option for Isabel, her middle sister decided that she wanted to attend school up in the Bay Area. Isabel helped make that reality happen for her sister by contributing to her school expenses from her own paychecks. A few years later, her youngest sister went to a public university in San Diego but got to live on campus, also through Isabel's financial support. Despite her parents still struggling to find consistent work, neither sister had experienced the family's crisis period as acutely as Isabel did.

Isabel and her parents decided that the best way to improve their collective lot was to hire a lawyer and have Isabel officially sponsor their application for lawful permanent residency; Isabel was twenty-two at that point. Beyond getting over the fear of making themselves known to the state, the cost of lawyers and fees was also a barrier. As Isabel noted, "It's a lot of money when you don't have any. And the money has to be upfront. Even though we couldn't pay for other stuff, we were like, 'It doesn't matter! We've got to use this money for that!'" It is clear from Isabel's inclusive "we" that she was a primary decision maker on the matter. Instead of returning to school, Isabel worked full-time and used her earnings to pay to secure her parents' status. In doing so, Isabel performed the ultimate brokering act with the state on behalf of her parents—helping them to get the secure immigration status that had eluded them for two decades.

Submitting the application, of course, was only the beginning of the process. While the application was out, it was extremely nerve-racking for the Clementes to know that the government had all of their information. They also had to stage her parents' applications over time; the lawyer deemed her mother's case to be more clear-cut, so they moved forward with hers first. Isabel's mother was extremely anxious about the process, which ended up taking nearly a year. Once her green card finally arrived, she said that "it felt really good . . . it was such a sense of relief." While the Clementes were exuberant about Paloma getting her papers, they were still nervous as they waited for her father's case to be resolved. Given that the lawyer deemed his case to be more complicated, it was even more stressful. Ultimately, though, his permit arrived too; when I saw her soon after, she stated, "Now that they have their permits to be here, we're all more at peace."

After a lifetime of worry about her parents' tenuous immigration status, Isabel was able to successfully broker her parents' inclusion. Since receiving their papers, Isabel's parents have still struggled to find jobs with good working conditions and wages. However, Isabel feels that the peace that her family now has—to drive legally, to maneuver around the area freely, to visit family members throughout California and in Tijuana, and to be free of fear over interactions with Border Patrol agents—has been well worth it. Isabel continued to live with her parents after they got their papers. When I asked her about her own future, it was clear that being the family broker all of those years had taken a toll on her. As she said at the time, "I'm twenty-four and I'm one of the oldest [cousins] that is not married, that does not have children. And I don't have any urgency to. I think I grew up too fast. I just don't feel the urgency of having my own family and having to worry about those things. I feel like I still have plenty of time to do that."

Even though she held significant authority within the household at that point—she was the highest wage earner and held substantial decision-making power—she still felt that her sisters did not respect her position within the family. As she noted, "Sometimes they forget that I do have the authority because it's me that's responsible. They don't respect that; they just see me as the sister. My mom realizes that, and she's like, 'You need to listen to her, too!' They had things different than I have. They haven't seen the struggle . . . or had to struggle like I have." Despite not being recognized by her siblings as an authority figure, she noted that many parent-like responsibilities fell on her even so. To exemplify this point, she shared, "My sister had a boyfriend and it was a really bad relationship. One time, there was a really bad situation. And who did she call? Me. My mom's working. My dad was out of state at that time. So what do I do? I ask for permission at work to leave early. I go and handle it." Though Isabel dutifully took care of the situation, it is clear that she has done more than her share of "handling" family crises.

Isabel's family was not the only one in which the oldest sibling sacrificed for the good of the family. Mateo also acknowledges very clearly the disproportionate contributions his two older sisters—and the eldest in particular—had to make for their family. Mateo is the youngest of three, with four years' space in between each sibling. When his eldest sister was little, their parents' status and economic situation was much less stable. He does remember some of the early years, saying, "I could tell from my dad growing up that there was definitely a lot of struggle." Consequently, he noted, "My oldest sister had to help out the family more. She's happy now, but she didn't have the opportunities that Lisa and I did." I asked if that sister's sacrifices ever caused any tension among them, and Mateo said, "No, she never rubbed it in our face or anything. But from time to time we think about, 'Hey, if she wants to go back to school and finish what she started, we need to support her. It's her turn now.'"

Mateo observed specifically how his parents' regularizing their status had really improved their overall family situation, saying, "By the time I came around to high school, my parents already had papers, so it made it easier for me. They were both U.S. citizens by the time I finished high school." Mateo got a job bussing tables when he was in high school, although it was not to help support the family. As he said, "I got my job in high school because I wanted to have money. When my eldest sister was that age, my parents didn't have their papers yet, so she got a job to help the family out. She *had* to have a job." Around this time, Mateo also started noticing that some of his other friends were working to save for pressing priorities. He said, "A lot of my friends have been working jobs, just working to save up money to apply for papers and get lawyers to speed up the process. I just couldn't imagine myself getting a lawyer at twenty just so I can get papers. I definitely understand their struggles a lot more now." By his early twenties, then, Mateo was clearly able to see how he benefited from his parents' improved immigration status and his sister's work in helping buffer the impact of their undocumented status.

Beto's transition into adulthood also highlights how gaining status can influence family economic circumstances and stability. Growing up, neither Beto nor any of his immediate family members had their papers. When he was nineteen, Beto recalled that it had been quite difficult for his family to establish itself in the United States initially, saying, "We lived in a small little one-bedroom apartment. We didn't have money to buy anything. My grandma would give her money or help us out with old clothes. But we didn't really have a lot. It took awhile for my dad to get on his feet." He characterized his family circumstances as challenging throughout the duration of his childhood, saying, "I saw them struggle financially, mentally, emotionally. As a kid, it's hard to see your parents struggle like I did."

Beto's father found a job with a landscaping company in the early 1990s and was employed there for nearly two decades, steadily managing to secure increases in his wages. Although the family found some financial security, Beto noted that "my dad worked hard, but couldn't come home like the traditional American father and take the kids to the park or to soccer practice. I understood as a kid that his job was hard." Beto's nuclear family has also benefited tremendously from the support of his dad's large extended family, many of whom live in the same neighborhood. Through one of these family connections,

Beto started working bussing tables when he was fourteen. As he noted when he was nineteen, "I've always had to work. I have to help my parents with bills and other things like that. I can't be at home being lazy." While many of his peers graduated and continued on to college, Beto was not able to because of his status and the prohibitive cost of attending school. Reflecting on that time, he said, "I knew I had the potential, but it was other factors that wouldn't allow me to go. I just had to accept it and move on because it's just part of life." Instead, he continued to work, sometimes at multiple jobs, while taking classes intermittently at community colleges.

Postgraduation, Beto also got married to his girlfriend from high school. At first, they continued to live with his parents, contributing some of their earnings to the household. During that time, Beto was able to get his green card and explore better employment options than were previously available to him. Eventually, though, Beto and his wife moved to New Mexico to live with her family, in part because of his father-in-law's worsening health. New Mexico was a growing experience for Beto, although he conveyed that he did not feel the same "sense of belonging" with his in-laws. Throughout his time in New Mexico, Beto still remained oriented toward his family back in San Diego. The previous few years had been really difficult for them. Beto's brother's deportation destabilized the family and introduced a new set of challenges—foremost among them that no one could see Luis, who had reestablished himself in Tijuana. Then Beto's marriage broke up, and in the aftermath he headed back to San Diego and moved in with his family again. There was one big difference in Beto's life at this point, though: he had made his way through the immigration maze and gotten his citizenship.

Once he became a citizen, Beto realized that the best way he could help improve his parents' circumstances was to try to help them get their papers as well. So he hired a lawyer and applied for both of them. Like Isabel, they were advised to stage each parent's applications separately, knowing that his mother's previous detention would complicate her case. Ultimately, Beto was only able to get a green card for his father, which was absolutely heartbreaking to him—and continues to weigh heavily on him. Beto's experience with his mother underscores that even adept brokers still face significant hurdles in taking on the state.

Ironically, getting his papers actually worsened his father's employment circumstances. His father lost his job of twenty years when he got his green card and tried to correct the paperwork with his employers, who were well aware of his status before. Though the company appreciated his strong work ethic and decades of loyalty, they had no way to transition him into his new legitimate status. This was an unexpected blow to the family, who envisioned his work circumstances improving. Around the same time, Beto's dad started experiencing chronic health issues that needed attention. Lacking insurance but now having the ability to cross the border, Beto took his father down to Tijuana to find care, which is what he had also been doing since he got his papers. Having a few more years of experience with trips to Tijuana by then, Beto ushered his father through the whole process. Beto, then, has transitioned into a caretaking role with his parents as he has continued into his twenties.

Indeed, multiple participants expressed firm commitment to taking care of their parents. Mateo also continues to live with his parents in the neighborhood in the same house where he grew up. Although he went away to college and lived in the dorms for his freshman year, Mateo made the decision to return home to live "because I was partying a lot and I decided, 'This is not very good for me!'" Living at home and commuting to school centered Mateo, and he was able to successfully complete his degree. Postgraduation, Mateo's intentions to remain in the neighborhood to be close to his parents were crystal clear, epitomizing the immigrant bargain. He recounted that as he looked toward graduation, "My thinking was, 'How am I gonna give back to my parents when I finish? How am I able to thank my parents for what they did, all of the struggles and sacrifices?'" For Mateo, part of thanking them was to continue to live with them at home and help out. As he shared when he was twenty-four, "I plan to stay in [name of neighborhood] for years to come. Either keep the same house that we have or tear it down and make a new one and retire my parents there."

As they continued into their twenties, other participants also continued to help their parents. After moving to L.A. for college, Paulina had stayed in the area afterward to work. However, an urgent call from her dad changed everything for her. As she recounted it, "My mom had a [serious health crisis] and my dad was freaking out. I've never seen my dad freak out so much—like not even when he was deported! He was just telling me that he needed me to come back home." Paulina dutifully returned to San Diego so she could help the family. The urgency of her mother's health crisis abated; as she said, "Luckily, she's doing really well right now." But Paulina remained in San Diego afterward, living initially with her family for a few more years before moving out and getting her own apartment when she was twenty-seven. Sal likewise continues to be there for his parents when they need him. When he was in high school, Sal's dad had returned to Tijuana to live after many years of working and living in the United

States. He struggled with finding work that paid well enough and with keeping up with household expenses in the new setting. When Sal himself first started living in Tijuana, he lived with his dad so that he would have more money coming in, even though he did not actually spend much time there. Even after he moved out subsequently, Sal continues to give his father money to help him out.

As they have gotten older, my participants' efforts to ensure their families' well-being have also involved new engagement with brokering activities. Victoria's brokering trajectory, for instance, has evolved as she continues into her mid-twenties. As the youngest of four children, Victoria did not have to expend as much effort on brokering as her older siblings did. When I first got to know both Victoria and Esperanza, the Medina family was fairly well situated economically; both parents had held their jobs for a long time and had steadily increased their earnings over the years. All family members' immigration statuses were also squared away; both parents and their two older siblings had regularized their statuses when the girls were young. By high school, her father was a citizen and her mother a resident. Victoria had not really witnessed the time period in which the family struggled, although Esperanza, who is three years older, remembers these struggles more markedly.

When Victoria married at age twenty-two, though, she encountered quite a different set of circumstances with her husband's family. Victoria's husband was also born in the United States, but his parents were undocumented. He was the oldest child with much younger siblings and had spent his childhood helping his parents; she noted, "He's very helpful to them, and they really appreciate that." Victoria reflected on the differences between their families, though, observing, "With my parents, they don't have a lot of money, but they're making it. They do have health insurance and things like that. But my husband's dad works in construction, and a lot of times he comes back home with a sore back. He doesn't have insurance to do anything about it. If something hurts and they have to go to the emergency room, it's a big problem."

Victoria has increasingly taken on some of the responsibility for her in-laws, particularly since some of her brothers-in-law are still minors and are not as able to perform these tasks. For instance, she has been trying to help her mother-in-law find a job, commenting, "I'm seeing how different it is for people who don't have papers. I've been trying to help her apply to the hospital to be housekeeping. She knew someone from there and she was like, 'Oh maybe they'll be able to help get me in.' So we did the application online. But the minimum requirement was high school and if you've house kept in a hospital or hotel.

She's only done offices and apartments, so she wasn't able to get it." Experiencing her in-laws' status limitations alongside them has also reanimated her desire to advocate for vulnerable immigrants; as she noted, "Since my parents had papers, I feel like I wasn't following things as much as I should. But now that I'm seeing the situation with my in-laws, I feel like, 'What can be done for them?! It's just wrong!'"

Victoria's husband has looked preliminarily into filing for his parents' papers but has found the process to be rather daunting. She knew that twenty-one was the magic age to "get the process moving" but was unsure of what exactly that would entail. Tomás likewise was aware of the possibility of filing on behalf of his mother, saying, "I have thought about trying to file for her. I know that you can do it when you're twenty-one, but that's just from my parents telling me." Recall that Tomás's family is quite isolated in the United States, with no extended family to assist them. While Isabel and Beto were able to find lawyers and initiate the process, there are significant obstacles for families who might be eligible—financial concerns and lack of knowledge about the process being two prominent ones.

Indeed, Victoria's question of "what can be done" for vulnerable immigrant families like her in-laws and Tomás's family factored in strongly to many of my participants' comments when I interviewed them as adults in 2014. Despite her frustration with her sisters not understanding their family's struggles as intimately as she does, Isabel and her middle sister often talk about what they could do to give back to other families in the same situation. She spoke several times of their dream project, telling me, "Once we have all our ducks in a row, we want to open up a nonprofit for the community. When we needed the help, we had it, in one form or another. We want to be able to help other immigrant families that, like us, sometimes have no way out. You just feel like you're stuck and there's nothing you can do. It was like that with my parents." Isabel remains incredibly grateful for the help of the center's staff for all of those years, but she sees the urgent need for more comprehensive social services. She is able to provide these to families in greater San Diego now, but also wants to serve the community in which she grew up more directly, too.

Beto likewise retains a strong commitment to the neighborhood and to youth in particular. Throughout his twenties, and as he was eligible for a wider range of jobs due to having his papers, Beto chose to work in community development, including as an AmeriCorps volunteer. Volunteering has been an important value to him for a long time; as he stated, "Since I was a kid, I've been giving back, because I know that's what needs to be done. In order to receive, at first you must give." Beto feels that he has many relevant experiences to share with neighborhood youth, stating, "I've been helping the youth in the middle schools and high school. I give them real-life problems and scenarios drawing from my experiences, and I mentor them with real-life solutions. The life mission for me is to keep kids out of trouble, to provide that support that I've been provided. I've been wanting to start a foundation for so long since I was a kid."

Beto also believes that financial literacy is a key component for these types of programs. As he transitioned to having status himself, Beto found that his parents had not been able to impart these skills to him because they did not have experience navigating mainstream financial institutions. Consequently, when he was first eligible to apply for credit cards, Beto ended up incurring a great amount of debt. As he noted, "My parents couldn't be a model for me because they never had them. There was a time where I got approved for two thousand, three thousand dollars. I just thought I could pay it off, but then those interest rates started kicking in and I'm in this financial hole, like, 'How do I get out of it now?' Finances is an issue I've been dealing with since I got my status." Like Isabel, though, he believes in the need for comprehensive services for immigrant families and the youth living within them. It remains to be seen if Isabel and Beto are able to actualize their dreams of opening nonprofit organizations in the neighborhood. What is clear, though, is that both experienced their families' struggles profoundly, greatly appreciate the assistance they received, and feel called to broker inclusion for youth like them.

Mateo also has a deep commitment to the neighborhood; Lisa echoed that he feels especially strong pride about where he is from, saying, "I talk to him about it, and I'm like, 'You're never gonna move out of the barrio, huh?' And he's like, 'Nope!' I guarantee my brother will stay there forever and ever." As the neighborhood has been gentrifying, Mateo and his mother have been attending the planning meetings so that they have a stake in the future of the neighborhood. He cares deeply about the neighborhood and says, "I'm always thinking of where I can give back or how I can give back." As he was preparing for his career as an EMT, Mateo went with the San Diego Fire Department to local schools. Tomás also volunteers for community safety awareness fairs in the neighborhood where he works, which is similar demographically to the neighborhood where he grew up and his parents still live. As adults, Esperanza and Victoria are still quite dedicated to their church, a prominent fixture in the community. Both sisters have been instrumental in starting a tutoring program at the church and a children's choir, with the intention of being role models for them in both their educational and musical pursuits.

"I LOOK BACK AT MY CIRCUMSTANCES AND THINK OF THEM AS AN ADVANTAGE": BECOMING PROFESSIONAL BROKERS

Beyond the support work they continue to provide for their families and the volunteer work they perform in the community, my participants also serve more formally as brokers through the careers they have pursued. They recognize that growing up in immigrant families has provided them with a set of concrete skills that serve them well in the working world. Casandra reflected on the complexities of "growing up immigrant," as she called it. On the one hand, she felt that "there were a lot of obstacles in our way. It definitely could be viewed as a struggle. As kids, I feel like from the get-go we were at a disadvantage, you know, system-wise, with my parents not being familiar with things." However, she continued by saying, "But now that I'm in the position that I am, I look back at my circumstances and think of them as an advantage. I'm bilingual. I'm confident in taking on challenges and solving problems. You learn not to take no for an answer, because you have to find another way. It just makes you get creative, be a problem solver." Casandra's list—bilingualism, confidence, challenge taking, problem solving, being creative—reflects unquestionably desirable job skills.

Luisa felt that she and her two siblings had benefited from the work ethic their parents had instilled in them, saying, "Growing up in an immigrant family gave me the notion that you've gotta work hard . . . dedication. I'm proud of that . . . it was definitely a good thing that we learned that." Carlos likewise felt that "both of my parents were very hardworking. They always pushed us to go to school and get a good job so that we wouldn't have to work like they did." Part of the Francos' strategy was to expose the children to their own challenging work environments. As Carlos recalls, "My mom would take us out to work with her cleaning houses. Even like two, three years ago, I still went to help her out. And my dad would take us to work [landscaping] in the summer outside. I don't know if he did it because he wanted us to work or he wanted us to see how hard it was working outside in the hot sun. But it was a good experience. All of my siblings and I have a strong work ethic because of that." It is also clear that Carlos gained humility and respect while working alongside his parents cleaning houses and landscaping.

When I interviewed participants in 2014 (when they were between twenty-two and twenty-eight), it was striking that they overwhelmingly worked in service professions that allowed them to draw from their advantageous knowledge bases and skill sets. Paulina, Casandra, and Wilson all worked in nonprofit organizations—Paulina and Casandra in a local chapter of a large national nonprofit social justice organization and Wilson in a smaller-scale nonprofit focused on bringing alternative energy to the neighborhood. Meanwhile, Isabel and Carlos worked as social workers specializing in low-income and Spanish-speaking clients. Esperanza and Victoria both worked in the legal field (Esperanza as a law student and Victoria, drawing inspiration from her older sister's career path, as a paralegal), dedicated to finding justice for members of their community. Mateo worked as an EMT in the barrio, while his sister Lisa and Luisa worked in early-childhood educational settings. Beto and Sal worked in customer service positions with well-known national companies in which their bilingualism was a plus and a core component of their professional identity. Tomás worked in security and also felt he was performing an important service to his community. Hearing them talk about their chosen fields and prior jobs, it was clear to me how much their childhood family and neighborhood experiences shaped their paths.

After high school, Casandra opted to attend a nearby public university, where she ultimately graduated with a degree in public administration. After graduation, she actually returned to the center, where I first met her, to work. She was welcomed back with open arms, as it was clear her experiences would be a great resource for families enrolled in the program. On coming back, she reflected, "I just felt really lucky to be able to give back by working there, by working with the parents and the students. I felt really comfortable in that atmosphere. And it made me appreciate it on a whole different level." While she was at the center, Casandra learned from Paulina of an opening at the nonprofit social justice organization where the latter had been working for a few months. The notion of working at the larger nonprofit appealed to Casandra because of its potential to help even more people and impact policy even further upstream. As she noted, "What I see is that sometimes immigrants are just not familiar with the system. We're trying to address that politically. I feel like it's worthwhile to try to tackle the problem on a whole other level."

Immigrant rights is a priority concern at her current organization and a topic she feels "most passionately about." She connects her enthusiasm about working there to her childhood: "As a kid, I knew there was something different about my parents' status, and I know that [my organization] had something to do with them being able to become legal residents in the 1990s. I'm like, 'Thanks to you guys, my parents were able to stick around and I'm here.' Had it been worse, maybe they would have been deported and I would have ended up back in Mexico with them." Instead, she recognized that "I'm a product of all those civil rights fights that have gone on since the 1960s. So now I'm like, 'Let me do my part and take part in it.' It's like a thank you–slash–let me give back to the next person, the next generation."

One of the ways in which she contributes in concrete terms is by being bilingual and bicultural; as she explained to me, "People turn to me for translation and turn to me for my Mexican background. They frequently tap into my resources." The fact that she characterized these as resources indicates that she has found being bilingual and bicultural to be workplace assets. But she ultimately sees putting these skills to good use as a means of giving back, explaining, "[My organization] has really given me that opportunity to give back and be involved in these important issues. I'm able to do my part."

Paulina likewise feels "so privileged to be able to work" at a nationally known nonprofit social justice organization. Part of what she appreciates about her job is being intimately involved with and able to focus on the range of issues that affect working-class families. As she pointed out, "There's so many issues that affect us, yet people don't see them because they're just trying to live their day-to-day life of work and being able to pay off bills." Paulina has substantially increased her knowledge of civil liberties and immigrant rights. As she asserted, "Immigrants really do have rights here in the United States. I didn't really know and appreciate that until I worked here." She also reflected that looking through an activist lens has allowed her to "see even more" about how immigrants were treated in different areas of San Diego County and the complexities of the Border Patrol and police enforcement that surrounded her growing up. This growing knowledge and insight has made Paulina better versed in the topics and better equipped to advocate for her family members and friends.

As a youth organizer, she has also become passionate about passing this knowledge on to youth from several high schools in different parts of the county, including her neighborhood high school. Paulina's office is particularly focused on low-income communities and communities of color; they conduct public education on a range of topics, including violations in the criminal justice system, immigrant rights, racial justice, LGBTQIA rights, and civic engagement. Paulina noted that the students with whom she has worked are particularly "connected to" immigration-related issues such as the DREAM Act, DACA, and driver's licenses for undocumented immigrants since many of them are immigrants themselves. But she also felt it was important to highlight a larger set of issues affecting communities of color, sharing, "We do our criminal justice school-to-prison pipeline and it just blows their mind. It absolutely blows their minds how they're targets." Paulina, then, has continued her work in spreading consciousness about the issues that frame the lives of youth from immigrant families.

Paulina is passionate about not only immigration and youth but also broader forms of injustice in the world, including global poverty and human rights. As we met up when she was twenty-five, we laughed about her "activist tendencies" and how she would often push the envelope *just* past where her mother was comfortable. Back in 2006, Paulina had participated actively in the immigrant protests behind her mother's back when the latter expressed concerns about potential dangers. Formal activism within a nonprofit social justice organization suits Paulina's outspoken personality well and has given her a productive vehicle through which to channel her passion and energies.

While no less committed to social justice, Esperanza's temperament has produced contributions that are quite different than Paulina's. She initially wanted to participate in the 2006 protests, but after debating it with her father, she "changed my view around it. I felt like I needed to do something and the easiest thing for me to do was to leave school and go protest. But I realized that wasn't the way to go." While Esperanza is not as outspoken as Paulina, when you talk to her it is clear she is equally committed to social justice issues that affect her neighborhood. Esperanza thought about going to University of California, Berkeley—where she believes she would have become much more of a public activist like Paulina and another good friend of hers from the program, Elena. But she has also come to recognize that her interpersonal style and approach to activism differs. Instead of being someone who protests on the streets, she fashions herself a "quieter" activist, working in support of social justice behind the scenes.

The seeds of this "quieter" activism were sown in high school, as she had her own interactions with agents of the state and experienced the deportation of one of her best friends, whose "wings were clipped" right before their senior year. However, she really cultivated her way of engaging with the immigrant rights movement when she went away to college. Deciding not to go to Berkeley in part because her church and family did not want her to go so far away, Esperanza initially started in San Diego as a premed major. Despite external pressure to major in the sciences as part of a program designed to help minority students become doctors, she decided to double major in ethnic studies and sociology. When she told the program that she was going to switch, "One of the doctors told me that I wouldn't get a job going down that line of work, but I was just following my heart at that point." She recalled, "I just started discovering all of these incredible things. I remember I would go to my ethnic studies professor's office hours every week. I'm sure I annoyed her, but I was just really fascinated by everything. The point for me was to take that lens and use it wherever I went." By her sophomore year, she "decided to go home, mainly because the money had run out. So I needed to save. But I also missed my family and my church activities." Being back in the community also enabled her to "stay grounded."

After graduating from college, Esperanza took a year off and then decided to go to law school, also in Southern California. I asked her when I interviewed her after her second year of law school whether she intended to go into immigration law specifically. She responded, "I'm not sure which realm I'll go into, but I see all of it as related to my community. Even in tax law, it's how school is funded through property taxes. That's a huge source of our problem here because we're underfunded. Even in business, developing small businesses, owners like my dad don't know how to develop them so they go bankrupt. In whatever area I select, there's an issue waiting to be resolved."

Esperanza's big motivation for going to law school was to be able to better advocate for her community. She noted that she was already receiving a number of phone calls for assistance, in particular from people from her church: "I'm still just a student and I'm getting calls for all sorts of things. I get calls from people who want to get their citizenship, not knowing that that's not what you learn in law school . . . that that's what you learn in your practice. There's a lot of work to do!" Esperanza ultimately aspires to be a judge, saying, "Those are the people who really have control over what the law is and how to interpret it through their positions of power—the positions where you can really make change on a large scale. That's my dream; that's where I want to get to."

Through all of these experiences, Esperanza has ultimately realized that "my approach is just not being out there protesting. I see Elena out there doing that a lot, but it's just not my style." This does not mean that she does not respect her friends who are active and vocal protesting in the streets; in fact, she matter-of-factly stated, "I think they're just different styles that work for different people." Esperanza has been able to craft her own approach to advocating for her community; as she stated, "I think my tactic will be to make subtle changes that will have a long-term positive effect. I just worry that if you do something to piss someone off, there you go. That's your cut and then you never get the chance to make the changes you want."

In the aftermath of the 2006 immigrant rights marches, scholars and public commentators were perplexed over what kind of legacy the protests would have in terms of formal electoral participation. There is some evidence that the energies behind the 2006 protests did translate into increased 2008 electoral participation (Bloemraad, Voss, and Lee 2011, 4). It is also the case that after 2006, youth of different immigration statuses propelled the DREAMer movement into the national spotlight and have continued to lead the broader immigrant rights movement (Nicholls 2013). Though my participants are not at the forefront of the DREAMer movement and may not participate regularly in protests or actions as adults, they are engaged in everyday political acts of brokering for their families and communities. While these brokering acts are less headline grabbing, they are nonetheless absolutely essential to ensuring the social inclusion of immigrants of all statuses. Thus it is crucial that we do not overlook the everyday work of advocating for immigrants being taken on by their children.

CONCLUSION

As exclusionary immigration policies and enforcement practices have expanded, citizen children have stepped up to broker the reverberations of them for vulnerable members of their mixed-status families and communities. Literature on transnational and mixed-status families divided by borders has chronicled the critical intergenerational caregiving roles of parents and grandparents (Dreby 2010; Horton 2009; Yarris 2017); however, intergenerational caregiving also operates in reverse in the U.S. context as children who are more secure in their immigration statuses come of age and come to take on increasingly important roles in their families and communities. As they transition to adulthood, my participants remain intimately involved with brokering on their family members' behalf and trying to promote their broader social inclusion; indeed, the values of sacrifice and solidarity inherent in these forms of intergenerational caregiving also flow in reverse between generations (141).

Individuals such as Isabel and Beto brokered for their parents and contributed to the household unit at a very early age in ways that were critical to the well-being of their families—and, indeed, to their continued existence as a family unit in the United States. Over time, their brokering work has only intensified and diversified as they made their best attempts to improve their parents' circumstances—efforts that have sometimes, unfortunately, fallen short. They have both taken on this brokering work as acts of commitment and loyalty to their families at the expense of their own interests and even their health and well-being.

Others, like Mateo and Tomás, described a broader commitment to their community that they have actualized though volunteer work, most often performed for youth growing up as they did. It is clear through these acts that their desire to "give back" to family and community has carried forward strongly into adulthood. It is also clear that they have particularly rich skill sets for performing this type of work. Still other participants, like Casandra and Paulina, have honed their brokering skills in ways that attempt to ensure the well-being of their community through professional employment in service capacities. Although none of my participants are full-time activists focused solely on immigrant rights or leaders of a youth-led immigration social movement, they remain committed to the political project of advocating for their family and communities. Indeed, doing this work has come to represent a core component of their adult identities.

The brokering roles of the children of immigrants in mixed-status families—in particular, those activities carried out relative to the state—have only taken on increased importance as the Trump administration has stepped up deportations, including through routine check-ins with immigration officials and broader immigration sweeps that extend far beyond those with criminal backgrounds. As I wrote this chapter, I heard the news of yet another mixed-status family being affected by the detainment of the parents and uncertainty about what would happen if the family was permanently separated. In this particular case, the eldest sibling, a nineteen-year-old college student, had to step up and assume guardianship for his three younger siblings who are minors. The family had a contingency plan in place for him to legally assume this responsibility, but he was nonetheless compelled to assume this very adult and complicated brokering role at a young age. This family also happens to live right around the corner from Beto's family; they are neighbors who unfortunately were unable to fend off the state's punitive reach into their family life. As I think of Beto's substantial brokering work over the last decades, I am saddened by the reality that yet another young adult who had dreams and aspirations of his own has been foisted into the role of a border broker, trying to accomplish the incredibly difficult task of being the glue that holds together the pieces of his family. In the next chapter, the conclusion, I return to the policy implications of brokering responsibilities for young adults in mixed-status immigrant families.

CONCLUSION

I ARRIVED AT the Garcías' house in San Diego one cool December afternoon in 2016, ready to join Beto for a trip to Tijuana to visit his older brother, Luis. The Garcías had moved away from the neighborhood where they lived when I first met them, which was Beto and his siblings' childhood home; Luis had been picked up and ultimately deported from not too far away from there, and the memory proved to be too intense for the family to confront on a daily basis.

Beto visits with his brother in Tijuana a few times a month, whenever he can squeeze it into a busy work schedule involving multiple jobs. Because Beto was able to successfully file for residency for him, Beto's father is able to cross the border and sometimes joins them. Beto's mother aches to see her oldest son again after seven years' absence, but she cannot cross due to her status. When I entered the house, Señora García greeted me and reported that she had just gotten off FaceTime with Luis; she expressed delight that he would have visitors from home that day. She then handed me a plastic grocery store bag containing various items, including a baseball cap, socks, paper towels, and oranges from a family member's tree. While the package contained nothing of particular significance, it had clearly been assembled with love. I assured her Luis would get it, all the while feeling conflicted that I was so easily able to cross the border to visit Luis in Tijuana when she could not.

Almost thirty years old at that point, Beto remained quite focused on his family members' well-being. A renewed commitment stems in part from the time when he was away from the family when he lived in New Mexico with his then-wife for several years to be closer to her extended family; as he reflected, "I loved my time there. I was really able to grow as an individual." He noted that when he moved to New Mexico initially, he intended to stay, saying, "I told myself once I opened my wings and flew away, then that was that. I'd be out there. I'd just live my life." Indeed, being able to move out of state at all was momentous for Beto, since he had spent his entire childhood undocumented and unable to move around freely. But it was also hard for him to be so far away from his own family during that period, especially as they were adjusting to their new circumstances once Luis was deported. When he split with his wife a few years after moving to New Mexico, Beto said he just knew, "I'm going back to my family."

Now several years later, Beto continues to live with his parents. He contributes significantly to the household expenses, which are still somewhat precarious given his father's challenges in working in landscaping as he gets older and his mother's limited work opportunities. He also worries more and more about his father's health, since he has performed physical labor his whole adult life and has developed chronic health conditions in recent years. Beto takes his father to doctor's appointments in Tijuana now that he is able to cross the border since he does not have—and has never had—health insurance in California. Beto also helps out his mother however he can. He frequently gives her rides to get together with family and friends who live in different parts of San Diego and regularly escorts her around to run errands like grocery shopping since she cannot drive. His presence—and secure status as a citizen—is also reassuring to her as she deals with increasingly aggressive enforcement actions and the embodied fear they produce. Beto explains his dedication to his parents, saying, "I'm not going to let my mom and dad suffer, because they've given us so much. That right there gives me a sense of urgency. That right there is what drives me to work, to start building."

Beto's statements reveal a deep and ongoing commitment—even "urgency," as he characterized it—to alleviating his parents' suffering. But as he looks toward his future, Beto also ponders, even dreams, about moving away from San Diego again—perhaps even back to New Mexico, where he still has close friends and knows he could live more affordably. He describes this situation as a "tug-of-war" in which he must balance his own desires and needs relative to those of the larger family unit. Family always wins this tug-of-war, in my and his own assessment, as he always ends up deciding to stay. His bottom line, as he has stated repeatedly, is that "I'll be here until things change with my mom." It haunts Beto that despite his best effort in filing on her behalf to regularize her status, he could not improve his mother's legal situation. The state clearly continues to wield significant power in shaping his family's circumstances.

I have witnessed numerous changes in the Garcías' lives over the past decade plus. When I first met them, all five had already been in the United States for more than a decade but nonetheless struggled without a pathway for regularizing their statuses. Their undocumented statuses hindered the García parents' employment options and economic stability, impeded Beto's and his brothers' educational trajectories, and affected all of their abilities to maneuver around safely and freely. Yet the Garcías also had a strong family bond and a larger extended family network upon which they could depend to help them make their way through those challenges. Beto's father found stable work, ultimately being employed by the same company for two decades. Eventually when they were teenagers, Beto and his brothers found jobs at restaurants as well, largely through their extended family connections.

Over time, some developments in their lives have been positive: Beto was able to get his papers and then his U.S. citizenship, and, in so doing, he was then able to help his father regularize his status, too. Beto's older brother, Luis, has found a community of fellow deportees in Tijuana and has started studying at the university there. Beto's younger brother, Felipe, was able to get DACA when the program came into being in 2012, and both brothers have been able to get far better paying and more satisfying jobs because of their change in status. They also both drive around officially licensed and are free to go wherever they want in San Diego, and Beto has a U.S. passport that enables him to come and go securely across the U.S.-Mexico border. When CBP agents ask him the ubiquitous question about his country of citizenship as he is crossing back from Tijuana at the port of entry, I observe him answering clearly and firmly, "U.S. citizenship," and self-assuredly handing his documents to the agent. Indeed, this is quite a change from when I first met Beto and crossing the border was not even remotely an option for him.

Yet the Garcías have encountered insurmountable obstacles along the way owing to their marginal immigration statuses and the vulnerabilities that accompany them. Beto's mother and his brother Luis both had encounters with immigration officials, resulting in her being held in a detention facility, with her petition for residency being stalled indefinitely, and him ultimately being deported to a homeland that he did not remember. Both they and the larger family unit bear emotional scars from these encounters with the state and the aftermath. Conditions of life in the United States have continued to deteriorate even more for Beto's mother as she deals with the increased insecurity and danger of simply walking down the street in a country in which she has lived for almost thirty years. Beto's younger brother now has to contemplate what his life in the United States might look like since DACA has been rescinded and he may find himself again without status. Given the increasingly hostile context for them in the United States, the García parents have even contemplated moving back to Mexico, either to Tijuana to be with Luis or to their hometown in Jalisco.

But in the midst of his family's worsening circumstances—or perhaps precisely because of them—Beto has emerged in an important role within his family: that of a border broker. He is the one who possesses the most secure status in his family now, who was able to successfully obtain papers for his father, and who is able to travel around in the United States and Mexico to see all the members of the family, deliver items to and from each of them, and ensure that they remain connected. He is the one who assists his family members in navigating their limitations by contributing his income to help cover their needs, driving them around so they feel safe, translating for them to ensure that their interests are protected, helping them remain healthy by navigating health-care systems on both sides of the border, and doing whatever else he can to try to minimize the impact of the state in dividing and compromising the well-being of his family.

PUNITIVE PUBLIC POLICIES AND YOUNG ADULTS FROM MIXED-STATUS FAMILIES

The more than 16.6 million members of mixed-status families like the Garcías have been aggressively targeted by and subjected to increasingly punitive immigration policies and enforcement practices over the last three decades. These policies and practices circumscribed my participants' lives pronouncedly as they grew up in a borderland San Diego neighborhood that for decades has been under the intense gaze of the state. In this book, I have demonstrated the damaging effects of these long-standing and intensifying policies and practices on

FIGURE 10. A Border Patrol sports utility vehicle stands guard at Friendship Park on the U.S. side of the U.S.-Mexico border.

this Gatekeeper generation—children from mixed-status families who grew up, came of age, and transitioned into adulthood in this milieu.

My focus on how these policies and practices affect children in mixed-status families during the transition from adolescence to adulthood enhances our understanding of their longer-term effects. I have highlighted not only how teenagers made sense of growing up in a mixed-status family but also how they have been (and continue to be) impacted by their family members' vulnerabilities over time, demonstrating the repercussive effects of illegality and deportability (Comfort 2007). Indeed, the structural vulnerability of their family units has subjected them to patterned physical and emotional suffering that constitute forms of legal violence (Menjívar and Abrego 2012; Quesada, Hart, and Bourgois 2011; Szkupinski Quiroga, Medina, and Glock 2014) and serve as multigenerational punishment (Enríquez 2015). Yet starting in their teenage years in the mid-2000s, I showed how my participants came to consciousness about the potential impact of anti-immigrant policies like H.R. 4437 and began advocating on behalf of their family members and friends through their participation in the immigrant rights protests. At the time, many people—in the media as well as in academic circles—wondered what the ultimate legacy of their burgeoning activism would be.

This book has answered that lingering question by examining the perspectives and lived experiences of these members of this H.R. 4437 generation over the subsequent decade as they became adults. As I have shown, my participants and their families continued to be deeply affected by immigration policies and enforcement practices into the 2010s. Some families (like the Clementes) became more stable as family members were able to regularize their statuses due to the actions of their adult (citizen) children, although others (like the Garcías) only became more and more vulnerable despite their children's best efforts. Even though my participants all come from and grew up in mixed-status families, these distinct familial trajectories underscore that legal status can also act as a stratifying factor between different families and over time as family members' circumstances change (Abrego 2014, 48). Legal status has come to serve as a central axis of stratification in U.S. society akin to race, class, and gender, tangibly marking immigrants and their children and limiting their incorporation pathways in the absence of comprehensive immigration reform (48; Dreby 2015a, 179; Menjívar 2010, 20). This book thus further bolsters calls for more "family-friendly policies" (Dreby 2015a, xiii) that acknowledge that family unity, a hallmark of U.S. immigration policy over the last fifty years that is currently being aggressively attacked, is also essential for promoting the incorporation, health, and well-being of immigrants and their children (Gubernskaya and Dreby 2017, 417).

THE BROKERING WORK OF THE ADULT CHILDREN OF IMMIGRANTS

Children in mixed-status families have shouldered a heavy burden in contending with the fallout of our broken immigration system, not only during childhood, as others have demonstrated (Dreby 2015a; Zayas 2015), but also into adulthood, as I have shown in this book. Yet despite the significant suffering and strain that the state has placed on their family units, my participants have remained committed to their families and actively engaged in contesting anti-immigrant policies and practices, even if it is not by marching in the streets as they did as teenagers. The focus of the literature on the brokering activities of children in immigrant families has principally been on the work that they perform as minor children. This book, however, highlights a range of new brokering practices that my participants cultivated into adulthood, in some cases taking on even greater prominence within their larger family units over time and across borders. It demonstrates that caregiving is not only a phenomenon transmitted down by grandparents and parents in transborder and mixed-status families (Dreby 2010; Horton 2009; Yarris 2017), but also a set of activities that young adults who have more secure immigration status perform as a commitment to family members who do not.

My participants engage in a range of everyday brokering activities for their families, such as contributing to the household income, helping family members navigate employment and other processes, translating for parents in medical appointments, and driving family and friends around in areas of high Border Patrol surveillance. They started performing these activities as teenagers, as I was first getting to know them, but have intensified the scope of what they do as they have gotten older and as deteriorating conditions have necessitated it. One of their most impactful brokering activities as adults has unquestionably been applying for and securing residency for their parents, as Isabel and Beto were able to do, albeit with only partial success in Beto's case. In addition to their parents, siblings have also benefited tremendously from my participants' brokering work; Isabel, for instance, sheltered her younger siblings from the worst of their parents' economic challenges and status vulnerabilities and ensured that their path to adulthood was much less hampered by their family's circumstances. Beto's older brother continues to benefit from his regular visits and transport of items from home that help keep him connected to the family he can no longer see in person in San Diego.

Beyond their families, most of my participants have chosen to pursue volunteer work and service-oriented professions, including social work, early childhood education, and nonprofit work. The seminal scholarship on the fate of the "new" post-1965 children of immigrants made negative prognostications about second-generation Mexicans in particular—that they were particularly "at risk" for downwardly assimilating (López and Stanton-Salazar 2001; Perlmann and Waldinger 1997) to the "new rainbow underclass" (Portes and Rumbaut 2001; Rumbaut and Portes 2001). Rather than constituting a burden on society as segmented assimilation might have predicted for them, my participants have achieved conventional measures of success (such as graduating from college and securing professional employment) but also continue to play important roles in their families and communities. Indeed, they have cultivated these roles *despite* growing up under the cloud of illegality and deportability that they "shared" with their family members and suffering from the embodied trauma of being directly and repeatedly subjected to ethno-racial profiling by the Border Patrol.

Much of the literature on mixed-status families has focused on the intense vulnerabilities their members face in their everyday lives as they navigate the repercussions of illegality. Though it is essential to illuminate these vulnerabilities and critique the far-reaching effects of these anti-immigrant policies and practices, this focus on vulnerability and suffering has often overshadowed the agency and capacity of children in these families (Gulbas and Zayas 2017, 54). Though I have similarly highlighted major constraints my participants have confronted throughout their lives, these constraints are not all that defines their lives; indeed, their resilience and abilities to maneuver around the socio-legal constraints their families face is quite remarkable (54). Looking over the life course, it is clear that they have blossomed into these roles with great courage and commitment to their families and communities. It is also clear that they are committed citizens (in the broadest sense of the term) who not only see forms of injustice around them but also strive toward their amelioration. Indeed, witnessing these developments over time is precisely what compelled me to write this book.

It is not only mixed-status family units who benefit from the brokering work of children in immigrant families; as Orellana (2001, 386; 2009, 124) highlights, teachers, medical professionals, social service workers, and broader U.S. society benefit from their contributions. The adult children of immigrants have even greater potential to leverage their skill sets to contribute to the social good and to change exclusionary social institutions in the process (122–23). Beyond being bilingual and comfortable going back and forth between the United States and Mexico, my participants described a range of skills that they cultivated in their immigrant families—problem-solving abilities, confidence in taking on challenges, and creativity in finding solutions. They have found these skills to be valuable assets in their adult careers—and, beyond that, in their lives.

I have also found that my participants have a "second generation advantage" (Kasinitz et al. 2008, 342) in the local borderland context that allows them to leverage their secure statuses, local knowledge bases, and transborder competencies into familial, professional, and social good. These second-generation border brokers have much to contribute to the U.S. society of the contemporary twenty-first century. Yet instead of buffering the negative effects of these immigration policies and enforcement practices, I would argue that their skills would be put to far better use in promoting the positive incorporation of their families and communities.

SHIFTING FOCUS FROM IMMIGRATION TO IMMIGRANT POLICY

Fueled by building anti-immigrant sentiment, immigration enforcement has progressively become the centerpiece of immigration policymaking over the last thirty years (Dunn 2010), garnering widespread bipartisan support. The growing and massive immigration enforcement infrastructure has been funded at record levels during this time, despite the steady decline in the rate of undocumented migration since 1990 (Massey and Sánchez 2010, 77). As I initially drafted this conclusion in late summer 2017, President Trump was leveraging anti-immigrant hysteria to seek even greater amounts of funding from Congress for his "super-sized" enforcement budget to pay for an expanded border wall, additional detention beds, thousands of new enforcement agents, and scores of new immigration judges and attorneys to prosecute immigrants (Breisblatt 2017).

By spring 2018, when I was revising the manuscript, he had, indeed, secured billions of dollars more from Congress to further bolster immigration enforcement, including a record-setting $7 billion ICE budget and an additional $1.6 billion for border security measures (Breisblatt 2018). He also remains focused on "building the wall"; indeed, the wall, laden with powerful symbolism, has been one of his most consistent policy positions since he kicked off his presidential campaign. But as this book has demonstrated, the border wall has already been a tangible—and menacing—presence in the lives of borderlanders for decades now, wreaking havoc on the lives of residents of all statuses and resulting in psychological distress and embodied trauma (Sabo and Lee 2015; Sabo et al. 2014; Szkupinski Quiroga, Medina, and Glock 2014).

Though his rhetoric against immigrants—and Mexicans in particular—is more unabashedly alarmist than his predecessors, Trump has been able to capitalize on an infrastructure that has been well-laid by both parties over the past thirty years for carrying out punitive attacks on immigrants and their children. These policies have resulted in a pervasive culture of fear in immigrant communities that is increasingly being recognized as a public health crisis by scholars (Dreby 2015a, 174; Lopez et al. 2017), physicians and health-care systems (Artiga and Ubri 2017; Stein 2017), and even those in the media (Richards 2017; Rodriguez 2018). By showing the consequences of the enforcement-heavy approach, this book contributes to the chorus of social scientists calling for the passage of comprehensive immigration reform and the opening up of pathways to legalization for undocumented and legally liminal immigrants—for the benefit of not only immigrants themselves but also their children (Bean, Brown, and Bachmeir 2015; Castañeda 2019; Dreby 2015a; Gomberg-Muñoz 2017; Gubernskaya and Dreby 2017; Gulbas and Zayas 2017; Schueths and Lawston 2015; Yoshikawa 2011; Zayas 2015).

Yet during these increasingly anti-immigrant times, children from immigrant families have become the fastest growing segment of children in the United States. The population of first- and second-generation children in the United States grew by 51 percent between 1995 and 2014 to 18.7 million, or one-quarter of all U.S. children (Child Trends 2014). These numbers tell us quite a bit about the profile of minors (children under the age of nineteen) living in immigrant families. But many children from the post-1965 wave of immigrants have now come of age, aged out of these statistics, and are living their adult lives. As the trajectories of my participants suggest, many of these young adults are well situated to serve as brokers, whether privately on behalf of their families or through more formal means in their professional lives. Children in mixed-status families in particular have had to cultivate maturity and savvy for dealing with their family unit's structural vulnerabilities. Illegality, deportability, and policeability have taken harsh tolls on these children and their families—and likely will continue to under Trump. Yet as I have shown in this book, we can also see second-generation young adults' resilience and the ways in which they can channel their skills and life experiences into becoming brokers, interceding attacks on their immigrant family members and communities as they mature and cultivate even more tools for contesting them.

Immigration policy has long received much more funding and bipartisan support in Congress than immigrant policy (Massey and Sánchez 2010; Padilla 1997). But what if the United States focused more on *immigrant* policy—the social, political, and economic incorporation of the immigrants who are already living, working, and contributing to economic, social, and political life here in the United States? While certainly a radical notion in the current sociopolitical climate, I would argue that, suitably empowered, the young adult children of immigrants—in particular, those from mixed-status families—are perfectly poised to serve in critical roles that would ultimately foster immigrant incorporation into U.S. society instead of buffering their family and community members' structural vulnerabilities. Indeed, many of these young adults are already serving in service professions as lawyers, social workers, and educators; in these capacities, they are dealing with the fallout of immigrants' lack of legal status, their reluctance to access services (including those for which they and their children are eligible), and the pervasive deportation fears and anxiety currently plaguing immigrant communities.

Yet in these very same positions with a different set of more inclusive immigration policies, these same individuals have the potential to broker the borders that have been erected between immigrants and broader U.S. society (Massey and Sánchez 2010). What if the knowledge bases and skill sets of young adults from mixed-status families were applied to helping family and community members adapt to life in the United States in concrete terms rather than dealing with the fallout of broken immigration policies and enforcement practices? Rather than simply buffering the impacts of our existing punitive immigration policies and enforcement practices, their brokering skills would be put to far better use in promoting the positive incorporation of their families and communities.

APPENDIX A

Conducting Research with Borderland Young Adults

THIS BOOK draws upon ethnographic fieldwork conducted over more than a decade, starting in 2004. My research consisted of an intensive period of dissertation fieldwork with a larger set of teenagers (n = 54) who were between fourteen and nineteen years old in 2005–2006, limited follow-up research with them during the subsequent eight years, and focused follow-up research on a smaller cohort of participants (n = 13) in 2014 when they were in their mid- to late twenties. As Boehm (2012, 26) emphasizes, ethnographic research is invaluable for explicating the distinct subjectivities of differently situated members of transnational and/or mixed-status families (see also Abrego 2014; Dreby 2010, 2015a). She also underscores that ethnography is a particularly apt approach for capturing immigrants' (and their children's) perspectives on the state and its imprint on their lives (Boehm 2012, 26).

The initial phase of my research project took place at a community-based nonprofit organization (which I refer to simply as the center) that serves neighborhood families (largely mixed-status in composition) in southeast San Diego. I volunteered at the center beginning in 2004, having gained permission to conduct my dissertation fieldwork there with the assistance of my sister, a leader in the organization at that time. I am not originally from San Diego, or even California; I was born and raised in the Washington, D.C., metropolitan area in a white, middle-class, U.S. citizen, English-speaking household. However, I was already quite familiar with the San Diego–Tijuana region before embarking on my research. San Diego is my second home; my closest family members have lived in Tijuana and in South Bay San Diego communities since the late 1990s. I also lived, worked, and taught there in the early 2000s, including work at a human rights advocacy organization focused on supporting immigrant rights, a local community college, and a community-based health clinic that housed a teen center I helped establish; the teen center served second-generation Mexican teenagers, allowing me to see just how vibrant a population they are, as well as some of the challenges that framed their lives.

The center where I conducted my fieldwork provides after-school college preparatory programing for neighborhood children, the majority of whom come from Mexican immigrant families whose parents are unfamiliar with the U.S. educational system. In 2004, the center served some two hundred children per year through after-school tutoring, mentorship, and technology programs. Activities took place in a centrally located converted warehouse that also served as an informal community center. Programs like the center that promote minority achievement provide youth from disadvantaged backgrounds with important forms of social capital (Smith 2008, 272). Youth benefit from exposure to extrafamilial mentors (Portes and Fernández-Kelly 2008; Smith 2008) and are able to develop positive support networks that enable them to overcome disadvantages (Gonzales 2011; Stanton-Salazar 2001).

At the time that I began my research, most studies on second-generation youth had been conducted in schools, with the logic being that they are a primary institutional site in which second-generation youth are introduced to dominant U.S. culture; adaptation to school is regarded as a predictor for a child's future well-being in society (Suárez-Orozco and Suárez-Orozco 2001, 3). Further, most of the foundational second-generation studies (e.g., Portes and Rumbaut 2001 and Rumbaut and Portes 2001) relied heavily on quantitative research designs. Suárez-Orozco and Suárez-Orozco (2001, 11–12) did point out, however, that survey-type questions were often not well-understood by the children in their sample of children of immigrants, meaning that "survey-like data, by themselves, tend to suggest a distorted picture." They therefore advocated a mixed-method research design that incorporates both quantitative techniques (such as surveys) and qualitative ones (like participant observation and interviews) (12). I employed a mixed-method approach in my initial fieldwork. Given that my focus was not on school experiences as such, the center provided an ideal place to get to know the teenagers where they would feel less constrained. Being able to participate in their daily lives and getting to know them over a longer period of time was also instrumental to understanding the complexities of their lives—both as teenagers in the first place and unquestionably as they became adults.

At the center, I encountered a group of teenagers who were not involved in behavior commonly ascribed to Mexican youth from the barrio, such as gang participation, dropping out of school, and teen parenthood (Dietrich 1998, 2). One could argue that the center served particularly high-achieving and self-motivated children; in actuality, though, some struggle in school throughout and end up leaving the program, while others complete it but do not continue on to four-year institutions, opting instead to attend community college on a part- or full-time basis. Regardless of their individual scholastic performance, I found that center participants faced similar cross-cutting structural circumstances, including their family members' immigration statuses and the challenges they introduced to the family unit, such as economic hardship, unstable housing, and food insecurity.

The center provided an opportune structure through which I could give back to the organization by serving as a full-time volunteer, by conducting evaluation activities, and by providing tutoring and mentoring to participants. During the summer of 2005, I began thirteen months of intensive fieldwork at the center with forty-two high school students. Throughout the entire year, I conducted participant observation—joining in the teenagers' daily activities each weekday afternoon, tutoring, mentoring, and just hanging out with them as they ate their snacks and interacted with each other. Though I helped them with their school assignments and college essays, we also talked informally about what was going on in their lives. Outside of the center, I participated in off-site special events such as community service projects and college visit trips, and I was fortunate enough to also attend family parties, events like *quinceñeras*, and graduation gatherings. I completed several months of participant observation at the center before embarking on other formal data collection activities. I felt it important to engage in intensive relationship and trust building given the age group with which I was working and the sensitivity of the topics I was investigating (see also Bejarano 2005, 68).

I was about to turn thirty when I started working at the center, placing me somewhere in age between my participants and their parents. Even though I was a clearly an adult, I proved to be an approachable adult from whom they could seek advice, academic and otherwise. Further, because I did not technically work at the center, I was an atypical authority figure. Like some of the other center staff, I was not from the community, which they clearly knew and even asked me about regularly; yet I found that they were largely open and receptive to me, despite our differences in age, racial/ethnic identity, gender (in some cases), and community of origin.

Given that the majority of my participants were minors, I had to obtain prior parental permission. Because parents were important "gatekeepers" (Dreby 2015a), I felt it necessary to be clear with them about the terms of their and their children's participation. I met individually with a parent/guardian of each child, reviewing the overall project and gaining their consent to conduct research with their children, all in Spanish. I also obtained the children's assent before conducting research, informing them that they could elect not to participate even if their parents had provided consent. No one declined to participate or withdrew from the study. Though I hoped to set up meetings with the parents quickly, it took several months to line up all of the meetings, as parents were quite busy with competing work and home responsibilities. I met with most of the parents at the center, in a quiet area not being used for programming. During my meeting with each parent/guardian, I also administered a household survey (also in Spanish) that provided demographic information (e.g., place of birth, level of education, employment history) as well as information about household composition and family characteristics, social network relationships, neighborhood dynamics, immigration experiences, and contact with Mexico. Completing the household survey first allowed me to better contextualize the family lives of the teenagers and the challenges their households faced.

I originally envisioned focusing more on the high school students than program alumni, given that I would have more regular access to them during my year of fieldwork. However, I had already spent significant time getting to know the previous two years of alumni (twelve individuals) by taking college field trips and doing evaluation activities with them. Program alumni were also around more than I anticipated, suggesting to me that involvement with the center was crucial not only in their adolescence but also in their transition to adulthood. Thus, I decided to include them in my study as well, bringing my total number of participants up to fifty-four. Given that the alumni were over eighteen, I was able to ask them directly for consent and did not systematically conduct household surveys with their parents (though several had younger siblings in the program, meaning their household information was included).

After gaining their parents' and their permission to proceed with conducting research, I embarked on my research activities, which included freelisting, focus groups, a survey, semistructured interviews, and PhotoVoice. All of these activities were conducted at the center. The research activities were mostly conducted in English, with scattered Spanglish throughout; I performed any translations featured in the book. Freelisting was one of my first activities with the teens, which I conducted as a means of discerning how they understood central concepts like *citizens* and *immigrants*. I held five focus group sessions with half of the high school students (twenty-one teens), displaying immigration-related media images as an elicitation technique to assess how they made sense of such public debates as border enforcement, driver's licenses for undocumented immigrants, and the Minutemen. In addition, I conducted a survey with all forty-two high school students, collecting information about their household composition and family characteristics, ethnicity and identity, the neighborhood, contact with Mexico, immigration, peer relationships, school and work experiences, and language use. Some questions in the survey deliberately paralleled the household survey so that I could compare information provided by the teens and their parents.

After completing this first set of research activities, I conducted semistructured interviews with half of the teens (twenty-one) and half of the alumni (six). The interview guide covered five general areas: family immigration history, relationship with Mexico, border crossing experiences, citizenship / national belonging, and identity. The alumni guide contained additional questions about college experiences, reflections on home, and changes in identity. I also conducted numerous impromptu interviews with teens and alumni specifically pertaining to immigration during the period of the protests between March and May 2006.

The final research technique I utilized in 2006 was PhotoVoice. Drawing on Freire's "critical consciousness," PhotoVoice involves having individuals photographically document their everyday life conditions in order to promote critical dialogue about issues of concern to the community (Wang and Burris 1994, 171). At the time, very few of the teenagers had access to digital cameras (let alone smartphones), so the opportunity to use them proved to be quite appealing. Definite themes emerged from our facilitated discussions of the pictures: daily life in the neighborhood, community fixtures (like taco shops, parks, and churches), negative forces in the neighborhood (like trash, alcoholism, and homelessness), the U.S.-Mexico border, hopes and dreams, celebrations, Mexican culture, family, history, and education. The teens identified and named these themes, and then took the lead on assembling a poster to represent them.

As a capstone to the PhotoVoice project, we held a series of public events to showcase the project—first for family members and friends at an event held in August 2006, and then for community members and others at the center open house event in November 2006.

After concluding my intensive fieldwork in 2005–2006, I returned three times in the subsequent year (2006–2007) to conduct follow-up research and participate in annual activities; the latter included an open house event in the fall, a week-long college-tour trip in the spring, and annual graduation ceremonies in the summer. During these return visits, I had the opportunity to check in informally with participants and catch up on their lives as they continued on to college, got and switched jobs, embarked on and ended relationships, started families, and moved away from (and returned to) their neighborhood.

In the years that followed, emerging social media platforms like Facebook also made it easy to keep up with my participants. As they entered their early twenties and I moved away and continued in my academic career, I kept in touch with participants via social media and in person during biannual trips back to San Diego. After several years of noting somewhat casually the developments in their lives, I was struck by the roles that they were taking on within their families and professionally; they remained quite dedicated to their families and many were settling into careers in service-oriented professions. I decided in 2014 to conduct follow-up participant observation and interviews with a cohort (thirteen; nearly a quarter) of original participants, who now ranged in age from twenty-three to twenty-eight. I selected participants with whom I had been in regular contact over the intervening years, with an eye toward including participants with variable family circumstances and who worked in different professional settings. Interview guides followed up on similar domains from my initial fieldwork while adding new questions exploring how their lives, family situations, and perspectives on immigration had changed.

I contacted participants via Facebook, an optimal mode of engaging millennials, and easily set times to meet. I conducted interviews with them largely in the neighborhood where we first met, in coffee shops and parks, though I conducted one phone interview since the participant no longer lived in San Diego. Over time, my focus has shifted from the place where I first met participants—the center—to the neighborhoods and workplaces where they now live. A longitudinal design such as the one I employed can help increase the validity of a research study; since ethnographers are better able to build on established rapport, it also sheds light on the compounded effects of social inequality as they unfold over the life course (Horton 2016, 11).

Scholars have described my research approach in different ways, including as a revisit study (Burawoy 2003) or a qualitative longitudinal case history approach (Thomson 2007). I decided to ground my analysis in a smaller set of individuals that would allow me to create biographical case analyses (Smith 2008) or case profiles (Thomson 2007) that provide greater depth of understanding of a smaller cohort of individuals. The book focuses principally on these individuals, but it also draws from the earlier fieldwork as well. *Border Brokers* follows the lives of this core set of participants to demonstrate how they have navigated immigration policies and border enforcement practices for themselves and their families over time.

I also embarked on this project nearly fifteen years ago as an engaged anthropologist, with the "twin aims" of cultural critique and advocacy for the well-being of vulnerable populations (Horton 2016, 187; Lamphere 2004). My intention was not only to understand the lives of the children in mixed-status families I studied in academic terms, but also to figure out mechanisms for more effectively advocating for them as it became clear that mixed-status families were becoming a critical public policy unit. Like Horton (2016, 11), I believe that it is our duty as ethnographers "to honor an unspoken ethical contract [we] establish with [our] participants through the very conditions of their entry." Indeed, my participants have entrusted me with their stories, and it is my ethical imperative to do something productive with them.

During these fifteen years, life for mixed-status families has gotten evermore challenging and the need for solutions to the long-standing immigration policy impasse ever more critical. Though I feel conflicted about sharing the pain and suffering of my participants and their family members, I do so to shine a light on these forms of patterned injustice and to advocate for their amelioration. As I have continued on with this research, I also see more and more clearly the role that children in mixed-status families themselves play in this effort—particularly those who have legal status, English-language skills, knowledge of U.S. social systems and political processes, professional credentials, and other forms of social capital. Thus, I believe it is important that we as social scientists not only seek to identify practical mechanisms for addressing pressing social problems ourselves but also find ways to support those who may just be better positioned to carry out this work than we are.

APPENDIX B

Participants

NAME (PSEUDONYM)	GENDER	BIRTH YEAR	GENERATION	FOLLOW-UP
Abby Ramos	F	1987	2	
Agustín de la Rosa	M	1991	2	
Alberto (Beto) García	M	1987	1.5	X
Alonso Correa	M	1990	2	
Amada Villanueva	F	1990	-1.5	
Ana Franco	F	1992	2	
Andréa Bustos	F	1991	2	
Andrés Martínez	M	1989	2	
Blanca Pérez	F	1989	2	
Carlos Franco	M	1986	1.5	X
Cármen Gómez	F	1987	-1.5	
Casandra Torres	F	1989	2	X
Claudio Torres	M	1991	2	
David Montero	M	1988	2	
Efraín Núñez	M	1988	2	
Elena Martin	F	1987	2	
Esperanza Medina	F	1988	2	X
Estéban Campos	M	1990	2	
Everardo Ortega	M	1992	2	

Federico Montero	M	1992	2	
Flor Bustos	F	1987	2	
Guillermo Espino	M	1990	2	
Hernando Ramos	M	1988	2	
Imelda Ortega	F	1989	2	
Isabel Clemente	F	1990	2	X
Juan Garza	M	1988	2	
Lisa Hidalgo	F	1987	2	X
Lola Jiménez	F	1987	2	
Lucía Mendoza	F	1987	1.5	
Lucy Duarte	F	1987	2	
Luisa Martínez	F	1988	2	X
Luz Díaz	F	1986	2	
Manuel Campos	M	1989	2	
Margarita Valencia	F	1990	2	
Marta Duarte	F	1990	2	
Mateo Hidalgo	M	1991	2	X
Miguel Méndez	M	1986	2	
Nadia Méndez	F	1991	2	
Nancy Acosta	F	1992	2	
Nayeli Molina	F	1987	2	
Nick Valencia	M	1989	2	
Noe Méndez	M	1988	2	
Pablo Fernández	M	1989	2	
Paloma Montoya	F	1990	2	
Paulina Santos	F	1989	-1.5	X
Paz Colón	F	1988	-1.5	
Pepe Ortiz	M	1989	2	
Raquel Cabrera	F	1991	2	
Salvador (Sal) Díaz	M	1988	2	X
Soledad López	F	1991	2	
Tomás Ramírez	M	1991	2	X
Valentino Correa	M	1992	2	
Victoria Medina	F	1991	2	X
Wilson Márquez	M	1989	2	X

ABBREVIATIONS

AEDPA	The Antiterrorism and Effective Death Penalty Act of 1996
CBP	U.S. Customs and Border Protection
CHIP	Children's Health Insurance Program
CILS	Children of Immigrants Longitudinal Study
DACA	Deferred Action for Childhood Arrivals
DAPA	Deferred Action for Parental Accountability
DHS	U.S. Department of Homeland Security
DREAM Act	The Development, Relief, and Education for Alien Minors Act
H.R. 4437	House of Representatives Bill 4437 (The Border Protection, Antiterrorism, and Illegal Immigration Control Act of 2005)
ICE	U.S. Immigration and Customs Enforcement
IIRIRA	Illegal Immigration Reform and Immigrant Responsibility Act of 1996
INA	Immigration and Nationality Act of 1965
INS	Immigration and Naturalization Services
IRCA	The Immigration Reform and Control Act of 1986
LIC	Low-Intensity Conflict doctrine
LPR	Lawful Permanent Resident
PRWORA	The Personal Responsibility and Work Opportunity Reconciliation Act of 1996
S.B. 1070	Arizona Senate Bill 1070 (The Support Our Law Enforcement and Safe Neighborhoods Act)
SWNA	Southwest North American region
TPS	Temporary Protected Status
T.J.	Tijuana
USCIS	U.S. Citizenship and Immigration Services

NOTES

INTRODUCTION

1. The technical term used by the Department of Homeland Security (DHS) and other federal agencies like Customs and Border Protection (CBP) and Immigration and Customs Enforcement (ICE) is *unauthorized*, defined as all foreign-born noncitizens who are not legal residents who entered the United States without inspection or were admitted temporarily and stayed past the date they were required to leave. I use the more common term *undocumented* to describe immigrants who do not have official status, except when referencing other works.
2. Though participants like Isabel, Carlos, and Beto live in mixed-status families, it is not an emic term they use to describe their family units; rather, the term is one coined by policy analysts and academics. As Gomberg-Muñoz (2017, 157–58) points out, the use of the term *family* can be critiqued in its privileging of hetero-patriarchal power structures and middle-class norms that are also codified in U.S. immigration processing. Despite these limitations in its usage, mixed-status family is still the term that best represents my participants' realities.
3. DeGenova (2002, 420) deploys quotes around both "illegal" and "legal" to "denaturalize the reification of this distinction." Many subsequent scholars have also put quotes around *illegality* to demonstrate that it exists as a historical configuration and social construction (Menjívar and Kanstroom 2014, 3). Hereafter, for readability and simplicity, I use *illegality*, and the related terms *deportability* and *policeability*, without quotes except when referring specifically to other sources. I do, however, retain the use of quotes around "illegal" immigration to delegitimize the concept and point out that it is historically, legally, and socially constructed.

4. Ortner (2005) defines subjectivity as "the ensemble of modes of perception, affect, thought, desire, fear, and so forth that animate acting subjects," which are molded by "cultural and social formations that shape, organize, and provoke" them (31). Subjectivity, she argues, is the basis of agency—"a necessary part of understanding how people (try to) act on the world even as they are acted upon . . . Agency takes shape as specific desires and intentions within a matrix of subjectivity—of (culturally constituted) feelings, thoughts, and meanings" (34).
5. A large body of anthropological scholarship has been focused on conceptualizing the state (Alonso 1994; Kearney 1991, 1995; Nagengast 1994; Sharma and Gupta 2006; Wilson and Donnan 1998). Field (1999, 2) defines the state as the "institutionalized, organizational apparatus that governs a group of individuals defined as citizens within a variously conceptualized spatial territory." Kearney (1995, 548) underscores that the state exerts its rule as "the guardian of national borders, the arbiter of citizenship, and the entity responsible for foreign policy." Though the state is an autonomous and powerful entity (Nagengast 1994), it is also understood to be a local assemblage of practices and people (Sharma and Gupta 2006, 6) as well as cultural and political forms, representations, and discourse (Nagengast 1994, 116). Regarding immigration specifically, state regimes, institutions, and agents do the work of interpreting, implementing, and extending immigration laws (Boehm 2012, 55; Coutin 2000; Heyman 1998, 2001). This work is accomplished through the targeting of immigrants (Fassin 2011; Inda 2006b) through coercive tactics as well as illegalized behaviors and practices (Heyman 2017, 49).
6. The children of immigrants encompass the second generation who were born in the United States (like Isabel); the 1.5 generation, who were born in Mexico but came at an early age and grew up in the United States (like Carlos and Beto); and the -1.5 generation, who were born in the United States but lived abroad for some of their childhoods (like Carlos's brother). Given that the majority of my participants would be most accurately characterized as second generation, I use that label as an umbrella term, highlighting when it does not technically apply.
7. I use the label *Mexican* because my participants most frequently self-identified as Mexican on the survey they completed as teenagers and in other situations that I observed. Their use of the label *Mexican* is significant in that it encompasses all the people of Mexican descent in their lives, including those born in Mexico and the United States.

CHAPTER 1

1. Padilla (1997, 595) distinguishes between immigration and immigrant policies. Immigration policies are centered on regulating which and how many persons enter a nation-state, while immigrant policies are those that facilitate the social and economic integration of immigrants into U.S. society once they have already entered a nation-state (see also Bean, Brown, and Bachmeir 2015, 196). The U.S.

government has historically tended to focus on immigration policy, while immigrant policy has not been as high of a national priority (Padilla 1997, 598).

CHAPTER 2

1. It should be noted that the distinction between "having papers" and "not having papers" is not unique to my participants, but is nonetheless the predominant way in which they cognitively mapped people's status and organized their understandings of belonging.
2. In Spanish, the green card is referred to as *la mica*, which is derived from the verb *enmicar*, which means "to cover in plastic" (Collins 1993).
3. The *n* for this category is thirty-nine; it is smaller because three of the households did not have resident fathers.
4. N = 19 mothers and 18 fathers.
5. Beto always spoke rather cryptically about not having papers, preferring to refer to his lack of papers as his "situation" or "problem."
6. A *cholo* (or *chola*, feminine) historically refers to a young person who participates in or identifies with gang subculture. Though it is often deployed as a stigmatizing label, some have also turned it on its head and embraced the label as a symbol of pride.

CHAPTER 3

1. Prior to January 2008, it was not mandatory to possess a passport or formal crossing document; alternate documents, such as a driver's license or school identification card, were adequate and were particularly acceptable for minors to use.
2. When speaking English, the teens (and other locals) refer to Tijuana simply as T.J.

CHAPTER 4

1. By stating that second-generation youth are entitled to these rights and protections as U.S. citizens, I am not suggesting that undocumented immigrants should be excluded from them. Indeed as Dunn (2010, 10) argues, an overriding focus on citizenship and national sovereignty at the border obscures the human rights, well-being, and dignity of noncitizens. Given that my participants were largely citizens, though, my purpose here is to demonstrate the effects of border enforcement practices on U.S. citizens of Mexican descent *in addition to*—and indeed in relation to—their undocumented friends and family members.
2. According to Heyman (1998, 166), the term *cotidianidad* was coined by the Immigration Law Enforcement Monitoring Project of the American Friends Service Committee (AFSC). AFSC is a Quaker-founded human rights organization that promotes social justice throughout the world. I conducted my master's research with AFSC's U.S.-Mexico Border Program in San Diego in 2000.

3. Though Lugo (2000) critiques the use of the academic and theoretical phrase *border crossing*, I use this terminology because it is, in fact, the emic term that many borderland residents use.
4. *La migra* is the colloquial term in Spanish used to refer to Border Patrol or other uniformed CBP or ICE officers.

CHAPTER 5

1. Since there were thirty-four families in my sample in 2005–2006, the number of birth fathers and birth mothers totaled sixty-eight. However, I was unable to gather information about the birth fathers from three families headed by single mothers. One teen's mother was from El Salvador and is therefore excluded from subsequent analysis. One mother was born in California. Thus of sixty-eight total parents, five (7 percent) are not included in the discussion about Mexican states of origin.
2. The regions are divided as follows: West (Aguascalientes, Colima, Durango, Guanajuato, Jalisco, Michoacán, Nayarit, San Luis Potosí, and Zacatecas); North (Baja California Norte, Baja California Sur, Coahuila, Chihuahua, Nuevo León, Sinaloa, Sonora, and Tamaulipas); Southeast (Campeche, Chiapas, Guerrero, Oaxaca, Quintana Roo, Tabasco, Veracruz, and Yucatán); and Central (Mexico City, Hidalgo, México, Morelos, Puebla, Querétaro, and Tlaxcala).
3. This includes common-law marriage, known as *unión libre* in Mexico and among Mexican-origin populations in the United States.
4. Very few of the teens' parents are originally from Tijuana; only two fathers and three mothers were actually born and raised in the city. One additional father and mother are from elsewhere within the state of Baja California Norte.

REFERENCES

Abrajano, Marisa, and Lydia Lundgren. 2015. "How Watershed Immigration Policies Affect American Public Opinion Over a Lifetime." *International Migration Review* 49 (1): 70–105.

Abrego, Leisy J. 2006. "'I Can't Go to College Because I Don't Have Papers': Incorporation Patterns of Latino Undocumented Youth." *Latino Studies* 4:212–31.

———. 2011. "Legal Consciousness of Undocumented Latinos: Fear and Stigma as Barriers to Claims-Making for First- and 1.5-Generation Immigrants." *Law and Social Inquiry* 33:709–34.

———. 2014. *Sacrificing Families: Navigating Laws, Labor, and Love Across Borders*. Stanford, CA: Stanford University Press.

———. 2016. "Illegality as a Source of Solidarity and Tension in Latino Families." *Journal of Latino/Latin American Studies* 8 (1): 5–21.

Abrego, Leisy J., and Roberto G. Gonzales. 2010. "Blocked Paths, Uncertain Futures." *Journal of Education for Students Placed at Risk* 15:144–57.

Aiken, Stuart C., and Vicky Plows. 2010. "Overturning Assumptions About Young People, Border Spaces, and Revolutions." *Children's Geographies* 8 (4): 327–53.

Alarcón, Rafael. 2005. "Mexican Migration Flows in Tijuana–San Diego in a Context of Economic Uncertainty." In *Ties That Bind Us: Mexican Migrants in San Diego County*, edited by Richard Kiy and Christopher Woodruff, 99–121. La Jolla, CA: Center for U.S.-Mexican Studies, UCSD.

Alba, Richard, Philip Kasinitz, and Mary Waters. 2011. "The Kids Are (Mostly) Alright: Second-Generation Assimilation." *Social Forces* 89 (3): 763–73.

Alba, Richard, and Victor Nee. 2003. *Remaking the American Mainstream: Assimilation and Contemporary Immigration*. Cambridge, MA: Harvard University Press.

Alba, Richard, and Mary Waters, eds. 2011. *The Next Generation: Immigrant Youth in Comparative Perspective*. New York: New York University Press.

Aleinikoff, T. Alexander. 1997. "The Tightening Circle of Membership." In *Immigrants Out! The New Nativism and the Anti-Immigrant Impulse in the United States*, edited by Juan Perea, 324–32. New York: New York University Press.

Allen, Brian, Erica M. Cisneros, and Alexandra Tellez. 2015. "The Children Left Behind: The Impact of Parental Deportation on Mental Health." *Journal of Child and Family Studies* 24:386–92.

Alonso, Ana. 1994. "The Politics of Space, Time, and Substance: State Formation, Nationalism, and Ethnicity." *Annual Review of Anthropology* 23:379–405.

Alvarez, Roberto R., Jr. 1991. *Familia: Migration and Adaptation in Baja and Alta California, 1800–1975*. Berkeley: University of California Press.

———. 1995. "The Mexican-U.S. Border: The Making of an Anthropology of Borderlands." *Annual Review of Anthropology* 24:447–70.

American Immigration Council. 2017a. Summary of Executive Order "Border Security and Immigration Enforcement Improvements." Last modified February 27, 2017. https://www.americanimmigrationcouncil.org/research/border-security-and-immigration-enforcement-improvements-executive-order.

———. 2017b. Summary of Executive Order "Enhancing Public Safety in the Interior of the United States." Last modified May 19, 2017. https://www.americanimmigrationcouncil.org/immigration-interior-enforcement-executive-order.

Andreas, Peter, and T. J. Biersteker, eds. 2003. *The Rebordering of North America: Integration and Exclusion in a New Security Context*. New York: Routledge.

Anzaldúa, Gloria. 1987. *Borderlands/La Frontera: The New Mestiza*. San Francisco: Aunt Lute Books.

Aparicio, Ana. 2006. *Dominican-Americans and the Politics of Empowerment*. Gainesville: University Press of Florida.

———. 2007. "Contesting Race and Power Through the Diaspora: Second-Generation Dominican Youth in the New Gotham." *City and Society* 19 (2): 179–201.

Artiga, Samantha, and Petry Ubri. 2017. "Living in an Immigrant Family in America: How Fear and Toxic Stress are Affecting Daily Life, Well-Being, and Health." Kaiser Family Foundation. Last modified December 13, 2017. https://www.kff.org/disparities-policy/issue-brief/living-in-an-immigrant-family-in-america-how-fear-and-toxic-stress-are-affecting-daily-life-well-being-health/.

Baker-Cristales, Beth. 2009. "Mediated Resistance: The Construction of Neoliberal Citizenship in the Immigrant Rights Movement." *Latino Studies* 7 (1): 60–82.

Balderrama, Francisco E., and Raymond Rodríguez. 1995. *Decade of Betrayal: Mexican Repatriation in the 1930s*. Albuquerque: University of New Mexico Press.

Barth, Frederik. 1969. *Ethnic Groups and Boundaries: The Social Organization of Culture Difference*. Boston: Little, Brown.

Basch, Linda, Nina Glick Schiller, and Cristina Szanton Blanc. 1993. *Nations Unbound: Transnational Projects, Postcolonial Predicaments, and Deterritorialized Nation-States*. Utrecht, The Netherlands: Gordon and Breach Publishers.

Bean, Frank D., Susan K. Brown, and James D. Bachmeir. 2015. *Parents Without Papers: The Progress and Pitfalls of Mexican American Integration*. New York: Russell Sage Foundation.

Behdad, Ali. 2005. *A Forgetful Nation: On Immigration and Cultural Identity in the United States*. Durham, NC: Duke University Press.

Bejarano, Cynthia. 2005. *¿Qué Onda?: Urban Youth Culture and Border Identity*. Tucson: University of Arizona Press.

———. 2010. "Border Rootedness as Transformative Resistance: Youth Overcoming Violence and Inspection in a U.S.-Mexico Border Region." *Children's Geographies* 8 (4): 391–99.

Benmayor, Rina. 2002. "Narrating Cultural Citizenship: Oral Histories of First-Generation College Students of Mexican Origin." *Social Justice* 29 (4): 96–121.

Bloemraad, Irene, and Christine Trost. 2008. "It's a Family Affair: Intergenerational Mobilization in the Spring 2006 Protests." *American Behavioral Scientist* 52 (4): 507–32.

Bloemraad, Irene, Kim Voss, and Taeku Lee. 2011. "The Protests of 2006: What Were They, How Do We Understand Them, Where Do We Go?" In *Rallying for Immigrant Rights: The Fight for Inclusion in 21st Century America*, edited by Kim Voss and Irene Bloemraad, 3–43. Berkeley: University of California Press.

Boehm, Deborah A. 2012. *Intimate Migrations: Gender, Family, and Illegality Among Transnational Mexicans*. New York: New York University Press.

———. 2016. *Returned: Going and Coming in an Age of Deportation*. Berkeley: University of California Press.

Breisblatt, Joshua. 2017. "House Committee Funds Administration's Super-Sized Immigration Enforcement." American Immigration Council. Last modified July 19, 2017. http://immigrationimpact.com/2017/07/19/house-committee-immigration-enforcement/.

———. 2018. "Congress Reaches a Deal to Fund Government for the Year Without Solution for Dreamers." American Immigration Council. Last modified March 23, 2018. http://immigrationimpact.com/2018/03/23/congress-deal-fund-government-dreamers/.

Brettell, Caroline B. 2006. "Political Belonging and Cultural Belonging: Immigration Status, Citizenship, and Identity Among Four Immigrant Populations in a Southwestern City." *American Behavioral Scientist* 50:70–99.

Briggs, Vernon M. 1987. "The Albatross of Immigration Reform: Temporary Worker Policy in the United States." *International Migration Review* 20 (4): 995–1017.

Bulmer, Martin, and Anthony M. Rees. 1996. "Conclusion: Citizenship in the Twenty-First Century." In *Citizenship Today: The Contemporary Relevance of T. H. Marshall*, edited by Bulmer and Rees, 269–97. Bristol, PA: UCL Press.

Burawoy, Michael. 2003. "Revisits: An Outline of a Theory of Reflexive Ethnography." *American Sociological Review* 68:645–79.

Cacari Stone, Lisa, Edna A. Viruell-Fuentes, and Dolores Acevedo-Garcia. 2007. "Understanding the Socio-Economic, Health Systems, and Policy Threats to Latino Health: Gaining New Perspectives for the Future." *Californian Journal of Health Promotion* 5:82–104.

Calavita, Kitty. 1992. *Inside the State: The Bracero Program, Immigration, and the I.N.S.* New York: Routledge.

Capps, Randolph, Rosa Maria Castañeda, Ajay Chaudry, and Robert Santos. 2007. "Paying the Price: The Impact of Immigration Raids on America's Children." Urban Institute. http://www.urban.org/UploadedPDF/411566_immigration_raids.pdf.

Capps, Randolph, Michael Fix, and Jie Zong. 2016. "A Profile of U.S. Children with Unauthorized Immigrant Parents." Migration Policy Institute. http://www.migrationpolicy.org/research/profile-us-children-unauthorized-immigrant-parents.

Capps, Randolph, and Karina Fortuny. 2006. "Immigration and Child and Family Policy." Urban Institute. Last modified September 14, 2006. http://www.urban.org/publications/311362.html.

Carrasco, Gilbert Paul. 1997. "Latinos in the United States: Invitation and Exile." In *Immigrants Out! The New Nativism and the Anti-Immigrant Impulse in the United States*, edited by Juan Perea, 61–77. New York: New York University Press.

Castañeda, Alejandra. 2006. "Roads to Citizenship: Mexican Migrants in the United States." In *Latinos and Citizenship: The Dilemma of Belonging*, edited by Suzanne Oboler, 143–65. New York: Palgrave Macmillan.

Castañeda, Heide. 2019. *Borders of Belonging: Struggle and Solidarity in Mixed-Status Immigrant Families*. Stanford, CA: Stanford University Press.

Castañeda, Heide, and Milena Andrea Melo. 2014. "Health Care Access for Latino Mixed-Status Families: Barriers, Strategies, and Implications for Reform." *American Behavioral Scientist* 58 (14): 1891–1909.

Chaudry, Ajay, Randolph Capps, Juan M. Pedroza, Rosa Maria Castañeda, Robert Santos, and Molly M. Scott. 2010. "Facing Our Future: Children in the Aftermath of Immigration Enforcement." Urban Institute. Last modified February 2, 2010. http://www.urban.org/research/publication/facing-our-future.

Chavez, Leo R. 1997. "Immigration Reform and Nativism: The Nationalist Response to the Transnationalist Challenge." In *Immigrants Out! The New Nativism and the Anti-Immigrant Impulse in the United States*, edited by Juan Perea, 61–77. New York: New York University Press.

———. 2001. *Covering Immigration: Popular Images and the Politics of the Nation*. Berkeley: University of California Press.

———. 2008. *The Latino Threat: Constructing Immigrants, Citizens, and the Nation*. Stanford, CA: Stanford University Press.

———. 2017. *Anchor Babies and the Challenge of Birthright Citizenship*. Stanford, CA: Stanford University Press.

Chávez, Sergio. 2016. *Fronterizos, Transnational Migrants, and Commuters in Tijuana*. New York: Oxford University Press.

Child Trends. 2014. "Immigrant Children: Indicators of Child and Youth Well-Being." https://www.childtrends.org/wp-content/uploads/2013/07/110_Immigrant_Children.pdf.

Cockburn, Tom. 1998. "Children and Citizenship in Britain: A Case Study for a Socially Interdependent Model of Citizenship." *Childhood* 5 (1): 99–117.

Cockcroft, James D. 1986. *Outlaws in the Promised Land: Mexican Immigrant Workers and America's Future*. New York: Grove.

Coe, Cati, Rachel R. Reynolds, Deborah A. Boehm, Julia Meredith Hess, and Heather Rae-Espinoza. 2011. *Everyday Ruptures: Children, Youth, and Migration in Global Perspective*. Nashville, TN: Vanderbilt University Press.

Cohen, Elizabeth F. 2005. "Neither Seen Nor Heard: Children's Citizenship in Contemporary Democracies." *Citizenship* 9 (2): 221–40.

Coleman, Mathew. 2007. "Immigration Geopolitics Beyond the Mexico-U.S. Border." *Antipode* 39 (1): 54–76.

Comfort, Megan. 2007. "Punishment Beyond the Legal Offender." *Annual Review of Law and Social Science* 3:271–96.

Cooks, Jamal, and Terrie Epstein. 2000. "Dissin' Democracy? African American Adolescents' Concepts of Citizenship." *Journal of Social Studies Research* 24:10–20.

Cornelius, Wayne A. 2001. "Death at the Border: Efficacy and Unintended Consequences of U.S. Immigration Control Policy." *Population and Development Review* 27 (4): 661–85.

Correa, Jennifer G., and James M. Thomas. 2015. "The Rebirth of the U.S.-Mexico Border: Latina/o Enforcement Agents and the Changing Politics of Racial Power." *Sociology of Race and Ethnicity* 1 (2): 239–54.

Coutin, Susan Bibler. 2000. *Legalizing Moves: Salvadoran Immigrants' Struggle for U.S. Residency*. Ann Arbor: University of Michigan Press.

———. 2016. *Exiled Home: Salvadoran Transnational Youth in the Aftermath of Violence*. Durham, NC: Duke University Press.

Coutin, Susan Bibler, and Phyllis Pease Chock. 1997. "'Your Friend, the Illegal': Definition and Paradox in Newspaper Accounts of U.S. Immigration Reform." *Identities* 2 (1–2): 123–48.

DeGenova, Nicholas. 2002. "Migrant 'Illegality' and Deportability in Everyday Life." *Annual Review of Anthropology* 31:419–47.

———. 2004. "The Legal Production of Mexican/Migrant 'Illegality.'" *Latino Studies* 2 (2): 160–85.

———. 2005. *Working the Boundaries: Race, Space, and "Illegality" in Mexican Chicago*. Durham, NC: Duke University Press.

———. 2006. "The Legal Production of Mexican/Migrant 'Illegality.'" In *Latinos and Citizenship: The Dilemma of Belonging*, edited by Suzanne Oboler, 61–90. New York: Palgrave Macmillan.

DeGenova, Nicolas, and Nathalie Peutz. 2010. *The Deportation Regime: Sovereignty, Space, and the Freedom of Movement*. Durham, NC: Duke University Press.

DeGenova, Nicholas, and Ana Y. Ramos-Zayas. 2003. *Latino Crossings: Mexicans, Puerto Ricans, and the Politics of Race and Citizenship*. New York: Routledge.

DeLaet, Debra L. 2000. *U.S. Immigration Policy in an Age of Rights*. Westport, CT: Praeger.

DeLeón, Jason. 2015. *The Land of Open Graves: Living and Dying on the Migrant Trail*. Berkeley: University of California Press.

Delgado, Richard. 1997. "Citizenship." In *Immigrants Out! The New Nativism and the Anti-Immigrant Impulse in the United States*, edited by Juan Perea, 318–23. New York: New York University Press.

Desjarlais, Robert, and C. Jason Throop. 2011. "Phenomenological Approaches in Anthropology." *Annual Review of Anthropology* 40:87–102.

Dietrich, Lisa. 1998. *Chicana Adolescents: Bitches, 'Ho's, and Schoolgirls*. Westport, CT: Praeger.

Dorner, Lisa M., Marjorie Faulstich Orellana, and Rosa Jiménez. 2008. "'It's One of Those Things That You Do to Help the Family': Language Brokering and the Development of Immigrant Adolescents." *Journal of Adolescent Research* 23 (5): 515–43.

Dreby, Joanna. 2010. *Divided by Borders: Mexican Migrants and Their Children*. Berkeley: University of California Press.

———. 2012. "The Burden of Deportation on Children in Mexican Immigrant Families." *Journal of Marriage and Family* 74:829–45.

———. 2015a. *Everyday Illegal: When Policies Undermine Immigrant Families*. Berkeley: University of California Press.

———. 2015b. "U.S. Immigration Policy and Family Separation: The Consequences for Children's Well-Being." *Social Science and Medicine* 132:245–51.

Dunn, Timothy. 1996. *The Militarization of the U.S.-Mexico Border, 1978–1992: Low Intensity Conflict Doctrine Comes Home*. Austin: Center for Mexican American Studies, University of Texas.

———. 2010. *Blockading the Border and Human Rights: The El Paso Operation That Remade Immigration Enforcement*. Austin: University of Texas Press.

Durand, Jorge, Douglas S. Massey, and Rene M. Zenteno. 2001. "Mexican Immigration to the United States: Continuities and Changes." *Latin American Research Review* 36 (1): 107–27.

Enríquez, Laura E. 2015. "Multigenerational Punishment: Shared Experiences with Undocumented Immigration Status Within Mixed-Status Families." *Journal of Marriage and Family* 77:939–53.

Eschbach, Karl, Jacqueline Hagan, Nestor Rodríguez, Ruben Hernández-León, and Stanley Bailey. 1999. "Death at the Border." *International Migration Review* 33 (2): 430–54.

Espiritu, Yen Le. 2003. *Homebound: Filipino American Lives Across Cultures, Communities, and Countries*. Berkeley: University of California Press.

Fassin, Didier. 2011. "Policing Borders, Producing Boundaries: The Governmentality of Immigration in Dark Times." *Annual Review of Anthropology* 40:213–26.

Field, Les W. 1999. *The Grimace of Macho Ratón: Artisans, Identity, and Nation in Late Twentieth-Century Western Nicaragua*. Durham, NC: Duke University Press.

Fix, Michael, and Wendy Zimmerman. 2001. "All Under One Roof: Mixed-Status Families in an Era of Reform." *International Migration Review* 35 (2): 397–419.

Fix, Michael, Wendy Zimmerman, and Jeffery S. Passel. 2001. "The Integration of Immigrant Families in the United States." Urban Institute. Last modified July 1, 2001. http://www.urban.org/publications/410227.html.

Flores, William V. 1997. "Epilogue: Citizens vs. Citizenry: Undocumented Immigrants and Latino Cultural Citizenship." In *Latino Cultural Citizenship: Changing Identity,*

Space, and Rights, edited by William V. Flores and Rina Benmayor, 255–77. Boston: Beacon.

Flores, William V., and Rina Benmayor, eds. 1997. *Latino Cultural Citizenship: Changing Identity, Space, and Rights*. Boston: Beacon.

Flores-González, Nilda. 2017. *Citizens but Not Americans: Race and Belonging Among Latino Millennials*. New York: New York University Press.

Foner, Nancy, ed. 2001. "Transnationalism, Then and Now: New York Immigrants Today and at the Turn of the Twentieth Century." In *Migration, Transnationalization, and Race in a Changing New York*, edited by Héctor Cordero-Guzman, Robert Smith, and Ramón Grosfoguel, 35–57. Philadelphia: Temple University Press.

———. 2009. *Across Generations: Immigrant Families in America*. New York: New York University Press.

Foucault, Michel. 1980. *Power/Knowledge: Selected Interviews and Other Writings, 1972–1977*. Edited by Colin Gordon. New York: Pantheon.

Fouron, Georges E., and Nina Glick Schiller. 2001. "The Generation of Identity: Redefining the Second Generation Within a Transnational Social Field." In *Migration, Transnationalization, and Race in a Changing New York*, edited by Héctor Cordero-Guzmán, Robert C. Smith, and Ramón Grosfoguel, 58–86. Philadelphia: Temple University Press.

Gans, Herbert. 1992. "Second-Generation Decline: Scenarios for the Economic and Ethnic Futures of the Post-1965 American Immigrants." *Ethnic and Racial Studies* 15 (2): 173–92.

García Bedolla, Lisa. 2000. "They and We: Identity, Gender, and Politics Among Latino Youth in Los Angeles." *Social Science Quarterly* 81 (1): 106–22.

———. 2005. *Fluid Borders: Latino Power, Identity, and Politics in Los Angeles*. Berkeley: University of California Press.

Getrich, Christina M. 2000. *The Deportee Monitoring Project*. Mandeville Special Collections Library, University of California, San Diego: The Register of American Friends Service Committee-United States-Mexico Border Program, 1974–2004.

———. 2008. "Negotiating Boundaries of Social Belonging: Second-Generation Mexican Youth and the Immigrant Rights Protests of 2006." *American Behavioral Scientist* 52 (4): 533–56.

———. 2012. "'Too Bad I'm Not an Obvious Citizen': The Effects of Racialized U.S. Immigration Enforcement Practices on Second-Generation Mexican Youth." *Latino Studies* 11 (4): 462–82.

Glick Schiller, Nina. 2003. "The Centrality of Ethnography in the Study of Transnational Migration: Seeing the Wetland Instead of the Swamp." In *American Arrivals: Anthropology Engages the New Immigration*, edited by Nancy Foner, 99–128. Santa Fe, NM: School of American Research Press.

Glick Schiller, Nina, Linda Basch, and Cristina Szanton Blanc. 1992. *Towards a Transnational Perspective on Migration: Race, Class, Ethnicity, and Nationalism Reconsidered*. New York: New York Academy of Sciences.

———. 1995. "From Immigrant to Transnational Migrant: Theorizing Transnational Migration." *Anthropological Quarterly* 68:48–63.

Glick Schiller, Nina, and Georges Fouron. 2001. *Georges Woke Up Laughing: Long-Distance Nationalism and the Search for Home*. Durham, NC: Duke University Press.

Golash-Boza, Tanya. 2006. "Dropping the Hyphen? Becoming Latino(a)-American Through Racialized Assimilation." *Social Forces* 85 (1): 27–55.

———. 2015. *Deported: Immigrant Policing, Disposable Labor, and Global Capitalism*. New York: New York University Press.

Golash-Boza, Tanya, and Pierette Hondagneu-Sotelo. 2013. "Latino Immigrant Men and the Deportation Crisis: A Gendered Racial Removal Program." *Latino Studies* 11 (3): 271–92.

Goldsmith, Pat, Mary Romero, Raquel Rubio-Goldsmith, Manuel Escobedo, and Laura Khoury. 2009. "Ethno-racial Profiling and State Violence in a Southwest Barrio." *Aztlán: A Journal of Chicano Studies* 34 (1): 93–123.

Gomberg-Muñoz, Ruth. 2017. *Becoming Legal: Immigration Law and Mixed-Status Families*. New York: Oxford University Press.

Gonzales, Alfonso. 2009. "The 2006 *Mega Marchas* in Greater Los Angeles: Counter-Hegemonic Moment and the Future of *El Migrante* Struggle." *Latino Studies* 7 (1): 30–59.

Gonzales, Roberto G. 2011. "Learning to Be Illegal: Undocumented Youth and Shifting Legal Contexts in the Transition to Adulthood." *American Sociological Review* 76 (4): 602–19.

———. 2016. *Lives in Limbo: Undocumented and Coming of Age in America*. Berkeley: University of California Press.

Gonzales, Roberto G., and Leo R. Chavez. 2012. "'Awakening to a Nightmare': Abjectivity and Illegality in the Lives of Undocumented 1.5-Generation Latino Immigrants in the United States." *Current Anthropology* 53 (3): 255–81.

Gonzales, Roberto G., Veronica Terriquez, and Stephen P. Ruszczyk. 2014. "Becoming DACAmented: Assessing the Short-Term Benefits of Deferred Action for Childhood Arrivals (DACA)." *American Behavioral Scientist* 58 (14): 1852–72.

Gramsci, Antonio. 1971. *Selections from the Prison Notebooks*. New York: International Publishers.

Griswold del Castillo, Richard. 2007. "Introduction: A Border Region and People." In *Chicano San Diego: Cultural Space and the Struggle for Justice*, edited by Richard Griswold del Castillo, 1–11. Tucson: University of Arizona Press.

Gubernskaya, Zoya, and Joanna Dreby. 2017. "U.S. Immigration Policy and the Case for Family Unity." *Journal on Migration and Human Security* 5 (2): 417–30.

Guelespe, Diana. 2015. "From Driving to Deportation: Experiences of Mixed-Status Immigrant Families Under 'Secure Communities.'" In *Living Together, Living Apart: Mixed Status Families and U.S. Immigration Policy*, edited by April Schueths and Jodie Lawston, 198–213. Seattle: University of Washington Press.

Gulbas, Lauren E., and Luis H. Zayas. 2017. "Exploring the Effects of U.S. Immigration Enforcement on the Well-Being of Citizen Children in Mexican Immigrant Families." *RSF: The Russell Sage Foundation Journal of the Social Sciences* 3 (4): 53–69.

Hagan, Jacqueline, Nestor Rodríguez, Randy Capps, and Nika Kabiri. 2003. "The Effects of Recent Welfare and Immigration Reforms on Immigrants' Access to Health Care." *International Migration Review* 37 (2): 444–63.

Haney López, Ian. 1996. *White by Law: The Legal Construction of Race*. New York: New York University Press.

Hardy, Lisa J., Christina M. Getrich, Julio C. Quezada, Amanda Guay, Raymond L. Michalowski, and Eric Henley. 2012. "A Call for Further Research on the Impact of Immigration Enforcement on Public Health." *American Journal of Public Health* 102 (7): 1250–54.

Harrison, Jill Lindsey, and Sarah E. Lloyd. 2012. "Illegality at Work: Deportability and the Productive New Era of Immigration Enforcement." *Antipode* 44 (2): 365–85.

Heidbrink, Lauren. 2014. *Migrant Youth, Transnational Families, and the State: Care and Contested Interests*. Philadelphia: University of Pennsylvania Press.

Hernández, Daniel M. 2008. "Pursuant to Deportation: Latinos and Immigrant Detention." *Latino Studies* 6 (1–2): 35–63.

Hernández, Kelly Lytle. 2010. *Migra! A History of the U.S. Border Patrol*. Berkeley: University of California Press.

Hess, Julia Meredith. 2009. *Immigrant Ambassadors: Citizenship and Belonging in the Tibetan Diaspora*. Stanford, CA: Stanford University Press.

Heyman, Josiah McC. 1991. *Life and Labor on the Border: Working People of Northeastern Sonora, 1886–1986*. Tucson: University of Arizona Press.

———. 1998. "State Effects on Labor Exploitation: The INS and Undocumented Immigrants at the Mexico-United States Border." *Critique of Anthropology* 18 (2): 157–80.

———. 1999. "United States Surveillance over Mexican Lives at the Border: Snapshots of an Emerging Regime." *Human Organization* 58 (4): 430–38.

———. 2001. "Class and Classification at the U.S.-Mexico Border." *Human Organization* 60 (2): 128–40.

———. 2002. "U.S. Immigration Officers of Mexican Ancestry as Mexican Americans, Citizens, and Immigration Police." *Current Anthropology* 43 (3): 479–507.

———. 2004. "Ports of Entry as Nodes in the World System." *Identities: Global Studies in Culture and Power* 11 (3): 303–27.

———. 2014. "'Illegality' and the U.S.-Mexico Border: How It Is Produced and Resisted." In *Constructing Immigrant "Illegality": Critiques, Experiences, Responses*, edited by Cecilia Menjívar and Daniel Kanstroom, 111–35. New York: Cambridge University Press.

———. 2017. "Contributions of U.S.-Mexico Border Studies to Social Science Theory." In *The U.S.-Mexico Transborder Region: Cultural Dynamics and Historical Interactions*, edited by Carlos G. Vélez-Ibáñez and Josiah Heyman, 44–64. Tucson: University of Arizona Press.

Horner, Pilar, Laura Sanders, Ramiro Martinez, John Doering-White, William Lopez, and Jorge Delva. 2014. "'I Put a Mask On': The Human Side of Deportation Effects on Latino Youth." *Journal of Social Welfare and Human Rights* 2 (2): 33–47.

Horton, Sarah B. 2009. "A Mother's Heart Is Weighed Down with Stones: A Phenomenological Approach to the Experience of Transnational Motherhood." *Culture, Medicine, and Psychiatry* 33:21–40.

———. 2014. "Debating 'Medical Citizenship': Policies Shaping Undocumented Immigrants' Learned Avoidance of the U.S. Health Care System." In *Hidden Lives and Human Rights in the United States: Understanding the Controversies and Tragedies of Undocumented Immigration*, edited by Lois Ann Lorentzen, 297–319. Santa Barbara, CA: Praeger.

———. 2016. *They Leave Their Kidneys in the Fields: Illness, Injury, and Illegality Among U.S. Farmworkers*. Berkeley: University of California Press.

Inda, Jonathan Xavier. 2006a. "Border Prophylaxis: Technology, Illegality, and the Government of Immigration." *Cultural Dynamics* 18 (2): 115–38.

———. 2006b. *Targeting Immigrants: Government, Technology, and Ethics*. Malden, MA: Blackwell Publishing.

Inda, Jonathan Xavier, and Julie A. Dowling. 2013. "Introduction: Governing Migrant Illegality." In *Governing Immigration Through Crime: A Reader*, edited by Julie A. Dowling and Jonathan Xavier Inda, 1–39. Stanford, CA: Stanford University Press.

Isin, Engin F., and Greg M. Nielsen. 2008. *Acts of Citizenship*. Chicago: University of Chicago Press.

Jonas, Susanne, and Catherine Tactaquin. 2004. "Latino Immigrant Rights in the Shadow of the National Security State: Responses to Domestic Preemptive Strikes." *Social Justice* 32 (1–2): 6–20.

Kasinitz, Philip, John H. Mollenkopf, and Mary C. Waters. 2004. *Becoming New Yorkers: Ethnographies of the New Second Generation*. New York: Russell Sage Foundation Publications.

Kasinitz, Philip, John H. Mollenkopf, Mary C. Waters, and Jennifer Holdaway. 2008. *Inheriting the City: The Children of Immigrants Come of Age*. New York: Russell Sage Foundation.

Katz, Vikki S. 2014. *Kids in the Middle: How Children of Immigrants Negotiate Community Interactions for Their Families*. New Brunswick, NJ: Rutgers University Press.

Kearney, Michael. 1991. "Borders and Boundaries of State and Self at the End of Empire." *Journal of Historical Sociology* 4 (1): 52–74.

———. 1995. "The Local and the Global: The Anthropology of Globalization and Transnationalism." *Annual Review of Anthropology* 24:547–65.

———. 2004. "The Classifying and Value-Filtering Missions of Borders." *Anthropological Theory* 4 (2): 131–56.

Kearney, Michael, and Carole Nagengast. 1989. *Anthropological Perspectives on Transnational Communities in Rural California*. Davis: California Institute for Rural Studies.

Kearney, Milo, and Anthony Knopp. 1995. *The Border Cuates: A History of the U.S.-Mexican Twin Cities*. Fort Worth, TX: Eakin Press.

Kibria, Nazli. 1993. *Family Tightrope: The Changing Lives of Vietnamese Americans.* Princeton, NJ: Princeton University Press.
Kiy, Richard, and Christopher Woodruff, eds. 2005. *Ties That Bind Us: Mexican Migrants in San Diego County.* La Jolla, CA: Center for U.S.-Mexican Studies, UCSD.
Lamont, Michèle. 2000. *The Dignity of Working Men: Morality and the Boundaries of Race, Class, and Immigration.* New York: Russell Sage Foundation.
Lamont, Michèle, and Virág Molnár. 2002. "The Study of Boundaries in the Social Sciences." *Annual Review of Sociology* 28:167–95.
Lamphere, Louise. 2004. "The Convergence of Applied, Practicing, and Applied Anthropology in the 21st Century." *Human Organization* 63 (4): 431–43.
Leiter, Valerie, Jennifer Lutzy McDonald, and Heather T. Jacobson. 2006. "Challenges to Children's Independent Citizenship: Immigration, Family and the State." *Childhood* 13 (1): 11–27.
Levitt, Peggy. 2001. *The Transnational Villagers.* Berkeley: University of California Press.
———. 2009. "Roots and Routes: Understanding the Lives of the Second Generation Transnationally." *Journal of Ethnic and Migration Studies* 35 (7): 1225–42.
Levitt, Peggy, and Nina Glick Schiller. 2004. "Conceptualizing Simultaneity: A Transnational Social Field Perspective on Society." *International Migration Review* 38 (3): 1002–39.
Levitt, Peggy, and Nadya Jaworksy. 2007. "Transnational Migration Studies: Past Developments and Future Trends." *Annual Review of Sociology* 33:129–56.
Levitt, Peggy, and Mary C. Waters, eds. 2002. *The Changing Face of Home: The Transnational Lives of the Second Generation.* New York: Russell Sage Foundation.
Library of Congress. 2005. H.R. 4437. http://thomas.loc.gov/cgi-bin/query/z?c109:H.R.4437:RFS.
López, David E., and Ricardo D. Stanton-Salazar. 2001. "Mexican Americans: A Second Generation at Risk." In *Ethnicities: Children of Immigrants in America*, edited by Rubén Rumbaut and Alejandro Portes, 57–90. New York: Russell Sage Foundation.
López, Nancy. 2004. *Hopeful Girls, Troubled Boys: Race and Gender Disparity in Urban Education.* New York: Routledge.
Lopez, William D., Daniel J. Kruger, Jorge Delva, Mikel Llanes, Charo Ledón, Adreanne Waller, Melanie Harner et al. 2017. "Health Implications of an Immigration Raid: Findings from a Latino Community in the Midwestern United States." *Journal of Immigrant and Minority Health* 19 (3): 702–8.
Lugo, Alejandro. 2000. "Theorizing Border Inspections." *Cultural Dynamics* 12 (3): 353–73.
Maira, Sunaina Marr. 2009. *Missing: Youth, Citizenship, and Empire After 9/11.* Durham, NC: Duke University Press.
Márquez, Raquel R., and Harriett D. Romo. 2008. *Transformations of La Familia on the U.S.-Mexico Border.* South Bend, IN: University of Notre Dame Press.
Martin, Philip L. 1999. "Unauthorized Workers in U.S. Agriculture: Old Versus New Migrations." In *Illegal Immigration in America: A Reference Handbook*, edited by David Haines and Karen Rosenblum, 133–56. Westport, CT: Greenwood Press.
———. 2002. "Mexican Workers and U.S. Agriculture: The Revolving Door." *International Migration Review* 36 (4): 1124–42.

Martínez, Lisa M. 2008. "'Flowers from the Same Soil': Latino Solidarity in the Wake of the 2006 Immigrant Mobilizations." *American Behavioral Scientist* 52 (4): 557–79.

———. 2013. "Politicizing the Family: How Grassroots Organizations Mobilize Latinos for Political Action in Colorado." *Latino Studies* 8 (4): 463–84.

Martínez, Oscar J. 1994. *Border People: Life and Society in the U.S.-Mexico Borderlands*. Tucson: University of Arizona Press.

Massey, Douglas S., Jorge Durand, and Nolan J. Malone, eds. 2002. *Beyond Smoke and Mirrors: Mexican Immigration in an Era of Economic Integration*. New York: Russell Sage Foundation.

Massey, Douglas S., and Magaly R. Sánchez. 2010. *Brokered Boundaries: Creating Immigrant Identity in Anti-Immigrant Times*. New York: Russell Sage Foundation.

Mendoza, Inzunza, Dina Jael, and Christian Fernández Huerta. 2010. "The Importance of Looking at the Border from a Young Person's Perspective." *Children's Geographies* 8 (4): 335–41.

Menjívar, Cecilia. 2000. *Fragmented Ties: Salvadoran Immigrant Networks in America*. Berkeley: University of California Press.

———. 2006. "Liminal Legality: Salvadoran and Guatemalan Immigrants' Lives in the United States." *American Journal of Sociology* 111:999–1037.

———. 2010. "Immigrants, Immigration, and Sociology: Reflecting on the State of the Discipline." *Sociological Inquiry* 80 (1): 3–27.

Menjívar, Cecilia, and Leisy Abrego. 2009. "Parents and Children Across Borders: Legal Instability and Intergenerational Relations in Guatemalan and Salvadoran Families." In *Across Generations: Immigrant Families in America*, edited by Nancy Foner, 160–89. New York: New York University Press.

———. 2012. "Legal Violence: Immigration Law and the Lives of Central American Immigrants." *American Journal of Sociology* 117 (5): 1380–1421.

Menjívar, Cecilia, Leisy J. Abrego, and Leah C. Schmalzbauer. 2016. *Immigrant Families*. Malden, MA: Polity Press.

Menjívar, Cecilia, and Daniel Kanstroom. 2014. *Constructing Immigrant "Illegality": Critiques, Experiences, Responses*. New York: Cambridge University Press.

Migration Policy Institute. 2015. "MPI Releases Detailed Data Profiles of Unauthorized Immigrants and Estimates of Deferred Action Populations for Top U.S. Counties." Last modified January 15, 2015. http://www.migrationpolicy.org/news/mpi-releases-detailed-county-profiles-unauthorized-immigrants-and-estimates-deferred-action.

Miroff, Nick. 2018. "Scanning Immigrants' Old Fingerprints, U.S. Threatens to Strip Thousands of Citizenship." *Washington Post*, June 13. https://www.washingtonpost.com/world/national-security/scanning-immigrants-old-fingerprints-us-threatens-to-strip-thousands-of-citizenship/2018/06/13/2230d8a2-6f2e-11e8-afd5-778aca903bbe_story.html?noredirect=on&utm_term=.8b9a10f5700b.

Murray, Royce. 2017. "Six Months of Immigration Enforcement Under the New Administration." American Immigration Council. Last modified July 21, 2017. http://immigrationimpact.com/2017/07/21/six-months-immigration-enforcement-administration/.

Nagengast, Carole. 1994. "Violence, Terror, and the Crisis of the State." *Annual Review of Anthropology* 23:109–36.

———. 1998. "Militarizing the Border Patrol." *NACLA: Report on the Americas.* Special Report on Militarization. 32 (3): 37–41.

National Council of State Legislatures. 2017. *State Laws Related to Immigration and Immigrants.* http://www.ncsl.org/research/immigration/state-laws-related-to-immigration-and-immigrants.aspx.

Nevins, Joseph. 2002. *Operation Gatekeeper: The Rise of the "Illegal Alien" and the Making of the U.S.-Mexico Boundary.* New York: Routledge.

Ngai, Mae M. 2004. *Impossible Subjects: Illegal Aliens and the Making of Modern America.* Princeton, NJ: Princeton University Press.

Nicholls, Walter J. 2013. *The DREAMers: How the Undocumented Youth Movement Transformed the Immigrant Rights Debate.* Stanford, CA: Stanford University Press.

Núñez, Guillermina, and Josiah Heyman. 2007. "Entrapment Processes and Immigrant Communities in a Time of Heightened Border Vigilance." *Human Organization* 66 (4): 354–65.

Oboler, Suzanne, ed. 2006. *Latinos and Citizenship: The Dilemma of Belonging.* New York: Palgrave Macmillan.

Ochoa O'Leary, Anna, and Azucena Sanchez. 2011. "Anti-immigrant Arizona: Ripple Effects and Mixed Immigration Status Households Under 'Policies of Attrition' Considered." *Journal of Borderland Studies* 26 (1): 115–33.

Ong, Aihwa. 1996. "Cultural Citizenship as Subject-Making: Immigrants Negotiate Racial and Cultural Boundaries in the United States." *Current Anthropology* 37 (5): 737–62.

———. 2003. *Buddha Is Hiding: Refugees, Citizenship, the New America.* Berkeley: University of California Press.

Orellana, Marjorie Faulstich. 2001. "The Work Kids Do: Mexican and Central American Immigrant Children's Contributions to Households and Schools in California." *Harvard Educational Review* 71 (3): 366–89.

———. 2009. *Translating Childhoods: Immigrant Youth, Language, and Culture.* New Brunswick, NJ: Rutgers University Press.

Orellana, Marjorie Faulstich, Lisa Dorner, and Lucila Pulido. 2003. "Accessing Assets: Immigrant Youth's Work as Family Translators or 'Para-Phrasers.'" *Social Problems* 50 (4): 505–24.

Ortiz, Isidro D. 2007. "'Sí, Se Puede!': Chicana/o Activism in San Diego at Century's End." In *Chicano San Diego: Cultural Space and the Struggle for Justice,* edited by Richard Griswold del Castillo, 129–57. Tucson: University of Arizona Press.

Ortner, Sherry B. 1996. *Making Gender: The Politics and Erotics of Culture.* Boston: Beach Press.

———. 2005. "Subjectivity and Cultural Critique." *Anthropological Theory* 5 (1): 31–52.

Osler, Audrey, and Hugh Starkey. 2003. "Learning for Cosmopolitan Citizenship: Theoretical Debates and Young People's Experiences." *Educational Review* 55 (3): 243–54.

Padilla, Yolanda C. 1997. "Immigrant Policy: Issues for Social Work Practice." *Social Work* 42 (6): 595–606.

Pallares, Amalia. 2015. *Family Activism: Immigrant Struggles and the Politics of Noncitizenship*. New Brunswick, NJ: Rutgers University Press.

Pallares, Amalia, and Nilda Flores-González. 2011. "Regarding Family: New Actors in the Chicago Protests." In *Rallying for Immigrant Rights: The Fight for Inclusion in 21st Century America*, edited by Kim Voss and Irene Bloemraad, 161–79. Berkeley: University of California Press.

Pantoja, Adrian, Cecilia Menjívar, and Lisa Magaña. 2008. "The Spring Marches of 2006: Latinos, Immigration, and Political Mobilization in the 21st Century." *American Behavioral Scientist* 52 (4): 499–506.

Park, Lisa Sun-Hee. 2005. *Consuming Citizenship: Children of Asian Immigrant Entrepreneurs*. Stanford, CA: Stanford University Press.

Pastor, Manuel. 2018. *State of Resistance: What California's Dizzying Descent and Remarkable Resurgence Mean for America's Future*. New York: New Press.

Perlmann, Joel, and Roger Waldinger. 1997. "Second-Generation Decline? The Children of Immigrants Past and Present—A Reconsideration." *International Migration Review* 31 (4): 893–922.

Pinkerton, James. 2008. "Border Patrol to Woo Black Recruits: Plan Part of Overall Staffing Boost." *Houston Chronicle*, January 12.

Portes, Alejandro. 2001. "Introduction: The Debates and Significance of Immigrant Transnationalism." *Global Networks* 1 (3): 181–93.

Portes, Alejandro, Cristina Escobar, and Renelinda Arana. 2009. "Divided or Convergent Loyalties? The Political Incorporation Process of Latin American Immigrants in the United States." *Sociology* 50 (2): 103–36.

Portes, Alejandro, and Maria Patricia Fernández-Kelly. 2008. "No Margin for Error: Educational and Occupational Achievement Among Disadvantaged Children of Immigrants." *Annals of the American Academy of Political and Social Science* 620:12–36.

Portes, Alejandro, and Rubén Rumbaut. 2001. *Legacies: The Story of the Immigrant Second Generation*. Berkeley: University of California Press.

Preston, Julia. 2010. "Report Faults Training of Local Officers in Immigration Enforcement Program." *New York Times*, April 2.

Pries, Ludger. 2004. "Determining the Causes and Durability of Transnational Labour Migration Between Mexico and the United States: Some Empirical Findings." *International Migration* 42 (2): 3–39.

Pulido, Laura. 2007. "A Day Without Immigrants: The Racial and Class Politics of Immigrant Exclusion." *Antipode* 39 (1): 1–7.

Pyke, Karen, and Tran Dang. 2003. "'FOB' and 'Whitewashed': Identity and Internalized Racism Among Second Generation Asian Americans." *Qualitative Sociology* 26 (2): 147–72.

Quesada, James, Laurie Kain Hart, and Philippe Bourgois. 2011. "Structural Vulnerability and Health: Latino Migrant Laborers in the United States." *Medical Anthropology* 30 (4): 339–62.

Ramos-Zayas, Ana Yolanda. 2003. *Nationalist Performances: Race, Class, and Space in Puerto Rican Chicago*. Chicago: University of Chicago Press.

———. 2004. "Delinquent Citizenship, National Performances: Racialization, Surveillance, and the Politics of 'Worthiness' in Puerto Rican Chicago." *Latino Studies* 2 (1): 26–44.

Reiter, Bernd. 2013. *The Dialectics of Citizenship: Exploring Privilege, Exclusion, and Racialization*. East Lansing: Michigan State University Press.

Richards, Sarah Elizabeth. 2017. "How Fear of Deportation Puts Stress on Families." *The Atlantic*. Last modified March 22, 2017. https://www.theatlantic.com/family/archive/2017/03/deportation-stress/520008/.

Roche, Jeremy. 1999. "Children: Rights, Participation, and Citizenship." *Childhood* 6 (4): 475–93.

Rodriguez, Nicole. 2018. "Trump's Immigration Crackdown Creating a Public Health Crisis Among Children, Analysts Say." *Newsweek*. Last modified January 4, 2018. http://www.newsweek.com/trump-immigration-crackdown-public-health-crisis-children-769486.

Romero, Mary. 2006. "Racial Profiling and Immigration Law Enforcement: Rounding Up of Usual Suspects in the Latino Community." *Critical Sociology* 32 (2–3): 447–73.

———. 2008. "Crossing the Immigration and Race Border: A Critical Race Theory Approach to Immigration Studies." *Contemporary Justice Review* 11 (1): 23–37.

Rosaldo, Renato. 1989. *Culture and Truth: The Remaking of Social Analysis*. Boston: Beacon Press.

Rosas, Gilberto. 2006a. "The Managed Violences of the Borderlands: Treacherous Geographies, Policeability, and the Politics of Race." *Latino Studies* 4 (4): 401–18.

———. 2006b. "The Thickening Borderlands: Diffused Exceptionality and 'Immigrant' Social Struggles During the 'War on Terror.'" *Cultural Dynamics* 18 (3): 335–49.

Rouse, Roger. 1991. "Mexican Migration and the Social Space of Postmodernism." *Diaspora* 1 (1): 8–23.

———. 1995. "Thinking Through Transnationalism: Notes on the Cultural Politics of Class Relations in the Contemporary United States." *Public Culture* 7 (2): 353–402.

Rumbaut, Rubén, and Alejandro Portes. 2001. *Ethnicities: The Story of the Immigrant Second Generation*. Berkeley: University of California Press.

Runsten, David. 2005. "Origins and Characteristics of Mexican Immigrants in San Diego: Evidence from the *Matrículas Consulares*." In *Ties That Bind Us: Mexican Migrants in San Diego County*, edited by Richard Kiy and Christopher Woodruff, 3–43. La Jolla, CA: Center for U.S.-Mexican Studies, UCSD.

Sabo, Samantha, and Alison Elizabeth Lee. 2015. "The Spillover of U.S. Immigration Policy on Citizens and Permanent Residents of Mexican Descent: How Internalizing 'Illegality' Impacts Public Health in the Borderlands." *Frontiers in Public Health* 3 (155): 1–9.

Sabo, Samantha, Susan Shaw, Maia Ingram, Nicolette Teufel-Shone, Scott Carvajal, Jill Guernsey de Zapien, Cecilia Rosales et al. 2014. "Everyday Violence, Structural Racism and Mistreatment at the U.S.-Mexico Border." *Social Science and Medicine* 109:66–74.

Sacchetti, Maria, and Nick Miroff. 2017. "How Trump Is Building a Border Wall That No One Can See." *Washington Post*, November 21.

San Diego Association of Government (SANDAG). 2017. *Demographics and Other Data*. http://www.sandag.org/index.asp?classid=26&fuseaction=home.classhome.

Sassen, Saskia. 1996. *Losing Control? Sovereignty in an Age of Globalization*. New York: Columbia University Press.

Schueths, April, and Jodie Lawston. 2015. *Living Together, Living Apart: Mixed Status Families and U.S. Immigration Policy*. Seattle: University of Washington Press.

Seif, Hinda. 2006. "'Wise Up!' Undocumented Latino Youth, Mexican-American Legislators, and the Struggle for Higher Education Access." In *Latinos and Citizenship: The Dilemma of Belonging*, edited by Suzanne Oboler, 247–72. New York: Palgrave Macmillan.

Sharma, Aradhana, and Akhil Gupta. 2006. *The Anthropology of the State: A Reader*. Hoboken, NJ: Wiley-Blackwell.

Sieff, Kevin. 2018. "U.S. Is Denying Passports to Americans Along the Border, Throwing Their Citizenship into Question." *Washington Post*, September 1. https://www.washingtonpost.com/world/the_americas/us-is-denying-passports-to-americans-along-the-border-throwing-their-citizenship-into-question/2018/08/29/1d630e84-a0da-11e8-a3dd-2a1991f075d5_story.html?utm_term=.9be813ffaad7.

Smith, Colin. 1993. *Collins Spanish Dictionary*. Glasgow, Great Britain: HarperCollins Publishers.

Smith, Michael Peter, and Luis Eduardo Guarnizo, eds. 1998. *Transnationalism from Below: Comparative Urban and Community Research*. New Brunswick, NJ: Transaction Publishers.

Smith, Robert C. 2002. "Social Location, Generation, and Life Course as Social Processes Shaping Second Generation Transnational Life." In *The Changing Face of Home: The Transnational Lives of the Second Generation*, edited by Peggy Levitt and Mary C. Waters, 145–68. New York: Russell Sage Foundation.

———. 2006. *Mexican New York: Transnational Lives of New Immigrants*. Berkeley: University of California Press.

———. 2008. "Horatio Alger Lives in Brooklyn: Extrafamily Support, Intrafamily Dynamics, and Socially Neutral Operating Identities in Exceptional Mobility Among the Children of Mexican Immigrants." *Annals of the American Academy of Political and Social Science* 620:270–90.

Smith, Robert C., Héctor R. Cordero-Guzmán, and Ramón Grosfoguel. 2001. "Introduction." In *Migration, Transnationalization, and Race in a Changing New York*, edited by Héctor Cordero-Guzmán, Robert C. Smith, and Ramón Grosfoguel, 1–32. Philadelphia: Temple University Press.

Stanton-Salazar, Ricardo. 2001. *Manufacturing Hope and Despair: The School and Kin Support Networks of U.S.-Mexican Youth*. New York: Teachers College Press.

State of California Department of Motor Vehicles. 2017. "AB 60 Driver License." https://www.dmv.ca.gov/portal/dmv/detail/ab60.

Stein, Fernando. 2017. "AAP Statement on Protecting Immigrant Children." Last modified on January 25, 2017. https://www.aap.org/en-us/about-the-aap/aap-press-room/Pages/AAPStatementonProtectingImmigrantChildren.aspx.

Stephen, Lynn. 2007. *Transborder Lives: Indigenous Oaxacans in Mexico, California, and Oregon*. Durham, NC: Duke University Press.

Suárez-Orozco, Carola, and Marcelo M. Suárez-Orozco. 2001. *Children of Immigration.* Cambridge, MA: Harvard University Press.

Suárez-Orozco, Marcelo, ed. 1998. *Crossings: Mexican Immigration in Interdisciplinary Perspectives.* Cambridge, MA: Harvard University Press.

Sunstein, Cass R. 2018. *#Republic: Divided Democracy in the Age of Social Media.* Princeton, NJ: Princeton University Press.

Szkupinski Quiroga, Seline, Dulce M. Medina, and Jennifer Glock. 2014. "In the Belly of the Beast: Effects of Anti-immigration Policy on Latino Community Members." *American Behavioral Scientist* 58 (13): 1723–42.

Taylor, Paul, Mark Hugo Lopez, Jeffrey S. Passel, and Seth Motel. 2011. *Unauthorized Immigrants: Length of Residency, Patterns of Parenthood.* Washington, D.C.: Pew Hispanic Center. http://pewhispanic.org/2011/12/01/unauthorized-immigrants-length-of-residency-patterns-of-parenthood.

Thomson, Rachel. 2007. "The Qualitative Longitudinal Case History: Practical, Methodological, and Ethical Reflections." *Social Policy and Society* 6 (4): 571–82.

Tsuda, Takeyuki. 2003. "Domesticating the Immigrant Other: Japanese Media Images of *Nikkeijin* Return Migrants." *Ethnology* 42 (4): 289–305.

———. 2012. "Whatever Happened to Simultaneity? Transnational Migration Theory and Dual Engagement in Sending and Receiving Countries." *Journal of Ethnic and Migration Studies* 38 (4): 631–49.

United States Census Bureau. 2016. "QuickFacts: San Diego County, California." https://www.census.gov/quickfacts/table/PST045216/06073,06.

United States Citizenship and Immigration Services (USCIS). 2016a. "Green Card." https://www.uscis.gov/greencard.

———. 2016b. "Lawful Permanent Resident." https://www.uscis.gov/tools/glossary/lawful-permanent-resident.

———. 2016c. "U.S. Citizenship." https://www.uscis.gov/us-citizenship.

———. 2016d. "Visit the U.S." https://www.uscis.gov/visit-united-states/visit-us.

United States Customs and Border Protection (USCBP). 2018. "Legal Authority for the Border Patrol." Last modified July 28, 2018. https://customs.custhelp.com/app/answers/detail/a_id/1084/~/legal-authority-for-the-border-patrol.

United States Department of Health and Human Services (USDHHS). 2012. *The Affordable Care Act: Coverage Implications and Issues for Immigrant Families.* ASPE Issue Brief. http://aspe.hhs.gov/hsp/11/ImmigrantAccess/Coverage/ib.pdf.

Urban Institute. 2016. "Visualizing Trends for Children of Immigrants." http://apps.urban.org/features/children-of-immigrants/.

Varsanyi, Monica. 2010. *Taking Local Control: Immigration Policy Activism in U.S. Cities and States.* Stanford, CA: Stanford University Press.

Vélez-Ibañez, Carlos G. 1996. *Border Visions: Mexican Cultures of the Southwest United States.* Tucson: University of Arizona Press.

Vélez-Ibañez, Carlos G., and Josiah Heyman. 2017. *The U.S.-Mexico Transborder Region: Cultural Dynamics and Historical Interactions.* Tucson: University of Arizona Press.

Vila, Pablo. 2000. *Crossing Borders, Reinforcing Borders: Social Categories, Metaphors, and Narrative Identities on the U.S.-Mexico Frontier.* Austin: University of Texas Press.

Viruell-Fuentes, Edna A. 2006. "'My Heart Is Always There': The Transnational Practices of First-Generation Mexican Immigrant and Second-Generation Mexican American Women." *Identities: Global Studies in Culture and Power* 13:335–62.

Voss, Kim, and Irene Bloemraad, eds. 2011. *Rallying for Immigrant Rights: The Fight for Inclusion in 21st Century America*. Berkeley: University of California Press.

Waldinger, Roger. 2013. "Immigrant Transnationalism." *Current Sociology Review* 61 (5–6): 756–77.

Waldinger, Roger, and Cynthia Feliciano. 2004. "Will the New Second Generation Experience 'Downward Assimilation'? Segmented Assimilation Re-assessed." *Ethnic and Racial Studies* 27 (3): 376–402.

Wang, Caroline, and Mary Ann Burris. 1994. "Empowerment Through Photovoice: Portraits of Participation." *Health Education Quarterly* 21 (2): 171–86.

Waslin, Michele L. 2013. "Driving While Immigrant: Driver's License Policy and Immigration Enforcement." In *Outside Justice: Immigration and the Criminalizing Impact of Changing Policy and Practice*, edited by David C. Brotherton and Daniel Stagement, 3–22. New York: Springer.

Waters, Mary C., Patrick J. Carr, Maria J. Kefalas, and Jennifer Holdaway. 2011. *Coming of Age in America: The Transition to Adulthood in the Twenty-First Century*. Berkeley: University of California Press.

Willen, Sarah S. 2007. "Toward a Critical Phenomenology of 'Illegality': State Power, Criminalization, and Abjectivity Among Undocumented Workers in Tel Aviv, Israel." *International Migration* 45 (3): 8–38.

———. 2010. "Citizens, 'Real' Others, and 'Other' Others: Governmentality, Biopolitics, and the Deportation of Undocumented Migrants from Tel Aviv." In *The Deportation Regime: Sovereignty, Space, and the Freedom of Movement*, edited by Nicolas DeGenova and Nathalie Peutz, 262–94. Durham, NC: Duke University Press.

Williams, Steve, Alan Bersin, Jose Larroque, and Gustavo de la Fuente. 2017. "It's Time to Make the San Diego-Tijuana Border More Efficient." *San Diego Union-Tribune*, May 5. http://www.sandiegouniontribune.com/opinion/commentary/sd-utbg-border-economy-tijuana-sandiego-20170501-story.html.

Wilson, Christopher E., and Erik Lee. 2013. *The State of the Border Report: A Comprehensive Analysis of the U.S.-Mexico Border*. Border Research Partnership. Last modified May 23, 2013. https://fronterasdesk.org/sites/default/files/field/docs/2013/05/23/mexico_state_of_border.pdf.

Wilson, Tamar Diana. 2000. "Anti-immigrant Sentiment and the Problem of Reproduction/Maintenance in Mexican Immigration to the United States." *Critique of Anthropology* 20 (2): 191–213.

Wilson, Thomas M., and Hastings Donnan. 1998. *Border Identities: Nation and State at International Frontiers*. Cambridge: Cambridge University Press.

Wong, Janelle, and Vivian Tseng. 2008. "Political Socialization in Immigrant Families: Challenging the Top-Down Parental Socialization Models." *Journal of Ethnic and Migration Studies* 34:151–68.

Wong, Tom K., Greisa Martinez Rosas, Adrian Reyna, Ignacia Rodriguez, Patrick O'Shea, Tom Jawetz, and Philip E. Wolgin. 2016. "New Study of DACA Beneficiaries Shows Positive Economic and Educational Outcomes." Center for American Progress. Last modified October 18, 2016. https://www.americanprogress.org/issues/immigration/news/2016/10/18/146290/new-study-of-daca-beneficiaries-shows-positive-economic-and-educational-outcomes/.

Yarris, Kristin E. 2017. *Care Across Generations: Solidarity and Sacrifice in Transnational Families*. Stanford, CA: Stanford University Press.

Yoshikawa, Hirokazu. 2011. *Immigrants Raising Citizens: Undocumented Parents and Their Young Children*. New York: Russell Sage Foundation.

Zavella, Patricia. 2011. *I'm Neither Here nor There: Mexicans' Quotidian Struggles with Migration and Poverty*. Durham, NC: Duke University Press.

Zayas, Luis H. 2015. *Forgotten Citizens: Deportation, Children, and the Making of American Exiles and Orphans*. New York: Oxford University Press.

Zayas, Luis H., and Mollie H. Bradlee. 2014. "Exiling Children, Creating Orphans: When Immigration Policies Hurt Citizens." *Social Work* 59:167–75.

INDEX

1.5 generation, as term, 222n6. *See also* second-generation young adults
-1.5 generation, as term, 222n6. *See also* second-generation young adults
9/11 attacks, effects of, 49–50
287(g) agreements, 19, 53

abandonment, children's feelings of, 94. *See also* family separation
Acosta, Nancy, 135
activism. *See* immigrant rights movement; protests; resistance to state power
AEDPA. *See* Antiterrorism and Effective Death Penalty Act of 1996 (AEDPA)
Affordable Care Act (ACA), 95
AFSC (American Friends Service Committee), 223n2 (ch. 4)
agency, as term, 222n4
Alabama, 53
American Friends Service Committee (AFSC), 223n2 (ch. 4)
"anchor baby," 48–49, 70. *See also* birthright citizenship
Antiterrorism and Effective Death Penalty Act of 1996 (AEDPA), 17, 48

Arizona, 25, 53
Arizona Senate Bill (S.B.) 1070, 53
Assembly Bill 60 (California), 101
assimilation theories, 11–13, 143–47, 204

belonging: 2006 student protesters on, 80–89; as "having papers," 72–73, 91–92, 223n1 (ch. 2), 223n5 (ch. 2); resistance to state power and, 134–37; through societal contributions, 74–79; transborder life experiences and, 140–43, 153–55, 159
birthright citizenship, 48–49, 68, 70, 88, 118. *See also* "anchor baby"
border crossing: description of, 117–18; Friendship Park, *201*; illegality and limitations of, 105–7; immigration inspections at, 124–31; mandatory documents for, 223n1 (ch. 3); at Otay Mesa Port of Entry, 27, 124; performing U.S. citizen identity at, 135–36; at San Ysidro Port of Entry, 27, *119, 124, 128,* 162; SENTRI pass for, 160; as term, 224n3 (ch. 4)
border enforcement practices: in 1990s, 45–47; in 2000s-2010s, 51–56; in borderlands, 131–34; of Bush, 49, 94;

ethno-racial profiling, 4, 50, 53, 118–24, 129–31, 204; inspections at ports of entry, 124–31; of Obama, 19, 51–52, 53–54, 94; Operation Blockade, 45, 122; Operation Gatekeeper, 9, 16–17, 45–47; search and seizure procedures, 131; of Trump, 54–56, 94, 137. *See also* border crossing; deportation fear; ports of entry; state power
border fencing, *46*
Border Patrol. *See* U.S. Border Patrol
Border Patrol checkpoints, 18, 103, 104, 131
Border Protection, Anti-terrorism, and Illegal Immigration Control Act of 2005. *See* H.R. 4437
"border wall" rhetoric of Trump, ix, x, 205–6
bracero program, 29, 40–41, 148, 162. *See also* guest worker programs
brokering roles of second-generation young adults: about, 10, 21–24, 171–73; active, decision-making, 175–77; in adulthood, 194–96, 203–5; community service, 187–89; gender and, 176; linguistic brokering, 21, 22, 170–75, 200, 203; in private sphere, 179–87; professional work, 22, 89, 170, 179, 189–94, 204; securing parents' status, 113–15, 162, 165, 172, 181, 184, 199; with state institutions, 177–78, 200–202. *See also* illegality experiences; second-generation young adults; transborder life
Bush administration, 49, 94

Cabrera, Raquel, 73–74
California: 2006 *mega marcha* protests, 9, 19, 29, 50–51, 59–62, 80–89, 178, 192; history of immigration and immigrant policies in, 16–17, 43–45, 49, 57, 80, 101; ports of entry in, 27, *119*, 124, *128*, 162; as "state of resistance," 56. *See also* San Diego, U.S.
Campos, Manuel, 159
CBP. *See* U.S. Customs and Border Protection (CBP)
Central Intelligence Agency (CIA), 50

"chain migration," as term, 56
Chandler, Arizona, 122
children. *See* second-generation young adults; third-generation youth; *specific personal names*
Children of Immigrants Longitudinal Study (CILS), 11–12, 14
Children's Health Insurance Program (CHIP), 47, 95
Chinese Exclusion Act of 1882, 37
chola/o, 223n6. *See also* gangs
CIA, 50
circular migration, 48, 146
citizen, as category, 9, 65. *See also* classification systems
"citizenship fraud," 39, 55
classification systems: about, 62–65, 71; inclusion/exclusion categories, 78–79; legal/formal categories, 65–68, 71–74; social/informal categories, 68–71, 75–78
Clemente, Isabel: on crossing the border, 3–4, 125–26, 135–36; education and work of, 169–71, 180–81, 187, 190; family history of, 3, 38, 91–93, 103; family responsibilities of, 109–10, 112, 166–67, 179–80, 195; on having a family of her own, 182; health episode of, 112, 169, 180; political views of, 78, 79, 86; securing her parents' status, 113–14, 181–82; transborder life of, 106, 163–67
Clemente, Paloma (mother of Isabel Clemente): green card process of, 113–14, 165; mobility restrictions of, 91, 103, 106; returning to Mexico of, 164–66; work of, 109
Clemente, Santos (father of Isabel Clemente), 103, 114, 164, 165, 166
Clinton administration, 47
cognitive development, 94
Colón, Paz, 74, 80, 126–27, 134
common-law marriage, 224n3 (ch. 5)
confinement. *See* detention programs
cotidianidad, 124, 223n2 (ch. 4)

DACA. *See* Deferred Action for Childhood Arrivals (DACA)
DAPA. *See* Deferred Action for Parental Accountability (DAPA)
Day Without an Immigrant, 81–82. See also *mega marcha*
deaths of immigrants, 47
Deferred Action for Childhood Arrivals (DACA): changes to, 88, 200; establishment and summary of, 19–20, 54; provisional residency regulations of, ix, 67; Trump on, 20, 54–55
Deferred Action for Parental Accountability (DAPA), 54, 55
deportability, as term, 96, 221n3
deportation fear: about, x, 3–5, 16–19; as embodied effect of illegality, 110–12, 122–31; during Operation Gatekeeper, 17; pyramid effects of, 96; Trump's elevation of, 55, 56, 94, 137. *See also* illegality experiences; mental health; state power
deportation programs. *See* border enforcement practices
depression, 73. *See also* mental health; trauma
detention programs, 50, 52
The Development, Relief, and Education for Alien Minors Act. *See* DREAM Act
DHS. *See* U.S. Department of Homeland Security (DHS)
Díaz, Luz, 159
Díaz, Porfirio, 40
Díaz, Salvador "Sal": on borderland surveillance, 132–33, 135; family responsibilities of, 101, 185–86; political views of, 73, 76, 78, 79, 82, 83, 84–85; transborder life of, 158–61; work of, 190
Disneyland, 18, 104
Diversity Immigration Visa Program, 56
downward assimilation, 11, 12–13. *See also* assimilation theories

DREAM Act (The Development, Relief, and Education for Alien Minors Act), 51, 192
DREAMer movement, 51, 71, 88, 194
driver's licenses, 18, 19, 51, 54, 73, 92, 100–101, 192
dual nationality status, 160
Duarte, Marta, 135

economy and anti-immigrant politics, 40–41, 109, 180
El Paso, Texas, 122
employer regulations, 50
empowerment, 84–85. *See also* protests; resistance to state power
Espino, Guillermo, 88
ethno-racial profiling, 4, 50, 53, 118–24, 129–31, 204
everyday violence, as concept, 138. *See also* legal violence

families. *See* mixed-status families
family, as term, 221n2
family crises and transborder life, 158, 185
family reunification policies, 43–44, 202
family separation: enforcement practices of, 48, 51, 53; as part of transnational life, 146–47, 162; prevalence of, 94; Trump's elevation of, 55, 95. *See also* border enforcement practices
FBI. *See* Federal Bureau of Investigation (FBI)
Federal Bureau of Investigation (FBI), 19, 50, 52
financial literacy, 183, 188
financial stress, 109, 152, 165, 180–81, 183, 203
Fox administration (Mexico), 49
Franco, Ana, 140
Franco, Camila (mother of Carlos Franco), 140, 150–51
Franco, Carlos: family history of, 4, 6, 38, 111; transborder life of, 25, 140–42, 150–52, 156; work life of, 189, 190

Franco, Luis (father of Carlos Franco), 140, 150–51
Friendship Park, U.S., *201*
funerals, 91, 106, 158

gangs, 13, 31, 145, 211, 223n6
García, Alberto "Beto": family history of, 4–5, 38; family responsibilities of, 166–67, 184–85, 195, 200, 203; on giving back, 187–88; marriage and citizenship of, 114–15, 184, 198, 199; on mother and family mobility, 106–7, 198–200; on "not having papers," 73, 183, 223n5 (ch. 2); transborder life of, 141–42, 161–63, 166; work of, 190, 199
García, Estela (mother of Beto García), 106, 162, 197
García, Felipe (brother of Beto García), 20, 199
García, Luis (brother of Beto García), 5, 141, 162, 184, 197, 203
gender: brokering roles and, 176; "gendered racial removal program," 52; migration patterns and, 33, 41, 148–49, 150
Georgia, 53
Gómez, Cármen, 83, 85, 86, 157
green cards, 113–14, 223n2 (ch. 2)
guest worker programs, 29, 40–41, 49, 66, 148, 162

H-2 visa, 66. *See also* guest worker programs
Hart-Cellar Act. *See* Immigration and Nationality Act of 1965 (INA)
"having papers," 72–73, 91–92, 223n1 (ch. 2), 223n5 (ch. 2)
health care access, 31, 45, 47, 95, 163, 186, 198. *See also* social services
Hidalgo, Lisa: education and work of, 136–37, 190; family and opportunities of, 109, 182; on fear, 104, 111, 133, 137, 139; on Mateo's commitment to barrio, 188
Hidalgo, Mateo: on adult responsibilities of siblings, 109, 182–83; community and work of, 31, 188, 190, 195; on limitations, 104, 107
high school debates on immigration, 84–85
home immigration raids, 51, 53
H.R. 4437 (Border Protection, Antiterrorism, and Illegal Immigration Control Act of 2005), 18–19, 50, 101
H.R. 4437 generation, 57–58, 80, 88, 89, 202
human rights organizations, 121–22, 223n2 (ch. 4)
human rights violations, 47, 51, 128–29

ICE. *See* U.S. Immigration and Customs Enforcement (ICE)
IIRIRA (Illegal Immigration Reform and Immigrant Responsibility Act of 1996), 17, 48, 53
illegal alien, as term, 42, 69–71, 75–78. *See also* unauthorized immigrant, as category
illegality experiences, 115–16; articulated effects by teens of, 99–100; effects of state power on, 96–98; effects on children's health and mental health, 95–96; family dynamics and, 107–10; in mixed-status families, 15–21, 38, 91–94; process of filing for citizenship and, 112–15; of second-generation youth, overview, 7–10, 62–64; subjective meanings of, 98–99; of transborder limitations, 105–7, 147; of travel limitations, 100–105. *See also* brokering roles of second-generation young adults; deportation fear
illegal *vs.* legal, as concept, 8, 42–43, 62, 221n3. *See also* classification systems
immigrant rights movement: 2006 *mega marcha* protests, 9, 19, 29, 50–51, 59–62, 80–89, 178, 192; on belonging, 79; Casandra in, 190–91; DREAMer activism, 51, 71, 88–89, 194; Esperanza in, 192–94; H.R. 4437 generation, 57–58, 80, 88, 89, 202; Paulina in, 191–92. *See also* resistance to state power

immigration: about, 29–30, 40–41; chain migration, 56; circular migration, 48, 146; criminalization of, 17–19, 48, 50, 52–53, 66, 82, 96; gender and, 33, 41, 148–49, 150; vs. immigrant policies, 205–7, 222n1; terms for, 224n3 (ch. 4). See also immigration policies; transborder life
Immigration and Nationality Act of 1965 (INA), 11, 42, 44, 56
Immigration and Naturalization Services (INS), 45, 49, 122
immigration policies: about, 37–39; of the 1900-1960s, 40–41; of the 1960s, 42–43; of the 1980s, 43–44; of the 1990s, 37–38, 44–49; of the 2000s, 49–53; of the 2010s, 52, 53–56; AEDPA, 17, 48; in California, 16–17, 43–45, 49, 57, 80, 101; guest worker programs, 29, 40–41, 66, 148, 162; IIRIRA, 17, 48, 53; vs. immigration, 205–7, 222n1; INA, 11, 42, 44, 56; IRCA, 4, 5, 16, 33, 38, 43–44, 67; Prop. 187, 17; PRWORA, 17; worker programs, 29, 40–41, 66, 148, 162. See also border enforcement practices; state power
Immigration Reform and Control Act of 1986 (IRCA), 4, 5, 16, 33, 38, 43–44, 67
INA. See Immigration and Nationality Act of 1965 (INA)
inclusion/exclusion classifications, 78–79. See also classification systems
Indiana, 53
INS. See Immigration and Naturalization Services (INS)
inspection stations. See border enforcement practices; ports of entry
integration pathways, 11–15. See also classification systems
interpreting and translating by children, 21, 22, 170–75, 200, 203
IRCA. See Immigration Reform and Control Act of 1986 (IRCA)
isolation. See social isolation

language skill development, 94. See also linguistic brokering by children
Las Palomas, Mexico, 155–58
lawful permanent residents (LPR), as category, 16, 17, 65
legal/formal classifications, 65–68, 71–74. See also classification systems
legal violence, 96–99, 121, 138. See also ethno-racial profiling; state power
legal vs. illegal, as concept, 8, 16, 42–43, 62, 221n3. See also classification systems
LIC (low-intensity conflict) doctrine, 45, 123
linguistic brokering by children, 21, 22, 170–75, 200, 203. See also language skill development
low-intensity conflict doctrine, 45, 123
lucha libre, 159

Márquez, Wilson: on 2006 protests, 83; family history of, 149; on illegality and immigrant terms, 75–77; on resistance to state power, 135; work of, 190
marriage, 5, 15, 149, 224n3 (ch. 5)
Martin, Elena, 192, 193
Martínez, Luisa: on barrio, 31–32; family history of, 149; on working hard, 189; work of, 190
mass deportation period, 51–52. See also border enforcement practices
media, 68–69, 83
Medina, Adán (brother of Esperanza and Victoria Medina), 127, 128, 154
Medina, Esperanza: on borderland surveillance and fear, 117–18, 132; on crossing the border, 127–29, 130–31; education and work of, 137, 172–73, 190, 192–94; opportunities of, 73; religious faith of, 153–54, 188; transborder life of, 152–55
Medina, Victoria: on border crossing, 131; on immigrant terms, 75; on in-laws' circumstances, 186–87; opportunities and brokering of, 118, 186–88; on paranoia,

133; religious faith of, 153–54, 188; transborder life of, 154; work of, 190
mega marcha (2006 protests), 9, 19, 29, 50–51, 59–62, 80–89, 178, 192
Méndez, Miguel, 82–83
Méndez, Nadia, 138
Méndez, Noe, 159
Mendoza, Lucía, 159
mental health, 51, 73, 95, 96. *See also* deportation fear; illegality experiences; trauma
"merit-based" system, 56
Mexican, self-identification as, 83, 222n7
Mexican-American War (1848), 40
"Mexican appearance," as legal grounds for inspection, 121. *See also* ethno-racial profiling
Mexican Independence Day, 31
Mexican Revolution (1910-1921), 29, 40
Mexico, regions of, 25, 148, 224n2. *See also* Tijuana, Mexico; U.S.–Mexico borderlands, overview
la mica, 223n2 (ch. 2). *See also* green cards
la migra, as term, 134, 224n3 (ch. 4)
military community in San Diego County, 28–29
mixed-status families: about, 3–7, 221n2; bidirectional political socialization model in, 87; crises and transborder life of, 158, 181, 182, 185; experiences of illegality in, 15–21, 38, 91–94; parental roles of children in, 109–10, 112, 166–67, 179–80; raids and trauma in, 51–53, 94, 127; statistics on, 5, 6, 11. *See also* brokering roles of second-generation young adults; second-generation young adults
Montero, Federico, 76
Montoya, Elena (mother of Sal Díaz), 158
Morelia, Mexico, 153, 154
Muslim American immigrants, x
"Muslim ban" executive order, x
MySpace, 61

NAFTA. *See* North American Free Trade Agreement of 1994 (NAFTA)
National Council of State Legislatures (NCSL), 53
National Day of Action, 81. *See also mega marcha*
national security issue, immigration as, 18, 49–50, 69
nation-state, as concept, 9, 222n5. *See also* state power
Naturalization Act of 1790, 37
nature, 156
nervios, 96. *See also* mental health
New Mexico, 25
New York, 147
nonimmigrant, as category, 65–66. *See also* classification systems
North American Free Trade Agreement of 1994 (NAFTA), 27

Obama administration, 19, 52, 53–54, 94
"obvious citizenship," 130–31, 138
Operation Blockade, 45, 122
Operation Gatekeeper, 9, 16–17, 45–47
Ortega, Imelda, 75
Otay Mesa Port of Entry, 27, 124

parental authority and brokering roles of children, 175–77
PATRIOT Act (2001), 50
Pérez, Blanca, 74, 86
permanent resident aliens. *See* lawful permanent residents (LPR), as category
The Personal Responsibility and Work Opportunity Reconciliation Act of 1996 (PRWORA), 17, 47, 95
policeability, as concept, 121, 221n3
ports of entry, 124–31; Otay Mesa, 27, 124; San Ysidro, 27, *119*, 124, *128*, 162. *See also under* border
prison corporations, 52

profiling. *See* ethno-racial profiling
Proposition 187 (California), 17, 44–45, 49
Proposition 187 generation, 57, 80
Proposition 209 (California), 45
Proposition 227 (California), 45
protests: (2006), 9, 19, 29, 50–51, 59–62, 80–89, 178, 192; (1994), 57. *See also* immigrant rights movement; resistance to state power
PRWORA. *See* The Personal Responsibility and Work Opportunity Reconciliation Act of 1996 (PRWORA)
public services access. *See* health care access; social services
public transportation surveillance, 101, 103

*quinceñera*s, 107, 140, 150, 157, 159

racial governance. *See* ethno-racial profiling
raids, 51, 53. *See also* search and seizure procedure
Ramírez, Luisa (mother of Tomás Ramírez), 103–4, 105, 107
Ramírez, Tomás: community service of, 188, 195; on deportation fear, 111, 133, 135; family history and responsibilities of, 103–4, 108, 110; on mother's papers, 105–8, 113, 187; work of, 190
Ramos, Hernando, 159
Reagan administration, 43–44
religion and identity, 153–54, 188
repercussive effects, as term, 98
research participants: about, 3–5, 10, 32–34, 223nn3–4, 224n1; list of, 217–18; summary of research method, 209–15. See also *specific personal names*
resistance to state power, 134–37, 139. *See also* immigrant rights movement; protests
retirement community of San Diego County, 28–29, 169, 171
rites of passage. *See quinceñera*s

San Antonio, Mexico, 140–41, 150, 151
San Clemente checkpoint, 18, 103, 104, 131
"sanctuary cities," 56
San Diego, U.S.: 2006 protests in, 9, 19, 29, 50–51, 59–62, 80–89, 178, 192; barrio in, 30–32; Friendship Park, *201*; Otay Mesa Port of Entry, 27, 124; overview of San Diego–Tijuana borderlands, 25–30; San Ysidro Port of Entry, 27, *119*, 124, *128*, 162. *See also under* border; California; Tijuana, Mexico
San Diego Union-Tribune, 28
Santos, Mari (mother of Paulina Santos), 155
Santos, Paulina: activism and political views of, 61–62, 65, 75, 78, 82, 86, 88–89; on border crossings, 130, 135; family responsibilities of, 185; transborder life of, 155–58, 160, 161; work of, 89, 190, 191–92, 195
San Ysidro Port of Entry, 27, *119*, 124, *128*, 162
Save Our State (SOS) Initiative, 45. *See also* Proposition 187 (California)
S.B. 1070. *See* The Support Our Law Enforcement and Safe Neighborhoods Act (S.B. 1070)
school surveillance, 133–34
search and seizure procedure, 131. *See also* border enforcement practices; raids
second-generation young adults: articulated repercussive effects of illegality by, 99–100; defined, 222n6; DREAMer movement, 51, 71, 88, 194; embodied effects of illegality on, 110–12, 124–31; H.R. 4437 generation, 57–58, 80, 88, 89, 202; illegality and family responsibilities of, 107–10; illegality and travel limitations of, 100–107; incorporation pathways, 11–15, 94; mental and physical health of, 51, 73, 95, 96; navigating illegality of, 7–10, 62–64; risks and vul-

nerabilities of, 6–7, 38–39; state power and influence on, 13–21, 131–34; state power resistance by, 134–37; statistics on, 11, 206. *See also* brokering roles of second-generation young adults; Deferred Action for Childhood Arrivals (DACA); DREAM Act; mixed-status families

Secure Communities program, 19, 52–53, 55

Secure Electronic Network for Travelers Rapid Inspection (SENTRI) pass, 160

segmented assimilation, 11–13. *See also* assimilation theories

selective acculturation, 12

September 11 attacks, effects of, 49–50

sibling relationships, 109–10

single mother households, 52, 94, 224n1

social belonging. *See* belonging

social/informal classifications, 68–71, 75–78. *See also* classification systems

social integration and illegality, 94

social isolation, 33, 35, 94, 103, 107–8, 115, 187

social media, 61, 71, 214

social services, 47–48, 95. *See also* health care access

South Carolina, 53

South Tucson, Arizona, 122

Southwest North American (SWNA) region, as term, 25

sports, 159

state, as concept, 9, 222n5

state power, 56–58; in borderlands, 24–25; brokering roles of children and, 177–78, 200–202; effects on second-generation young adults, 13–21; as legal violence, 96–98; navigating pervasiveness of, 124–34; resistance to, 134–37, 139. *See also* border enforcement practices; deportation fear; immigration policies

stigmatization of Mexican immigrants, 74, 75–76

structural violence, as concept, 138. *See also* legal violence

student walkout, 81. *See also mega marcha;* resistance to state power

subjectivity, as term, 222n4

The Support Our Law Enforcement and Safe Neighborhoods Act (S.B. 1070, Arizona), 53

surveillance. *See* border enforcement practices

taxes, 65, 78

Tel Aviv, Israel, 122

temporary protected status (TPS), as category, ix, 66–67

Texas, 25, 45, 54, 122, 150

third-generation, 12, 94, 104. *See also* second-generation young adults

threat narratives, 69. *See also* national security issue, immigration as

Tijuana, Mexico: nickname to, 223n2 (ch. 3); overview of San Diego–Tijuana borderlands, 25–30; resident deportees in, 28, 157, 199; transborder lives and, 105, 158–61, 162–64, 197–98. *See also* San Diego, U.S.

Torres, Casandra: on 2006 protests, 83; on "growing up immigrant," 189, 190–91; on paying taxes, 78; work of, 190, 195

transborder life: belonging and, 140–42; as concept, 142–47; hometown engagement, 150–55; illegality and limitations in, 105–7, 147; local engagement, 155–61; parents' regions of origin and, 148–49; state-mediated engagement, 161–67. *See also* San Diego, U.S.; Tijuana, Mexico

transborder region. *See under* border; U.S.–Mexico borderlands, overview

translating and interpreting by children, 21, 22, 170–75, 200, 203

transnationalism, as concept, 142, 143–47

trauma, 51, 94, 127. *See also* deportation fear; illegality experiences; mental health

travel limitations, 100–107

Treaty of Guadalupe Hidalgo (1848), 40
Trump administration: border wall rhetoric by, ix, x, 205–6; on DACA, 20, 54–55; enforcement policies of, 54–56, 94, 137

unauthorized immigrant, as category, 65, 66, 221n1. *See also* classification systems; illegal alien, as term
undocumented, as concept, 9, 71, 221n1. *See also* classification systems
unión libre, 224n3 (ch. 5)
United States v. Brignoni-Ponce, 121
U.S. Border Patrol: agent demographics of, 129–30; establishment of, 40; Operation Gatekeeper, 9, 16–17; surveillance by, 101–2, *102*; term for, 224n3 (ch. 4). *See also under* border
U.S. citizen identity performance, 135–36, 153
U.S. Citizenship and Immigration Services (USCIS), 22, 65–66
U.S. Congress, 4, 17, 42, 45, 47–50, 56, 205

U.S. Customs and Border Protection (CBP): enforcement practices of, 9–10, 24, 125, 129, 178, 199; fear of, 127, 129, 130, 139; terms of, 221n1, 224n3 (ch. 4)
U.S. Department of Homeland Security (DHS): establishment of, 18, 49; legal terms of, 221n1; Secure Communities program, 19, 52–53, 55
U.S. Immigration and Customs Enforcement (ICE), 55, 205, 221n1, 224n3 (ch. 4)
U.S.–Mexico borderlands, overview, 24–32, 131–34. *See also* San Diego, U.S.; Tijuana, Mexico
U.S.–Mexico Border Program (AFSC), 223n2 (ch. 4)
Utah, 53

Villanueva, Amada, 107, 129, 133, 157, 159

Wilson, Pete, 49
workplace raids, 51, 53

ABOUT THE AUTHOR

Christina M. Getrich, PhD, is an assistant professor in the Anthropology Department at the University of Maryland, College Park. Her research examines the incorporation of mixed-immigration status families into U.S. society and the production of Latinx health disparities. She explores the lived and embodied experiences of U.S. immigration policies and enforcement practices in order to determine how immigrants, their children, and advocates (including health care providers) maneuver to fight for broader social inclusion. Her research has been published in journals including *Social Science and Medicine*, *Medical Anthropology Quarterly*, *The American Journal of Public Health*, *American Behavioral Scientist*, and *Latino Studies*.